Musing the Mosaic

THE SUNY SERIES IN

POSTMODERN CULTURE

Joseph Natoli, editor

Musing the Mosaic

Approaches to Ronald Sukenick

Edited by

Matthew Roberson

State University of New York Press

Published by
State University of New York Press, Albany

Printed in the United States of America

For information, address State University of New York Press,
90 State Street, Suite 700, Albany, NY 12207

Production by Diane Ganeles
Marketing by Michael Campochiaro

Library of Congress Cataloging-in-Publication Data

Musing the mosaic : approaches to Ronald Sukenick / Matthew Roberson, editor.
p. cm. — (SUNY series in postmodern culture)
Includes bibliographical references and index.
ISBN 0-7914-5727-3 (alk. paper) — ISBN 0-7914-5728-1 (pbk. : alk. paper)
1. Sukenick, Ronald—Criticism and interpretation. 2. Postmodernism (Literature)—United States. I. Roberson, Matthew. II. Series.

PS3569.U33 Z78 2003
813'.54—dc21 2002029231

10 9 8 7 6 5 4 3 2 1

Contents

Photographer: Andi Olsen

Ronald Sukenick

Introduction

Matthew Roberson

For thirty-odd years, novelist and critic Ronald Sukenick has actively participated in the reshaping of the American literary tradition. His has been for not one but two generations among the strongest, most creative, and most intelligent voices insisting that fiction can no longer perform its traditional functions in the contemporary age, that in an ever more dynamic world fiction can no longer rely on conventions. Of the many American writers to emerge in the late 1960s—what in his essay for this collection Charles Harris calls a "watershed [moment] in contemporary American fiction"—Ronald Sukenick is one of the very most important.

He has published six novels, three collections of short fiction, four books of nonfiction/theory (and played a pivotal role in the creation and growth of the publishing houses the Fiction Collective and FC2, as well as the journals the *American Book Review* and *Black Ice Magazine*). Distinguishing Sukenick's texts: their constant struggle to open language, metaphors, and form—to take the seams out of writing before restitching it in ways that are truly novel. As a result, Sukenick's revolutionary work "comes closer to the dissolving fragmentary nature of lived experience, [and] its lack of finality and closure" than perhaps anything written before it (Tatham 2).

Frequently *too much* for our usual categories, Sukenick's books resist labels (constantly challenging Sukenick critics to come up with neologisms that *will* fit). They juggle storytelling at the same time as they consider artistic and aesthetic questions, which they do while raising and acting out theoretical speculations that emerge at the same time as political topics that impinge on personal concerns (and this in all his books, fiction and non). Containing fragmented, nonlinear narratives, recurrent self-reflexivity, typographical play, fictions within fictions, experiments in mixed-media and graphic designs, and an insistent blurring of boundaries between fiction and "the real," they are knotted and complicated books, and the best way to trace their threads is by seeing the big picture—integrating studies that grapple with all of Sukenick's fiction and nonfiction, and maybe even some of his "real" life.

With the partial exception of Jerzy Kutnik's 1986 study of Sukenick and Federman, nothing before *Musing the Mosaic* has taken such a comprehensive view.[1] This is in part because—although revered in certain circles—Sukenick has never drawn broad attention. And this is in part because, at times, he's not only *too much* but *way too much*—too unusual, too challenging, and too contrary in his undermining of the idea of the book as traditionally conceived. His texts frequently subvert every expectation, narrative and otherwise, a reader might bring to them, as well as the very systems of rational thought, language, and categories supporting critical analysis and a wider discussion of his work. Like a joke one either "gets" or doesn't, Sukenick's texts speak to a certain mindset or mood, and a willingness to play along, and this they haven't fully received.

Often, Sukenick's books so deeply offend the average sensibility that they revolt and repel. Several years ago, in a senior seminar, one of my female students claimed that being assigned *98.6*—and having to read its portrayal of a rape scene—left her feeling violated. Fortunately, she went on to discuss several reasons why Sukenick might want his texts to confront readers as they do. It seems, however, that too few readers—and even potential critics—take that extra step.

Although it's unfortunate that certain factors have marginalized Sukenick, some advantages come from the deferral of a far-reaching, comprehensive study of his work. Coming out in 2003, this collection can effectively examine Sukenick's importance to American letters while also stressing how the protean and interdisciplinary attitude developed in large part by Sukenick, and which we've come to know as postmodernism, is not only alive and kicking, but perhaps more expansive than anyone imagined it could be.

There's been much talk of the death of postmodernism. Even Sukenick declared it a goner in recent years. Declaring postmodernism dead, however, is about as easy and effective as defining it, which few have had luck doing, and these few because they have perspectives open to indeterminacy. Among these, whatever his recent words, Sukenick must be counted, if not via more literal attempts to "define" postmodernism, then through his texts' performances of a pomo attitude. What is this pomo attitude? It's an attitude that embraces contradiction. It's an attitude, as Sukenick argues in his most recent book, *Narralogues*, that believes we must use fiction as a medium for telling the truth, which is by its very nature (truth, that is) a provisional beast. It's an attitude that wants to cross borders between genres and disciplines and traditions and texts and lives, and it's an attitude that is ever increasingly more necessary and inescapable.

Why necessary and inescapable? In a contemporary moment shaped by the shallow and inebriating cultural logic of spectacle and simulation (a postmodernism of sorts, to be sure, but not exactly the pomo one would associate with Sukenick), Sukenick's texts exemplify how writing can be "the blunt instrument of power" rather than hollow facsimile (*Narralogues* 5). Their form of imaginative writing provides, as Sukenick himself says, "a way of salvaging experience from overbearing and intrusive discourses whose aim [is] to manipulate one's sense of the world in somebody else's interest" (5). As the kind of reflective discourse that demands from the reader an interactive response not generated in narrative as entertainment, they, and fictions like them, can again take their place among what Sukenick calls "serious discourses of knowledge in our culture" (6).

These are goals toward which Sukenick has always worked. Several years ago, Paul Maltby labeled Sukenick's work dissident fiction, feeling that its primary function is to expose and struggle against the ideologies and conceptual limits of the restrictive postmodern language modes of late capitalism. Marcel Cornis-Pope has made similar arguments, claiming that Sukenick's texts operate as "revisionistic exercises of cultural imagination . . . questioning our perceptual and discursive systems, reinventing the rules by which reality is projected" (182). Both Maltby's and Cornis-Pope's discussions also agree with Charles Russell's claim that the implicit ideal of Sukenick's fictions:

> Is a state of pure presentness. More directed against the constraints of the past than positing an ideal future of significant difference, the postmodern work is rarely concerned with an aesthetics of sustained development. In fact, it is unable to foster such an aesthetics, since any rigorously ordered work must be subject to the same process of demystification of established meaning that generated the original creative impulse. (257)

Sukenick's texts, in other words, don't do the work of The Novel. They do not aspire to represent a rational reality or a psychological subject; they instead see the novel as a performance of ideas/ideals that can teach readers. As working models of the sort of perpetually present, generative writing (of the self, among other things) described by Maltby, Cornis-Pope, and Russell, Sukenick's work provides useful lessons to his readers, since this kind of "thought is . . . a powerful form of discourse if only because we all make use of it as we create our own life stories from our experience" (*Narralogues* 6).

Sukenick's books, therefore, valuably extend the ways that we can consider our world. They do contain narrative; in fact, Sukenick insists that even his most "argumentative" books cannot work without narrative, as narrative is to him the only "mode of understanding that uniquely is quick enough, mutable enough, and flexible enough to catch the stream of experience" (1). They do not, however, let themselves be taken as only their narratives, and certainly not as narratives that aspire to only mimetic, dramatic representation. According to Sukenick, "When you define fiction by representation you end up confining it to realism at some level and arguing that fiction, as a form of make-believe, is a way of lying to get at the truth, which if not palpably stupid is certainly roundabout and restrictive" (2).

As he goes on to say in *Narralogues*, if one wants to find "truth" in fiction, then there has to be a struggle against the the prevailing belief that while literature must be about "reflecting" reality, it must not in any consequential or thoughtful way practice another kind of "reflection," raising issues, examining situations, and meditating on solutions in ways that generates an "illuminating angle of vision of its own" (3). The novel must give accord to its rhetorical qualities, allowing itself to be an "ongoing persuasive discourse that [is] agonistic, sophistic, sophisticated, fluid, unpredictable, rhizomatic, affective, inconsistent and even contradictory, improvisational, and provisional in its argument toward contingent resolution that can only be temporary" (1). In this way, a fiction becomes like any other discourse. You would not say that an argument represents anything other than the argument, and so with fiction.

A more detailed explanation of Sukenick's theories of fiction begins this collection. Steve Tomasula's piece, "Taking the Line for a Walk," examines Sukenick's 1985 collection of critical essays, *In Form: Digressions on the Act of Fiction*, in order to understand Sukenick's early sense of the place of the novel—what it could mean—during "postModernism," which Tomasula places between 1972 and 1985. Sukenick's thoughts were, as Tomasula puts it, part of a "vital, if marginalized conversation for anyone interested in the viability of literature at the time Sukenick began writing it down," and not only because they confronted the breakdown of modernist assumptions, and the void they left, but because they dealt practically with "the increasing influence of mass-marketing on literature." Tomasula also turns to Sukenick's most recent text, *Narralogues*, which he sees as offering a retrospective look at the period in question, as well as a discussion of how the novel can remain vital when the "nascent trends in literature identified in *In Form* have themselves grown to maturation: a publishing industry dominated by a handful of conglomerates; a time that has seen the resurgence of the realist novel and autobiography even as the Modernist 'self' has given way to the postmodernist 'subject'; a time when the digitalization of culture and the rise of alternative media have forced conceptually driven authors to reevaluate the value and form of the written word."

Charles Harris's piece, "At Play in the Fields of Formal Thinking," also takes an interest in Sukenick's theories of writing, focusing on Sukenick's book-length study of Wallace Stevens—*Wallace Stevens: Musing the Obscure*—and *In Form*. According to Harris, *Wallace Stevens* and *In Form* explain Sukenick's sense of how reflexively writing (about) himself exemplifies a process of interpretation, a depiction of how the human mind works as it makes sense of the reality of self and culture, as well as how it reminds "the reader of how he himself thinks and what he is thinking, and thereby . . . activate[s] his imagination so that he himself can look at the world, not necessarily my [Sukenick's] version of it—in his own versions of it" (*In Form* 146). These of Sukenick's ideas can be connected, according to the piece, to the ways that all contemporary metafiction, which Harris sees as a literature in large part defined by the "deployment of reflexive techniques," works in the interest of postmodernist concerns—in this case, the creation of an oppositional politics. Harris's essay then analyzes how Sukenick's first novel, *Up*, illustrates "as it extends Sukenick's earliest formulation of an aesthetic theory and represents an excellent example of the novelist 'at play in the fields of formal thinking' " (inner quote from *In Form* xvii).

In her study of Sukenick's first collection of short stories, *The Death of the Novel and Other Stories*, Nancy Blake takes up Lacanian ideas to suggest that not only does Sukenick's fiction pose "the question of the authority of the Other," but that in his work "art sets as its goal the construction of its own Other." If, that is, language is the "Other" into which we are born, and by which we are defined, then Sukenick takes onto himself the project of reconstructing that Other by pursuing a generative mode of thought—a sort of positive ignorance of what (language) has come before—that can result in an openness to experience, to the multiplicity of possibilities that exist if we can only tune in.

To back her argument, Blake focuses on the "collage-like pieces" in *The Death of the Novel*, stressing how their surrealistic interplay of writing and "found object" make Sukenick's project possible, as well as how, as this project is developed, it disturbs "all standard notions surrounding ego identity."

The concept of ego identity is also taken up by Ursula K. Heise, in "Sukenick's Posthumans." Concentrating on Sukenick's second novel, *Out*, with some reference to Sukenick's most recent novel, *Mosaic Man*, Heise discusses Sukenick's style of character construction, how he persistently refuses "to grant his fictional characters any plausible psychology, or, indeed, any coherent identity that would remain recognizable over the duration of the text." Noting, however, that this method of character construction is not unique to Sukenick, but shared by a number of postmodernist writers, Heise's piece claims that what is distinctive to Sukenick's postmodern characters, and what in part makes his work relevant to the contemporary moment, is the way that his "questioning of human identity . . . is associated with a suprisingly realistic conception of place and geography on the one hand, and with the exploration of how new technologies of information and communication alter the experience of space and the configuration of human identity, on the other." The broader question approached by Sukenick, according to Heise, is "how the human subject should be reconceptualized in its systemic relations to planet-wide non-human spaces, whether these be the webs of global ecology or the networks of international information technology."

In "Interruption Discontinuity Imperfection It Can't be Helped," Cam Tatham examines episodes of shocking sex and violence in Sukenick's third novel, *98.6*, wondering how these moments represent an attempt to reach the "extraordinary," a place or experience beyond custom, beyond language and literature, a place of pre- or post- or nonlinguistic feelings. Tatham further wonders in what ways these attempts can be considered successful. Is part of their success that they affect the reader in some ways that are close to extraordinary? To the last question Tatham argues yes; that like Carlos Castenada's don Juan, Sukenick teaches by tricking—in *98.6* manipulating the reader into a startled "disruption of ordinary, routine perception" that leads to the "deliberate cultivation of a willingness to see—and experience—the world anew." Case in point, "Interruption Discontinuitiy Imperfection It Can't be Helped" recognizes in a critifictional way how Tatham himself, as the critic and professor, can not remain and has not remained aloof from what he studies. Weaving his own story through the discussion of Sukenick, Tatham shows, "more or less, how deeply he is implicated in what he is saying," and how *98.6* has been for him "one of those life-changing experiences, becoming over all the years virtually a sacred text."

Situating *98.6* and *Long Talking Bad Conditions Blues*, as well as Sukenick's third collection of stories, *Doggy Bag,* within a broader scheme of postmodern arts, Charles Russell's "Explorations of Post-modern Time, Space, and Image" compares Sukenick's works to those of painter David Salle, a young neo-expressionist visual artist of the 1980s, in order to "illuminate many of the core aesthetic issues of this period known as the postmodern." Never ignoring the challenges involved in comparisons between literary and visual arts, or the particular differences in tone and attitude between Sukenick and Salle, Russell focuses on "the affinities that justify" this specific comparision: Sukenick's and Salle's shared interest in making "the act of creation a central subject" in their works, and the ways they develop "highly self-conscious formal and thematic strategies that explore the processes and challenges of meaning-making." Russell studies how Sukenick and Salle "validate the organization of narrative time in the novel and compositional space in self-revealing terms" in order to operate in "the absence of wholes," or "the apparent lack of coherence to both external reality and personal experience upon which the aesthetic artifice can be based." Also of interest to Russell is how both artists are entangled in what they understand to be a highly-mediated popular culture, which they approach comically, ironically, and critically as they mine it "for their iconography." Where the individual is concerned, says Salle, both "indicate the ceaseless creation and loss of personal identity within [the] competing codes of meaning" under examination in their works.

Brian McHale's essay, "Sukenick in Space, or, The Other Truth of the Page," also examines how Sukenick makes the act of creation a central interest of his poetics. Contextualizing this interest within a culture of spontaneity "that arose in the United States immediately after the Second World War" and embraced a "range of cultural practices, from abstract-expressionism, collage, and assemblage in the visual arts, through Beat and Black Mountain writing, to bebop and free jazz," McHale looks at *The Endless Short Story*, *Long Talking Bad Conditions Blues*, *Doggy Bag*, *Blown Away*, and *Mosaic Man* to explain an improvisational Sukenickian "writing that preserves the trace of the writer's actual activity in real time and real space, writing that registers the process by which the page itself was inscribed." This "truth of the page," according to McHale, corresponds to the "underlying orality of spontaneous prose." There is, however, he goes on to say, a second "truth of the page" that Sukenick recognizes, one that recognizes the reality of the written word, its "*materiality*, its existence as a structure of real objects: the white space of the page, the shapes that typography makes, the concrete 'technological reality' of the book." In a way linking literary and visual arts, McHale says this materiality emerges in formal and typographical experiments that result in Sukenick's "palimtexts," whose "spaced out prose" create postmodern, archeological ruins of print.

Sukenick's sense of the technological reality of fiction is further explored in Lance Olsen's "Graphiction." Looking to three works—*98.6*, *Doggy Bag*, and *Mosaic Man*—from two different decades of Sukenick's career, Olsen explores how Sukenick uses graphics to destabilize, complicate, and make self-conscious traditional reading assumptions and processes. "What is the advantage of such a graphictional strategy," he asks. "What does one gain—and what does one lose—by employing it? By learning to think about the novel as a concrete structure rather than an allegory, do we thus banish the notion of allegory altogether, or simply displace it and reintroduce it at another level of meaning-making? Is it ever really possible to demystify a text without engendering another kind of mystification—here, perhaps, of the technological reality of the text itself?" How are these questions further complicated, and illuminated, the piece wonders, by its own self-reflexive, formally inventive graphictional nature? To what extent does it matter if Sukenick's (and Olsen's and others') graphictions are all in some ways proto-hypermedia texts, anticipatory of electronic environments?

Mark Amerika's piece, "The Artist Is The Medium Is The Message: A Ron Sukenick Re-Mix," follows. Like Olsen, Amerika puts together a collage that illustrates its ideas in visually striking ways as he connects "Sukenick's fiction and theory-digressions" with "emailings and personal conversation" (between the two writers) with Amerika's own digressions on how Sukenick's work "anticipate[d] the arrival of more multi-disciplinary, networked-narrative environments being created on the World Wide Web." Amerika illustrates while discussing, in other words, the kind of "rhetorical remixing" he sees in Sukenick's creation of a "not-fiction," a type of writing whose "purpose is to gather data in pleasurable complexes, yield information, and argue truths," as well as to manipulate the "the narrative interface" between the page and the self, the page and the world of experience. As this "interventionist not-fiction" writing practice leaves behind "both the [traditional] book and literary sense and sensibility," Amerika argues, it suggests the contemporary need of writing to upgrade "to the latest version. In this case, the latest version would be one you could apply to your web browser, personal digital assistant, mp3 player, or email program, because in this ever-morphing new media environment that writers finds themselves in, what was once a narrative practice in search of an audience of sophisticated readers, has transformed into a networking practice that uses the intuitive (Sukenick might even say "prophetic") role of the writer as a medium, or shamanic filterer. A kind of DJ Deconstructionist or Network Conductor whose disintermediating practice as Cultural Producer leads to a Reconfiguring of the Author into a Virtual Artist."

Examining the cultural context that in part bred Sukenick, JR Foley's essay is on *Down and In: Life in the Underground*, Sukenick's nonfiction remembrance of life in the American avant-garde "underground" of the 1950s, 1960s, and 1970s. Foley examines how this text, ostensibly an autobiography, is actually a collective memoir, or "collective autobiographical experience . . . an experiential history out of which an art-literary movement came," that "succeeds in placing *l'hypocrite lecteur* vicariously at a crowded table in every dark, teeming bar in '40s–'60s Greenwich Village, eavesdropping on everyone, famous, brilliant, and otherwise." The more recognizable in Sukenick's cast of characters: Allen Ginsberg, Gregory Corso, Judith Malinea, Robert Creeley, Ted Joans, Ed Sanders, Diane Wakoski, Jackson Pollock, Franz Kline, Willem DeKooning, and Andy Warhol. At stake in this world: how to remain "free," intellectually, artistically, personally, in the face of an ever-increasingly pervasive American status quo that reveres "The Golden Calf," and functions according to "caution, conformity, and mercenary values." "Defining what the underground was" (and is), Foley writes, and "how 'adversary artists' must redefine or re-realize it in changing circumstances is what Sukenick [orchestrates] his subterranean voices to address."

In "Unwriting/Rewriting the Master Narratives of 'Bankrupt' Modernity," Marcel Cornis-Pope outlines what he calls Sukenick's revisionistic poetics, which works to unwrite "what has been formulated as an experience," before continuing on "with an imaginative rewriting that allows "a new sense of experience" to evolve.[2] Cornis-Pope looks briefly at the whole of Sukenick's oeuvre in order to explain how Sukenick has "arrived at this concept of 'interventive' fiction gradually, in an unremitting struggle with narrative conventions and epistemologies" associated, in particular, with "the seductive economy of narration that for Sukenick functions as the chief illusion-building mechanism of modernity." Cornis-Pope's primary interest, however, is *Mosaic Man*, which, according to him, is Sukenick's "most important work to date," reconfiguring "not only Sukenick's previous work . . . but also the poetics of post-Holocaust/post-Cold War fiction," and the "dominant narratives that have shaped his destiny as a writer: the existential picaresque, the western quest, the gauche-pornographic novel, the family chronicle, the political thriller, and even the grand narratives of the Hebrew Bible." In its reconfigurations, it further develops Sukenick's "collective" memoirs, submitting "the author's cultural heritage . . . to a thorough reexamination, discarding one-sided definitions in favor of new cross-cultural interactions."

In a new interview, Larry McCaffery covers a great deal of territory as he wonders with Sukenick about the novel today. Tracing changes in the world that have affected Sukenick's current "task as a fiction writer," they discuss their common feeling that what in the 1950s was a favorable democratization of art led to a loss of integrity in creative works, where "art got completely confused with the entertainment industry, which meant it totally lost its adversarial position."[3] One result of this loss of integrity is contemporary postmodernism, which Sukenick feels has no "coherency, no morality, no real aesthetic purpose beyond that of grabbing people's attention," and is part of a system of commodification that has moved away from the kind of work done by literary artists of the 70s, which, whatever its deconstructive impulses, also had a reconstructive "impulse that was just as crucial, some recognition that new values, new sets of aesthetic assumptions would have to be erected." Turning to *Narralogues*, they weigh possible "solutions" to this situation, in particular Sukenick's feeling that if fiction is to tell the "truth" nowadays, if it is to have any constructive power, it has to return to rhetoric, because only when writers are able to "accept that the novel is rhetorically-based" can they reestablish fiction as an intellectual activity that moves beyond a mind-numbing representational realism dominating American literature and culture. The novel, Sukenick says, can also take advantage of the electronic communication technologies that make "writing a very kind of plastic activity" that allows one to "literally see how writing emerges from drawing as a graphic art . . . and work with a new conception of the space [and sound] of the page." Fittingly, the conversation also takes up the shared work they have done toward restoring an integrity to the American novel, focusing on the Black Ice Books series they started to publish writers with positions opposed to the middle-class and popular cultures of America, writers who like Sukenick are deeply political in that they find genuinely inventive ways to "open up new experiences for [their] audience[s]."

What does Sukenick finally add up to? Nothing simple or straightforward, writes Jerome Klinkowitz in "8½ Ronnies," since at the start of Sukenick's career there were already five Ronnies: "critic, novelist, fictively-inclined scholar, scholastically inclined fictionist, and the publicized image of a fifth figure who does all these things and more"—and Sukenick didn't stop expanding. Despite emerging in the tough literary and academic times of the late 1960s and 1970s, says Klinkowitz, "like a Fellini self-portrait Sukenick survived, projecting at least three and a half more identities until by century's end his magic number was attained." Analyzing in turn each Ronnie emerging over the past thirty years, Klinkowitz pays attention to the various texts that have defined each character, moving from *Wallace Stevens* and *Up* to *Mosaic Man* and *Narralogues*, situating them in the American cultural conditions that helped make them. The sixth Ronnie? "The combative (if not embattled) figure of the 1970s, writing three novels which are defiantly countercultural," as well a collection of critical and theoretical essays on the state of art at the time. Number seven? A "figure concerned with cultural power—concerned to the extent of being willing to broker it" via his championing of personal power over mass market. And eight? A "transitional figure who writes just one book, *Doggy Bag*, which examines all he has made of himself before moving on to more work by a Ronnie still in progress, the eighth and one half," who assembles all the parts that have come before into new "wholes" that are the beginnings of something else.

Although, as is already clear, I took one obvious route in organizing these essays, putting them (roughly) in order according to a chronology of Sukenick's works, I hope it's also clear that other logics of organization connect the pieces, and that juxtaposed works are bound by shared topics and styles. Similarly, although this collection is about providing a comprehensive study of Sukenick, it is much more than dutifully so; instead, it offers coverage of Sukenick's life and work via sharp new perspectives, ones that work over perennial aesthetic and cultural debates, and ones that move beyond literary criticism and theory, tying Sukenick to other contemporary fields: art history, ecocriticism and autobiographics, psychoanalytic theory, and technology and hypertext studies.

Notes

1. Kutnik's book is titled *The Novel as Performance*.

2. I also discuss this narrative/political method in my dissertation, "Moinous Li(v)es," using Deleuze and Guattari's ideas in *A Thousand Plateaus* to frame my discussion.

3. As an example of this democratization, McCaffery and Sukenick turn to Andy Warhol, who, according to Sukenick, "destroyed a lot of crap that was coming out of the painting style and gallery scene, especially the mystique of the artist and the addict and all that shit." They also mention, it must be noted, that Warhol was among the first to turn his situation into pure commercialism.

Works Cited

Russell, Charles. *Poets, Prophets and Revolutionaries: The Avant-Garde from Rimbaud to Postmodernism.* Oxford: Oxford University Press, 1985.

Sukenick, Ronald. *In Form: Digressions on the Act of Fiction.* Carbondale: Southern Illinois University Press, 1985.

———. *Narralogues: Truth in Fiction.* Albany: State University of New York Press, 1999.

Tatham, Campbell. "Mo-Sukenick." *New Novel Review.* Forthcoming.

Taking the Line for a Walk: *In Form* to *Narralogues*, A History *in Medias Res*

Steve Tomasula

or to begin in the middle—"What is everyone everywhere all the time?" This is the "funnymental" question that drives Ronald Sukenick's *In Form: Digressions on the Act of Fiction* and his *Narralogues: Truth in Fiction*. And probably Ron Sukenick himself. For if, as Sukenick says, his work is an "ongoing conversation with himself" that readers are allowed to listen in on, what we hear in these two books is a demonstration of the centrality to literature of an inextricable link between form and experience (*In Form* xi). Not life experience, per se. Indeed, these two collections of prose on writing differ from other such books by offering little in the way of maxims or autobiography in "the writing life" even as they take up literary form in a variety of forums: art and the underground; film; the politics of language; and always, the relation of fiction, especially formally innovative fiction, to its wider culture.

Rather, *In Form* offers a "theory of composition . . . continuous with the art, leading into it and coming out of it without claiming any privilege of authority over the poems or fictions" it brings into being—a principle embodied in his "narralogues," which Sukenick defines as a synthesis of "narrative plus argument" (*In Form* ix–x; *Narralogues* 1). For the goal Sukenick sets out in these two books is to continue, not conclude. To continue means to reinvent, not emulate, and form is simply the manifestation of this process. In other words, experience is cognate with process and process is cognate with thought, with the self. Process that strives to achieve art is necessarily resistant to conventional thought, be it today's propaganda or yesteryear's form of the novel. "Experience" and therefore literary form is by nature, then, individual, i.e., by Sukenick's lights, unconventional.

This was a vital, if marginalized, conversation for anyone invested in the viability of literature at the time Sukenick began writing it down: back in the period when modernism was ending and with it modernist assumptions of the self and the aesthetics that art and literature rested upon; back when the increasing influence of mass-marketing on literature motivated Sukenick and other authors to bypass traditional publishing institutions by founding their own cooperative press; back when many authors were mourning what then seemed to be the exhaustion of literature: that is, the transition from high modernism to postmodernism dated here as 1972–85, the years in which the forward-looking essays of *In Form* were originally published. This conversation has grown in importance if only because the nascent trends in literature identified by *In Form* have themselves grown to maturation: a publishing industry dominated by a handful of conglomerates; a time that has seen a resurgence of the realist novel and autobiography even as the Modernist "self" has given way to the postmodernist "subject"; a time when the digitalization of culture and the rise of alternative media have forced conceptually-driven authors to reevaluate the value and form of the written word; a climate, in short, that has created a need for the retrospective look of *Narralogues: Truth in Fiction*, published in 2000.

"When I first started writing fiction," Sukenick states in *Narralogues*, "I had no sense that my writing career would span a breakthrough to a new rhetoric of narrative" (*In Form* 4). But it did. And therein lies the importance of *In Form* and *Narralogues*, a diptych of essays and narralogues addressed to a particularly American problem from a particularly American point of view. As Stanley Cavell has made the question of what it means to be a philosopher in America an inherent component of his intellectual project, so Sukenick has asked what it means to be a writer, especially an avant-garde writer, in America during the transition from modernism to postmodernism. Like Alain Robbe-Grillet's essays on the *nouveau roman* and its relation to French culture, Sukenick's insights on this transitory moment in literature are seminal. Unlike Robbe-Grillet, his revisitation of these insights well after the passing of the avant-garde offers a perspective that speaks to the role of any future literature of opposition in an era of corporate conglomeration and shifting aesthetics. That is, the Janus-like nature of the twenty-six prose pieces collected here forms a kind of history of what American "experimental" writers like Sukenick were reacting against, as well as a polemic for what literature with roots in the avant-

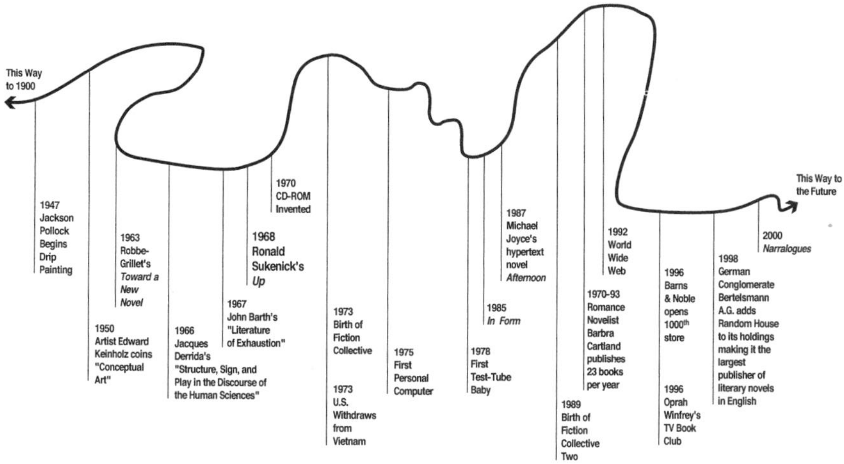

garde could become if it were to be more than reactionary. Put simply, in Sukenick's work we hear an avant-garde author at the collapse of modernism questioning the assumptions of his day by asking what form in the novel can mean. And he concludes that for literature to be vital, to become more than a commercial product, it is vital for authors to return to the fundamental nature of their medium: to write with a high awareness of the dual nature of the literary text as both an architecture of words and a performance of writing/reading.

The Sukenick Project/Aesthetic

Most of Sukenick's conclusions descend from his theory of composition, which circulates throughout the essays of *In Form*, and are revisited in *Narralogues*. In fact, it is only through the eternal return of formal issues and their bearing on politics, the underground, and other key Sukenick themes that one arrives at this theory. For theory should be "part of the story, rather than about it," Sukenick writes, typifying his dismissal of a writing theory apart from practice (*In Form* 5). In *In Form* his theory of composition is usually broached obliquely, and most clearly seen when in action, that is, when Sukenick performs his conception of theory and practice through their necessary fusion. Or as his essay/performance "The Finnegan Digression" first put it in the middle of *In Form*, written in the middle of his career in the in-between time of post- and modern:

<table>
<tr>
<td>
went down trucking
to the blah blah
zork uh uuh
onna saddy nite
and why not
lokka me ma ahma
vant gard a sperry
mentalist
w
  h
    e
      e
        e
          e
            but to
return to the nar
was there a nar uh yes
so I was out berg wat
chin ono dio glasses
train on thisyere two
f two faced dickey
and this was pitt. . . .
</td>
<td>
G
E
N
R
E
</td>
<td>
What is everyone everywhere all the time?
Finnegans Wake. The funnymental novel
of our error.
  What is it: myth, dream, vision joke?
The content of multiple myth (including
the private myth of James Joyce in person).
The techniques of dream. The omniscience
of vision. The tone of a joke. A sacre-
ligious joke. *The Bible,* starring
James Joyce as God the Father paring his
fingernails on the chamberpot while he makes.
Makes what? His mock-epic of creation in
one movement, bowel, macrocosm through
Mickrocosm. A dirty joke? It always
is. Is the novel out of ordure? Dream,
vision, joke? All of these? None of
these? Art is finally art, not second-
hand life. A record of creation (and
all of creation) is a bible. And a
bible is a book. And a book is just a
book. An edition to creation. Break
down restrictive ideas of fiction;
suggest concrete reality of book as
artifact.
</td>
</tr>
</table>

(*In Form* 99)

Written as a parody/homage to James Joyce's modernist icon, "The Finnegan Digression" is what Sukenick claims all written art must be—both theory and performance—or narralogue, a narrative fused to argument embodied in its form, one inseparable from the other. Strategically placed after *In Form's* discussion of the use of typographic play and the breakdown of genres, "The Finnegan Digression" functions as a pivot point between theory and practice by serving as, to use a central Sukenick Yeats-ism, both dance and dancer (*In Form* 227). Immediately we see the resistance to convention that is so central to Sukenick; it is there on a sentence-by-sentence level, embodied by this passage's resistance to be controlled, that is, quoted in the traditional academic style. As in much of Sukenick's work, any quote that doesn't include the white space is a misquote; to quote only the words (themselves a play of black and white space) is to separate the dance from dancer, to paint a still life in the original sense of the word: *natura mort*, i.e., dead nature.

Conversely, the heart of Sukenick's intellectual project is to unleash the life of a text, to let it be a bull in the china shop of conventional syntax and diction, both clown and scholar in Mikhail Bakhtin's carnival. The use of *jouissance* of the text, is not out of "ordure" as genres, sentences, even words break down. "If Stevens uses the phrase 'dew-dapper clapper-traps' to describe the lids of smokestacks," Sukenick writes in his essay "Wallace Stevens: Theory and Practice," it is because he likes the way it sounds regardless of its obscurity" (*In Form* 184). Clearly the same logic applies to Sukenick's own work. Moreover, the layers of meaning he evokes through an emphasis on the phonological quality of words is compounded by their status as visual objects. Conventional syntax departs the stage as sentences run diagonally down the page. In the above passage, for example, the word "GENRE" printed (vertically) between dominant, and gloss-like columns, invites the reader to read not just left to right, but also up and down and across columns. The architecture of the page forces readers to read in a nonlinear fashion, backtracking, retrofitting the pieces of text into "a web of interconnecting associations" or "attention structures" that pulls them to "a particular way of seeing things," as Sukenick describes this process of "narrative thinking" (*Narralogues* 72). Its presence changes the context in which the two columns are read, linking them in such a way that one changes the meaning of the other, and by so doing opens up a multiplicity of other meanings that simply wouldn't emerge had the text been laid out in straight lines. Thus experimental writing—"ahma vant gard a sperry mentalist"—is conceived as a GENRE. But GENRE also is the subject of the question, "What is it? . . . ." Through spatial play, these few lines take on the polysemous density of poetry, simultaneously asking: What is *Finnegans Wake*?; what is fundamental about the novel?; what is novel about our mistaken ideas of the novel?; what is experimental writing? It implies that *Finnegans Wake* is the fundamental novel of our times, seeing how it "went on trucking," spawning a tradition, including the "me" writing this "Finnegan Digression," which is an error, for this path, especially with the commercialization of literature and the exhaustion of the avant-garde, leads nowhere but down. So is it, like Bloom's bowel movement in *Ulysses*, a dirty joke by Joyce?—laid on all writers throughout posterity? Is the error in taking *Finnegans Wake* as a "funnymental" (fundamental? mentally funny?) bible. Or is our error in treating bibles as cookie-cutters on life and art instead of as guides back to the "nar"—narrative—the primal source of all bibles, including *Finnegans Wake*?

Of course, exegesis focused only on the artifact of the text expunges the fact that it is not only an artifact but, as Jerzy Kutnik points out, an experience (72). That is, exegesis of Sukenick's work is often an act of paraphrasing a joke. In place of belly laughs, the reader gets an explanation. What is also left out are the paths the reader's eye takes as he or she executes choices among possible readings. As Roland Barthes and others have shown, any act of reading is performative in that readers are always co-composers, bringing their own background and understanding to bear on textual meaning. But as exemplified in the "Finnegan Digression," Sukenick's columns and word games and spatial arrangement of type make the readerly performance gymnastic. While readers execute linguistic flips (puns) and somersaults (assonance) and sssssplits (onomatopoeia), they can't help but become aware of their role as co-author, a role easily submerged in the traditional "readerly" text, to uses Barthes's term (4). Since the "writerly" function of the reader is much of the subject of the Sukenick text, moving through the space of the page, i.e., reading, becomes its performance. Sukenick's analogy of dance and dancer for this process is well chosen, for reading this work is like waltzing with its author—a movement through narrative time and space. But there is another level to this analogy in terms of its composition.

Theories of Composition

Just as the reader is in effect assembling pieces of a collage in a writerly manner, so Sukenick, in his role as author, composes the novel through improvisation and collage as he tries, and fails, to keep up with his own thoughts (*In Form* 86–87). In the manner of M. H. Abrams's formulation of poetry genres, Sukenick lays out in his "Thirteen Digressions" a taxonomy of the controlling ideas authors employ when imagining a text. Like Abrams, he labels them imitative, expressive, illuminating, and adds generative. One by one he dismisses the first three as modes of mimesis, out of step with contemporary culture. Imitative theories of composition, he explains, the most pervasive and deeply embedded of these, make of the novel a second-hand view, a counterfeit in the Platonic sense of the poem as a simulacrum of reality, rather than a bit of reality real in its own right (*In Form* 22). Expressive theories, or more accurately, self-expression as in the confessional or autobiographic novel, are other distorting mirrors in that they place the self at the center of a world rather than incorporating personal experience into fiction "at the same level as any other data" (*In Form* 24). Self-expression, he claims, is another version of Narcissus, transfixed by his own reflection to the exclusion of everything else: a view that rings particularly hollow when "all over the world societies are moving more in the direction of collectivization instead of individualism" (*In Form* 124). At the other pole, novels of illumination in a world where Reality has become "realities" can only illuminate other mirrors. Or nothingness. "Even for Joyce," he writes, "epiphany becomes inadequate as first social reality, then culture," dissolving as it does into the language of *Finnegans Wake*. Still, he continues, "it may be that the mind at its most illumined confronting the world at its most obscure is able to generate extensions of experience that alter and unify the field of experience itself" (*In Form* 27–28). And this, he asserts, is the beginning of a generative theory of composition and its interdependent form.

The Geometry of Generative Composition

Form to Sukenick is a way of thinking that contrasts with formulas, or techniques for writing. He draws on Emerson's conception of form as "a manner of thought so 'passionate and alive' that it creates 'an architecture of its own, and adorns nature with a new thing' " (*In Form* xv). Although the affinities between *In Form* and Robbe-Grillet's *For a New Novel* are many, he cites a variety of influences for his theory itself, especially those where, as in Ezra Pound's *The Cantos*, "the continuity of art and experience . . . is so obvious" (*In Form* 17). The influence of Jackson Pollock's action paintings as a "record of his own composition" is also so evident in Sukenick's theory of composition that his texts can be thought of as an attempt to execute abstract expressionism in prose (*In Form* 228). He also cites Paul Klee "taking the line for a walk"; Charlie Parker's jazz improvisation; Charles Olson's projective verse; Laurence Sterne's composition by "digression"; John Cage's "open-ended, chance [musical] composition"; William S. Burroughs' cut-up method of composition; Allen Ginsberg's "exploitation of his own personality in his poems"; Jack Kerouac's "Essentials of Spontaneous Prose," William Carlos Will-

Influences on Sukenick's Theory of Composition:
1. Abstract Expressionism; 2. Nouveau Roman; 3. Automatic Writing; 4. Klee's Line; 5. Sterne's Line; 6. Skyline of Rome; 7. Jazz Improvisation; 8. Spontaneous Prose; 9. Finnegans Fake; 10. Ideograms; 11. The Tape Recorder; 12. Dance/Dancer; 13. The Bossa Nova; 14. Hieroglyphics; 15. The Beats/Underground.

iams, Jack Spicer, Robert Duncan—Sukenick acknowledges his debt to a number of poets, but especially Wallace Stevens (*In Form* 227, 148, 18, 21, 18–19).

"For Stevens," Sukenick writes, "poetry is a way of saying things in which the way of saying yields the meaning and in which the way of saying is more important than, but indistinguishable from, the thing said." In this manner, according to Sukenick, poetic imagination was for Stevens, not so much a "way of creating, but of knowing." The poem offers a persuasive way to think about reality by offering up a persuasive way of looking at a pre-existing, if often chaotic reality. The poem, then, is foremost an " 'act of mind' "(*In Form* 176–79, 17).

More specifically, Sukenick makes the text into a nexus between the mind of the reader and that of the author. Working back from the poem to the mind of the author, he extends this conception of poetry into a theory of composition for himself as novelist. Following Stevens's lead, he sees the text as a vehicle to show "how abstractions operate in experience, how they transmute, how they contradict one another, how they repeat and vary and interact with other kinds of experience, how they feel" (*In Form* 17). That is, at the heart of any story is the story of how it "embodies the progression of the mind as it confronts and affects experience" (*In Form* 14). He privileges "unmediated experience without intervention of premeditated form"—"pre-established order" as Robbe-Grillet called it—over the widespread practice of casting new thought in pre-existing molds, e.g., the conventions of the realist novel (*In Form* 17, Robbe-Grillet 73). His is a literature of "non-constraint," then, and the reason is simple: " 'Nature does not use *pi*,' " Sukenick explains, quoting Hugh Kenner (*In Form* 28). Bubbles and other spheres are generated by the play of forces, not their description by theorists. Likewise, the novel is only a true product of its generative force, the force of an author's thoughts, when its form both generates and is generated by the text, embodied thought. The activity of writing generates its own problems and solutions, or as he says of Stevens, "the mind orders reality not by imposing ideas on it but by discovering significant relationships within it, as the artist abstracts and composes the elements of reality in significant integrations that are works of art" (*In Form* 28, 171). By so doing it becomes a movement both from and into "fuller consciousness" (*In Form* 87). When form is instead treated as *a priori,* be it the fixed forms of a sonnet, or the conventions of the realist novel, the work suffers. Poems become petty entertainments, novels a form of escapism.

Conversely, when an author allows form to mirror thought, the page becomes a "record . . . of the way the mind works, the way we experience things, including the way we experience creative thought" (*In Form* 29). The novel written in this fashion becomes not an imitation of the world, or a form of escapism from it, but a force in the way that other texts, laws for example, or the Declaration of Independence, effect the real lives of real people. Because, in this view, the experience of composition is allowed to become a part of whatever other story is told, because form is the embodiment of thought, and because experience is inherently unique, the story that emerges from this generative theory of composition inherently breaks down the "old fictions, the old constructs"—the metaphoric formulations of reality that may have served previous generations well but are no longer valid. Or as he tells Larry McCaffery in *In Form's* extended interview:

> It's like cutting a log in a new direction: a new grain opens up, literally a new content appears when you cut something in a new way from the way it usually gets cut. You see different things; words then begin to surrender their meanings in different ways and begin to reveal all that huge amount of accumulated wisdom that language contains from the whole history of the culture. (110)

The Novel as Conceptual Art: The Nexus of Epistemology/Artifact/Performance

For Sukenick, there's a clear answer to the question, If a tree falls in the forest and there's no one there to hear, does it make any sound? The answer is in both the falling and the log:

<table>
<tr>
<td>. . . is with stale
matzoballs that
Dooky ordered spe
cial from Rapopor
ts I tella you
this man stop at
nothing senor one
time traveling wi
a french pimp in
the Yucatan got a
terrible yen for
a blow job surrou . . .</td>
<td>V
E
R
Y</td>
<td>S
I
M
I
L
I
T
U
D
E</td>
<td>Finnegans Fake: is it real?
It's not imitation. It's life in
process, thought in process, process
in process. But not real life—it's
static: the more it changes the more
it stays the same. If it moves it's
alive, if it stays still it's art.
If it does both it's Finnegans Wake.
It's a fake. But it inCORPorates. A
symbol indicates, a pun inCORPorates.
Some business. Is this corpse dead?
Wake up. Similitude? Very.</td>
</tr>
</table>

(*In Form* 100)

Narrative is how humans relate to the world, Sukenick explains, with the novel in particular being a main vehicle for this "normal . . . epistemological procedure" (*In Form* 153). Its "compelling statements" are the means by which humans organize the chaos of the world into some sense (*In Form* 171). Or, as critic Joseph Tabbi reminds us, the novel is the vehicle best suited to "organizing vast amounts of information into patterns possessing cognitive value and coherence" (3). Conversely, Sukenick writes, the blank page is "the void where everything is called into question" (*In Form* 15). Thus the novel becomes "the most self-conscious of forms," the "most supple and powerful replay technology," as well as "an instrument for arguing truth" (*In Form* 87, *Narralogues* 4). Its power derives not only from its ability to relate intricate social, linguistic, and ontological relationships in coherent patterns, but its ability to shape content so that reading is a reenactment of those relationships. The novel is suited to its role as epistemological laboratory, then, because every novel serves as its own best example: every novel embodies, not just holds, a way of understanding. Every reader approaches this example *experientially* as well as intellectually. Experiencing the world through a book is experiencing the world as it is construed by that book. Being persuaded by a novel means being persuaded by the novel to accept the world as figured by the assumptions inherent in the novel's form, to share its "attention structure," as Sukenick puts it, where the "argument is the action," the "story line . . . a form of reasoning" (*Narralogues* 70, 71, 3).

Here he echoes Robbe-Grillet's belief that narrative structure cannot be considered apart from the "anecdote it serves to report" (*In Form* 41). In his novel *The Tunnel*, William Gass makes a similar point about form and content by asking if it is possible to write a tragedy in limerick. The difficulty in doing so is the reason Dennis Barone claims that "every realist work is conservative no matter who writes it"—a direct way to phrase Sukenick's skepticism of the efficacy of radical content in conservative form: the attempt by authors to effect change in perception by depicting the world through ready-made templates, be they the conventions of the realist novel or the stock importation into literature of jazz improvisation (*In Form* 172, 118). Instead, he claims, attention to the relation between form and the experiential component of reading reveals how conventional forms encourage conventional thought: reading any novel written in traditional form is to reenact traditional assumptions as to how the world is construed, e.g. a belief in closure a reader might *experience* by being able to, through a character, draw the disparate details of a fictive world into a rational conclusion. Or faith in common-sense empiricism, as for example, readers might reenact by implicitly putting trust in what a character learns through sense perception.

Conversely, the "normal" orientation for an author, as it is for a philosopher, as it is for a scientist, is toward innovation. They don't call it "novel" for nothing, he writes, dismissing categories such as "experimental" out of a belief that all artistic work is an experiment in so far as it is art and not mere craft or entertainment. In individual works, then, authors are always in the process of redefining the novel—or at least they should be. As a genre, the novel is perpetually in the process of being redefined—if, as Sukenick maintains, form carries the burden of expressing (or of creating) the relationship between people and their world. If the world changes, so must our expression of it. If the novel is to be the vehicle for this expression, its form must evolve or die. For like the scientist, historian or philosopher, the novelist formulates "contingent statements about the world . . . whose main virtue is that they displace even more contingent . . . statements while at the same time recognizing their own contingency" (*Narralogues* 71). In a reciprocal exchange with being in the world, the author takes his or her cue from the world and hands back a world remade.

It's not difficult to see an agreement between a number of early modern authors and Sukenick's articulation of the relationship of form to world. Yet by 1968, the year Sukenick published his first novel *Up*, the modernist insistence on inner consciousness as the ultimate yardstick had begun to seem as out of touch with the world as the picaresque plot was to José Ortega y Gasset. This modernist orthodoxy, i.e., the "new conventional novel," did mirror a reality, Sukenick wrote of the novel at this time, but "things did not seem to happen to me the way they happened in [those] books . . ." (*Narralogues* 5). That is, to Sukenick the then dominant modernist form had come to seem as rigid and artificial as the grid lines of perspective painting to a surrealist; just as eighteenth century conventions of novelistic form began to slew out of synch with a society impacted by the telephone and the assembly line, the modernist novel that supplanted it had in turn became an anachronistic tradition in a society that was becoming organized, as Sukenick says of his novel *Long Talking Bad Conditions Blues*, around:

> discontinuity, interactivity, ellipse, eclipse, non-sequitur, incompletion, association, chance, coincidence, achronicity, synchronicity, improvisation, intervention, self-contradiction, overlap, mosaic, modularity, graphic composition, sonic formation, rhythmic symmetry, vortextualization and eddyfication, rhizomatic interconnection, hypertextual hopscotch,

> paradox, wordplay, and in conclusion, inconclusion, all of it fluctuating faster than thought. (*Narralogues* 19)

Or, as Sukenick states early in *In Form*, "the traditional novel is a metaphor for a society that no longer exists" (3).

The American New Novel

While some critics mourned the corpse the novel had become, others had given up on its relevance in an age of film and television. Marshall McLuhan among others proclaimed an end to not just the novel, but the whole Gutenberg galaxy. Yet Sukenick characterizes this time as a moment of exciting possibility, noting that "genre is traditional," i.e., a matter of how literary conventions were conceived, while "medium is technological" (88). If the novel were to reinvent itself, as he maintained every novel that aspires to art must, it would have to do so by revisiting these two defining characteristics—the tradition that allowed some works, but not others, to be thought of as "novels," and the nature of the novel as a print medium. The two were interrelated with the possibility of both being expanded, not narrowed, by technology. In fact, he writes, "this is typically what happens when a new medium is introduced. The new medium . . . creates more options, and the older ones become more essentialized because they no longer need to be concerned with what the new mediums do better. Monet didn't stop painting with the advent of photography and take up the camera," for example, "he just became more painterly" (*Narralogues* 43).

Drawing a parallel between the collapse of illusionistic space in painting and the collapse of illusionistic time in realist fiction, he effectively noted that once mimetic representation ceased being a valid goal for painters, painters began to work against the illusion of space in their canvases in two ways. Some flattened the surface, bringing into existence cubism and other forms of abstract painting. Others moved off the canvas completely, thereby ushering in performance art, earth art, body art, and a variety of other nontraditional genres. Both trajectories were significant to Sukenick.

Why should the novel be limited to pages, he asked, any more than visual art was limited to hanging on a wall? Anticipating electronic books, books on the Internet and CD-ROM, he wrote "if electronics discovers a technique (through a laser disc system perhaps) might it not also be possible to incorporate the moving image?" (*In Form* 97). Apparently having taken note of movements such as Fluxus in the visual arts, he envisioned novels "printed on scrolls, on gloves, on moebius strips . . . on video tape, or acted on stage" (*In Form* 204). In his essay "The New Tradition" he concluded that "to complain that the novel can't escape its binding . . . is like complaining that the mind can't escape from its skull" (*In Form* 206). But given the existence of film and theater, this was also to ask, why work in print at all? What justified printed novels?

The answer was revealed partly by the fact that what some authors were doing in the novel, e.g. scenic description, could be done better in film. To state the matter bluntly, "The pleasure of description in the novel is the pleasure of linguistic skill, not that of genre painting," i.e., whatever it was that distinguished "literature" from "writing" was in the language (*In Form* 31). Furthermore, "once the 'mirror of reality' argument for fiction crumbles, possibilities long submerged in our tradition open up, and in fact a new rationale for fiction becomes necessary" (*Narralogues* 3). His innovation was to take this starting point as a way to think the novel through as a medium. To recognize the hypertextual nature inherent in this medium and how a conception of print as a medium could maximize this potential. As he explains in his "Film Digression," the "technology of the page is still more powerful than any other, including that of the computer, for communicative and creative purposes in language because of the page's 'retrieval system,' scanning, paging, availability visually of information through simple eye movement on any page in any order" (*In Form* 97). Anticipating scrolling with a mouse, hotlinks, and other characteristics of the hypertext novel, he continues:

> what about an electronic scroll . . . whose configuration could be changed [to examine] . . . a macrosection projected onto a larger broadsheet or, at the other pole, could be broken down into fiche for detailed examination of another kind, fiche that could contain segments of information of any size, from paragraph to sentence to word to syllable? Suppose we could arrive at the electronic equivalent of a page with its concrete material advantages and still under the control of the eye and hand moving in any direction at any speed at the will of the reader, either in successive stills or in controllable motion depending on the pace and purpose desired? (97)

The importance here isn't the physical mechanics of reading (a justification made problematic, in any case, by empirical studies) so much as the recognition of what was essential in reading. Like impressionist painters who decided that what was essential about their art wasn't the mimetic representation of fields but the fleeting impression of those fields on the mind, Sukenick concluded that what was essential to the novel was the mind in the process of composing the novel: a "record—not of 'reality'—but of the way the mind works" (*In Form* 29). Like abstract painters who decided that what was essential about painting was paint, Sukenick concluded that what was essential to the novel was its materials—thought embodied as language: the broadsheet of the mind, the scrolling capacity of the mind, the ability to quickly zoom in or zoom out. And all at the reader's whim.

Gertrude Stein's effort to capture "moments of consciousness" echo here. But Sukenick cites an American source even closer to home. Calling action painting the fundamental artistic development of the second half of the century, he saw in it qualities that could be brought into the novel, especially its ability to situate the art act within the world (*In Form* 121–22). Jackson Pollock didn't want to paint nature, he wanted to "be nature." Conversely, referring to his attempts to embody experience in his paintings, Pollock also claimed to want the viewer to "lose himself in their delirium" (Hughes 486; Sandler 111). Rather than bringing to his painting "a subject matter or preconceived idea," he wanted to make the world immediate in the paint by remaining receptive to "what the painting has to offer. The more immediate the artist works with the material," he said, "the . . . greater the possibilities of making a direct . . . statement. . . ." (Pollock 23–24). For Sukenick, this was a reality and a statement that pigment in genre painting could only indicate—a reality that Sukenick believed the novel should make immediate on the page. Like Pollock, his goal was to subvert any tendency of a viewer/reader to get lost in a "quasi hypnotic level of the make

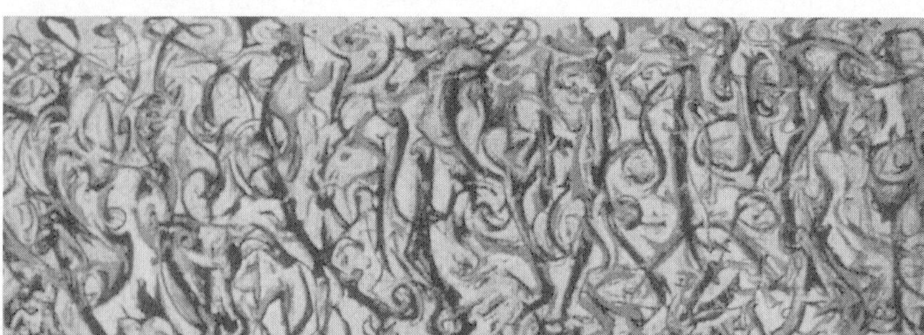

Jackson Pollock, *Mural*, 1943 (detail). The University of Iowa Museum of Art. Gift of Peggy Guggenheim (1959.6), copyright The University of Iowa Museum of Art. Photo: Steve Tatum.

believe" (*Narralogues* 3). Like Pollock he saw that a way to do so was by making the page/window opaque. For as Sukenick writes: "Opacity implies that we should direct our attention to the surface of a work, and such techniques as graphics and typographical variation, in calling the reader's attention to the technological reality of the book, are useful in keeping his or her mind on that surface instead of undermining it with profundities" (*In Form* 212).

That is, if mimesis is best left to genre painters, the movies and antique novels, if the point of a novel is to serve as a record of how the mind thinks, and by so doing trigger thought in the reader, this record would have to be abstract—the way an action painting could only represent a trace of the painter's thought by ensuring that a viewer couldn't use it as a window on the world, directing the viewer's gaze to a "place" other than the paint. On this point, Sukenick quotes an insightful example from William Gass:

> Think, for instance, of a striding statue; imagine the purposeful inclination of the torso, the alert and penetrating gaze of the head and its eyes, the outstretched arm and pointing finger; everything would appear to direct us toward some goal in front of it. Yet our eye travels only to the finger's end, and not beyond. Though pointing, the finger bids us stay instead, and we journey slowly back along the tension of the arm. In our hearts we know what actually surrounds the statue. The same surrounds every other work of art: empty space and silence. (*In Form* 38)

Similarly, Sukenick came to see novels as "concrete objects"—a type of objectivist prose. A novel was a thing the reader actually holds in his or her hands. It should also be a part of the reader's actual experience, and not a facsimile of some exterior reality, negating its status as print by inviting readers to enter a dream state as does the traditional novel in which the story is conceived of as a kind of virtual reality that lulls readers into forgetting that the words they are reading are a construction on a page. Or as he put it, as in action painting, "the truth of the page is on top of it, not underneath or over at the library" (*In Form* 212).

Unlike the paint in an action painting, or the bronze of a statue, though, the materials of novels—its words—are inherently referential. "Reference," Sukenick writes, is what "language couldn't avoid," even if "representation was quite another—mimetic—matter" (*Narralogues* 63). So the essential novel was to him essentially split, given that its materials had a dual nature as both a graphic shape and a semantic entity—two qualities at war. We may encounter every book, as Michel Butor says, as a diptych, its left-hand page, separated by a gutter from its other panel, the right-hand page (55). But to take note of this formal quality, the reader has to suspend reading. Likewise, considering the printed word as a visual shape, a graphic entity, necessitates that the forward motion of the narrative stops. Or as Simonides noted, a poem is a speaking painting, whereas a painting is a mute poem (Mitchell 192). Yet as Joseph Frank points out, this division is permeable, with paintings often suggesting temporality, whereas literature incorporates "painterly" elements, such as description, which arrest the forward motion of the story (Klinkowitz 37–38).

The key for Sukenick was to transform "the visual element of fiction from an implicit and inert compositional factor to an expressive one" (*In Form* 45). To do so he sought to acknowledge the visual nature of the printed word without mistaking language as a visual medium, as do the authors of Concrete Poetry, or "Cement Poetry," as Sukenick calls what he sees as a confusion of the essential nature of language by the attempt to make it into a literal picture. What was needed instead was a way to make page arrangement and the visual aspects of print foreground the "discursive aspect of language" (*In Form* 45).

An insight into how this could be achieved is an ur moment in Sukenick's own creation myth of himself as an author. Specifically, he relates sitting at his desk when "for no good reason" he "wrote a line":

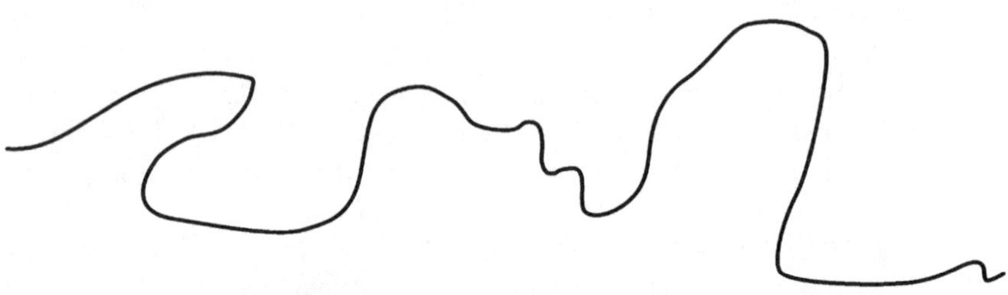

At first, he relates, "he didn't know what he meant." But then he realized that the line itself was what he meant: "It was about freedom." A freedom related to the absolute freedom valorized by abstract expressionists. It represented "freedom for the writer and liberation for the reader"—a Stern-like breakout from the dictates of justified type, an opening up of the semantic field of the novel to non-linguistic elements. He continues:

> It [also] graphed a moment of violent emotion, of quick ups and downs in feeling, of radical instability . . . a profile . . . of Lyndon B. Johnson about whom he had violent feelings because this was written at the height of the Vietnam war. . . . the Western landscape . . . and on and on. . . . What it all came to . . . was that there is such a thing as writing without language, and that . . . this writing without language is even a significant part of writing in language . . . The look of writing is part of its meaning. It's part of the argument. (*Narralogues* 82–84)

This epiphany in which Sukenick recognized the potential for a semiotic reading of form led him to ask, "Isn't it about time to broaden the frame of reference we're used to in written language to include the range of meaning that graphics can refer to?" (*Narralogues* 84). Poets have always used the white space of the page to "score written language" for reading, as Sukenick puts it—but we often think of their use of space as stanzas, not the architecture of an artifact (*In Form* 96). According to him, this is what Pound meant in regard to Chinese ideograms, or "e.e. cummings with his page arranged poems," or John Cage's "nonsyntactical 'demilitarized' language" (*In Form* 84, Rasula and McCaffery 281). Aligning his own novels within this tradition, he summarizes Sharon Spencer's rationale for what she calls the "architectonic" novel, the novel characterized by the spatialization of its form:

> the spatialization of form serves as an alternative to the old novel's sequential organization in plot and narrative. Through such techniques as juxtaposition and manipulation of the print on the space of the page, the novelist can create a structure which communicates by means of pattern rather than sequence in a manner approaching the plastic arts. (*In Form* 204)

By using spatial arrangement as an element of rhetoric, Sukenick believed, the novel could approach the richness and fluidity of thought. The novel itself would be a hybrid where the visual aspect of the text modifies meaning. To do so, the novel would have to be abstract even though it retained its discursive nature. It must retain its discursive function—being careful to not cross over into the visual arts—because the mind is discursive. Furthermore, it must be read, as opposed to heard, since a true essentialized system of writing would be "abstract enough to bypass speech and get directly into an extension of the process of thinking" (*In Form* 94). He quotes Burroughs: '"The study of hieroglyphic language shows us that the [written] word is an image. . . . However, there is an important difference between a hieroglyphic and syllabic language . . . . A syllabic language forces you to verbalize in auditory patterns. A hieroglyphic language does not' " (*In Form* 95). The lesson Sukenick draws here is that by breaking the link to sound, a reader's mind would naturally form thought at a pre-auditory level. For an author working in English, this meant a return to the fact that the essential novel was discursive and spatial. If it wasn't discursive, then the author would be better off writing expressionist poetry or creating visual art. If a novel's meaning wasn't dependent on its status as text, that is, if the discourse wasn't spatial, but auditory, then film or theater would be a more fitting medium. Only writing that draws on its nature as a graphic entity, only writing that has "severed . . . its relations with the auditory world" can be "abstract enough to bypass speech and get directly into an extension of the process of thinking" (*In Form* 95, 94). Only a reader moving spatially around a page, not compelled to "pronounce," even silently, the fleeting connections of mind will allow word combinations to offer up cascades of associations without the intermediate modulations of sound. Thus, in an essential novel, i.e., a novel that draws its power from its essential nature, language is primary, and "words should no more have a sound than images" (*In Form* 94).

Music without sound, Mallarmé's conception of the musician who bypasses "the senses as much as possible to address the mind more directly," serves as Sukenick's ideal model for literature as well: " 'Reading creates a solitary, tacit concert played in the mind, which grasps its meaning through the slightest vibration. . . . Poetry close to the idea is music *par excellence*' " (*In Form* 98).

With the eye ranging over the page the way it might move across a painting, the text becomes more fluid, more dependent on a reader who is engaged in thinking as opposed to one who is immersed in thought. Quoting Emerson, Sukenick characterizes thought as " 'a prison . . . because thought, once formulated, becomes an impediment to thinking,' " whereas the goal of his New Novel was to keep thought (and therefore meaning) perpetually "in process" (*Narralogues* 63–64). Like the drips in an action painting, the word play of an abstract novel encapsulated for Sukenick what he saw as an "essential story" of all fiction: the story of "motion and stasis" (*In Form* 9)—just as Robbe-Grillet before him concluded that the interest of description is no longer the thing described but the movement of the description (147–48). Indeed, although Sukenick's New Novel is generated by the associations of the author, it is composed as a structure that will exploit the fact that its materials, words, as Cary Nelson notes, preceded any one novel and therefore conjure all sorts of associations outside the text (Nelson, in Klinkowitz 37). By using spatial arrangement to organize these materials, reading becomes more flexible than it can be when a reader's eyes are compelled to ride the Gutenberg rails of type set in straight lines. The text becomes more hypertextual as readers arrange and rearrange textual elements of the page and new patterns offer up new associations. The words form a matrix that forces readers to actively engage with the text rather than passively absorb the meaning an author has preordained.

As Robbe-Grillet championed the *nouveau roman* as a novel of pure surfaces, "fiction as fiction," an entity in its own right, Sukenick championed this American New Novel as "the river rather than its containing banks": both a "concrete structure and an imaginative structure"—a novel that is essentially both a process and artifact (101, 204–05):

dialects of demo
tic Afrikaans tha
mean ladies crapp
er get the scene
blug zork well I
was told he was a
charming swine bu
turn out he wasn'
t charming prego
urp outrageous my
dear suked over b
a tamarind tree y
darn and now to t
a ttack tic attic
webby old bottles
dead love notes o
costumes granpa
brani granulated
by voyage at end
wavign cane I tel
you boy we're not
going to stand fo
this kinda thing . . .

NEW NOVEL

Yes or no?
Not either/or, but/and. Indeterminate
meaning = multiple possibility. Don't
negate, include. Synthesize, don't
anal lies. Simultaneous multiplicity.
Say yes. Anyone can do it. It's a dead
end that implies a new beginning, aWake.

LANGUAGE

What's it made of?
Words. Not narrative. Not description.
Not observation. Not characterization.
Not comment. Not detail. Words. The
river rather than its containing banks,
the water rather than its course, which
is in any case circular. The Medium
itself, language, words as concrete
objects. A cure for schizophrenia:
no more division between abstraction
and sensation, thinking and feeling.
Word as magic. Language is a thing to
be seen and heard, is real, not facsimile.
(*In Form* 101)

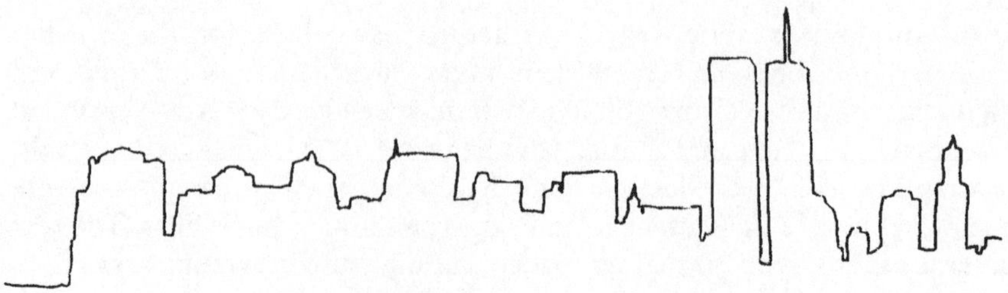

The Skyline of Wall Street, or Literary Markets and the Politics of the Bossa Nova

Sukenick's emphasis in the New Novel on the individual, his insistence that "every form" of the novel "should be idiosyncratic," that the novel was that "instrument that undercuts official versions of reality" carries with it an assumption that aesthetics are political. It arises from an assumption that individual readers would appropriate this form in order to invent their own worlds, and this stance puts it inherently at odds with mainstream, i.e., commercial literature (*In Form* 67). The politics in his theory of composition come partly from his belief in a "necessary conflict between art and the status quo" (*In Form* xix). That art conceived as business as usual isn't art at all but decoration or entertainment, or less benignly, an endorsement of conformity. More generally, he writes that the politics of the New Novel are the politics implicit in the aesthetics of the Bossa Nova, or the lifestyle of hippies, beats and the underground—an implicit questioning of who owns the rule book, who owns the language—a politics that works against the poetics of the minuet, mass market, mass politics, or any heuristic for thought that strives to bring individuality into the fold of group think. Thus he takes to task critics like Gerald Graff who attack poststructuralism for eroding authority, claiming that this leads to totalitarianism. Isn't it the reverse, Sukenick asks, "acceptance of political dogma and consumerist cliché?" (*In Form* 235). In America, he argues, this could be understood as the dogma *of* consumerism—the continual pressure on Americans by their culture to make their reality "a corporate one, mediated by the profit drive . . . in almost every aspect . . ." (*Narralogues* 57). A formulation in which realist novels participate, even those that espouse radical content.

"Giving a bad conscience to the literature of mass consumption" has always been one role of the "avant-garde" according to Robbe-Grillet (26). To see the degree to which Sukenick's New Novel was an extension of this aspect of the avant-garde in America one only needs to note the contrast between it and the state of the novel at the time of *Narralogues*. At the turn of this century, conventional realism comprises the basis for the novels that dominate bestseller lists, literary reviews, and course curriculums. Although their authors often exhibit a high interest in craft, typically the work exhibits little interest in formal innovation. It is as if, Sukenick says, authors today were engaged in a "counter-revolution of the oldfangled" (*In Form* 209).

If the novel were no more than entertainment, its homogenization into an easily consumed product would be of no more consequence than any matter of taste or fashion. But if as Sukenick argues, aesthetics serve class interests, then a literature grounded in " 'standards' based on the clichés of consumer manipulation and the static effect of tradition" is a political issue for everyone (*In Form* 67). It becomes a code that "might be in the interest of some literary people to maintain, and of others to break," some literary people being everyone involved in the "circumstances of publication, the publishing situation, the condition of the market, the structure of production and distribution, socioeconomic and political considerations" that come to bear on "literary composition, style, criticism, literary history and evaluation" (*In Form* 49).

As the influence of mass marketing bore down on the idiosyncratic novel, the conception of the literary began to shift. And shift according to parameters other than literary ones, as Sukenick notes, especially when the literary parameters they moved away from questioned the status quo (*Narralogues* 62). Books that defy genre categories, as Sukenick claims all quality books do, also defy marketing categories for, from the publishing industry's perspective, what is required is a "language and form that is standardized so that it can be merchandised to the largest number of people" (*In Form* 33, 35). As "nonstandard" novels vanish from the stores, novels that do translate easily into movies or mass paperback sales come to be thought of as literature; thus, as Sukenick concludes, "no one takes novels seriously until they become movies, which is to say no one takes novels seriously" (*In Form* 241). In fact, Sukenick writes, when it comes to publishing, "literary values are besides the point" (*In Form* 55). But more to his point, and indeed the importance of his work "in the margins of literature," is his core belief that:

> the validation of serious fiction as against the flood of junk from the conglomerate entertainment giants is not an 'academic' matter to me. I am not engaged in a theoretical struggle with imaginary windmills but in an uneven battle with real monsters. This kind of battle, fought by too few against odds that are too great, has real consequences in determining whether a free intellectual discourse will be able to continue in this country. (*Narralogues* 6–7)

Once you begin to examine how contingent reality can be, he tells Abádi-Nagy, then claims for realism are revealed to be not about reality but authority. In other words, "the going literary forms" don't represent reality so much as they represent the power of the "status quo" (*In Form* 147, *Narralogues* 5). It is only by acknowledging this actuality, he argues, that we can begin "dealing with our fate in a much more direct way." That we can begin "talking about who controls our imaginations or what controls our imaginations, what has the authority to do so, whether it is proper authority, whether we want it to control our imaginations" (*In Form* 147). Yet seeing the glass half full, he concluded that by acknowledging the subtle though powerful politics of the marketplace, the "closing [of] the market to quality books," did not necessarily have to be all bad—and in fact could mean in Emerson's words, '"freedom from baser places."' At the least it represented a recognition of the fact that "the democratic impulse of our literary populism matches all too well the common denominator marketing necessities of publishing conglomerates"—and the consequences for literature inherent in mass publishing (*In Form* 52, xiv). It made clear the consequences for individual expression, and the importance of individual response.

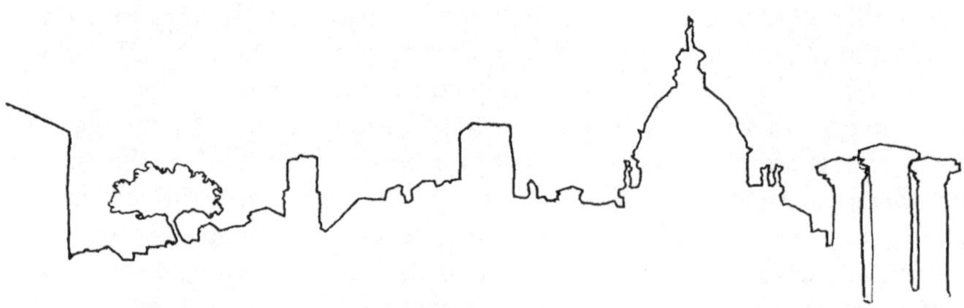

The Skyline of Rome, or to Continue, not to Conclude

Near the end of *Narralogues*, Sukenick as a character in his own work looks out over the skyline of Rome and sees the history of civilization in bricks: "a history of voracious looting and scavenging, culture feeding on itself in a progressive comedy of transformation, the spoils of conquest ornamenting the Roman Empire, Roman columns used to build Christian churches, Romanesque frescos ripped off for Baroque buildings, the Pantheon robbed to decorate St. Peter's, antique monuments as marble quarries for newer palazzi" (*Narralogues* 113). But despite the soot-blackened statues and losses he also sees "something vivacious" about this "ongoing cultural cannibalism"—the "vitality of an ecosystem that . . . flourishes by feeding on itself, every loss representing also a gain" (*Narralogues* 114). And likewise, it is not a good idea to force a consistency upon Sukenick that does not exist.

The cannibalism is certainly there; the "skyline" he drew at the inception of his Ur myth is a first cousin to the case for freedom Corporal Trim makes in *Tristram Shandy* by using his cane to write a flourish in the air that Sterne records as:

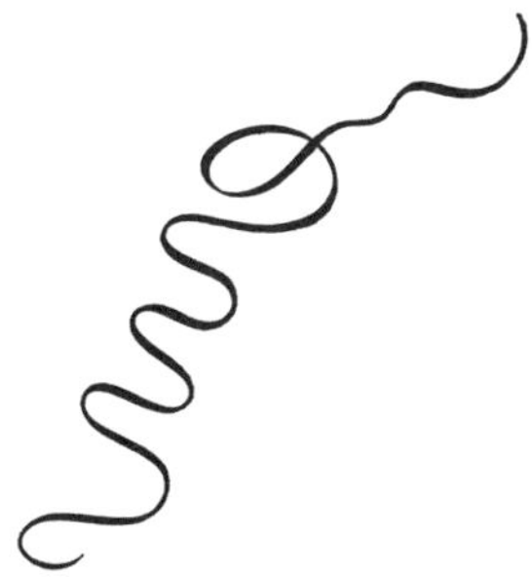

(629)

So are Sukenick's digressions—beginning with, as he is first to point out, the "Laurencesternean" subtitle of *In Form* (*Narralogues* 76). As a Beatrice-like character in his own work, he leads his fictionalized protégé Waldo through *Narralogues*, explaining, "That was the way it was supposed to work. . . . You take some predecessor's way of working the material, and maybe the material itself, and you work it your own way" (*Narralogues* 80). Indeed, in this archeology, Sukenick's collected writings on the novel becomes the jawbone of an evolutionary link. It exhibits too many affinities with modernist assumptions to be squarely postmodern: affinities with "happenings" and action painting, for example, or a dependence on schizophrenia as an operative metaphor, growing as it does from a modernist assumption of an essential individuality—even as he tries to use the self as a socially constructed conduit through which culture speaks itself. Yet as Sukenick repeatedly stresses, he works from experience, and since his experience is of the same world that poststructuralist thinkers experience, they both deal with many of the same critical issues, the difference being that his examination is conducted through his fiction.

That is, despite its modernist affinities, *In Form* works against a modernist aesthetic, placing an emphasis on diegesis at the expense of mimesis while eschewing hermeticism, psychological depth, and many of the other characteristics associated with many modernist works. His displacement of the modernist self as the center of the novel by the postmodern subject especially looks forward to the period of literature first intimated in *In Form*. The ramifications for form, namely his insistence that fiction is a form of argument, not "dramatic representation," and the consequent return to the "rhetorical tradition" in fiction is, by *Narralogues*, perhaps the defining characteristic of the postmodern novel (*Narralogues* 4). His insistence on the endless mutability of the novel, the role of form in the novel, and the case he makes for the novel's resistance to the homogenization of culture—an insistence that "marketplace success" shouldn't be confused with "artistic success"—is perhaps the single most important case that can be made today for the novel as an art form (*Narralogues* 62).

And what was the point?—not to be postmodern. Not to be anything. "The point," as Waldo figures it, "was to move progressively into virgin territory where there were no rules, where a practice was not yet a discipline" (*Narralogues* 74). Listening in on Sukenick's conversations with himself that make up these two books, the reader comes to understand that the point of this progression is not to "make it new," to resurrect the avant-garde, or improvise for improvisation's sake—"all that old beatnik stuff, we've heard it before," as Sukenick puts it (*In Form* 7). He implies, time and the tide of events themselves will sweep away yesterday's literature no matter what authors do—a forecast that seems especially valid given recent advances in e-book technology, online bookstores, and other developments about to once again revolutionize publishing, or given the dawning biotech age, to cite just one nonliterary development sure to impact upon how people think of themselves, relate to each other, and, of course, write.

What is important for authors is to write (a way of thinking) novels (the most comprehensive medium for recording thought) that matter: novels that embody something readers can believe about their time and place. His theory of writing is a translation of the avant-garde, then, to the new cultural climate. For authors and readers at the start of a new millennium, there could perhaps be no more valuable "rule of thumb" than the Sukenick position that writers should be critics of society and not accessories to institutions and markets (*In Form* 140). Given the commercial nature of this international cultural climate, much of Sukenick's enduring importance is that he shows another way—a way to live in Rome and not do as the Romans: a way for authors, and people, and literature to remain vital in the face of hegemonic commercialization and radical cultural change. To continue, not to conclude, as he says: to remain connected to an ever-changing world by looking forward not backward as do commercially driven novels that continually rehearse yesteryear's form. Thus he casts his cannibalism, appropriations, speaking in tongues, and recyclings not as a collage—what he calls the modernist way of dealing with disparate parts—but Mosaic, which takes "disparate parts and turns them into new wholes"—"the beginning of something else" (91). In sum, he offers himself as an author who is neither modern nor postmodern, but a mosaic of each. An exemplar mosaic man.

Works Cited

Barone, Dennis. "What's in a Name? The Dalkey Archive Press." *Critique: Studies in Contemporary Fiction* 37.3 (1996): 222–40.

Barthes, Roland. *S/Z*. Trans. Richard Miller. New York: Hill and Wang, 1974.

Baumbach, Jonathan. "Who Do They Think They Are? A Personal History of the Fiction Collective." *In the Slipstream: An FC2 Reader*. Eds. Ronald Sukenick and Curtis White. Normal, Ill.: Fiction Collective Two, 2000. 9–19.

Bérubé, Michael. "Teaching Postmodern Fiction Without Being Sure That the Genre Exists." *Chronicle of Higher Education*. 19 May 2000: B4–5.

Becker, Howard S. *Art Worlds*. Berkeley: University of California Press, 1982.

Butor, Michel. *Inventory*. Ed. Richard Howard. New York: Simon and Schuster, 1968.

Hughes, Robert. *American Visions: The Epic History of Art in America*. New York: Alfred A. Knopf, 1997.

Kutnik, Jerzy. *The Novel as Performance: The Fiction of Ronald Sukenick and Raymond Federman*. Carbondale: Southern Illinois University Press, 1986.

Klinkowitz, Jerome. "The Novel as Artifact: Spatial Form in Contemporary Fiction." *Spatial Form in Narrative*. Eds. Jeffrey R. Smitten and Ann Daghistany. Ithaca, N.Y.: Cornell Univeristy Press, 1981. 37–47.

Mitchell, W. J. T. *Picture Theory: Essays on Verbal, and Visual Representation*. Chicago: University of Chicago Press, 1994.

Ortega y Gasset, José. *The Dehumanization of Art and Other Essays on Art, Culture, and Literature*. 1925. Princeton, NJ: Princeton University Press, 1968.

Pollock, Jackson. *Theories and Documents of Contemporary Art: A Sourcebook of Artists' Writings*. Eds. Kristine Stiles and Peter Selz. Berkeley: University of California Press, 1996.

Rasula, Jed and Steve McCaffery, eds. *Imagining Language: An Anthology*. Cambridge, Mass.: MIT Press, 1998.

Robbe-Grillet, Alain. *For a New Novel: Essays on Fiction*. 1963. Trans. Richard Howard. New York: Grove Press, 1965.

Sandler, Irving. *The Triumph of American Painting: A History of Abstract Expressionism*. New York: Harper & Row, 1970.

Sterne, Laurence. *The Life and Opinions of Tristram Shandy*. [1759]. New York: Random House, n.d.

Sukenick, Ronald. *In Form: Digressions on the Act of Fiction*. Carbondale: Southern Illinois University Press, 1985.

———. *Narralogues: Truth in Fiction*. Albany: State University of New York Press, 2000.

Tabbi, Joseph. *Reading Matters: Narrative in the New Media Ecology*. Ithaca, N.Y.: Cornell Univeristy Press, 1997.

Watt, Ian. *The Rise of the Novel: Studies in Defoe, Richardson and Fielding*. Berkeley: University of California Press, 1957.

"At Play in the Fields of Formal Thinking": *Up* and Postmodernist Metafiction

Charles B. Harris

In a recent essay, Ronald Sukenick declares that postmodernist fiction "has come and gone" ("Not-fiction" 3). More recently, critic Michael Bérubé argues that it was never here to begin with. With all due respect to both positions, I want to propose that "postmodernist fiction" remains a vital aesthetic category, that one of its defining characteristics is the deployment of reflexive techniques in the interest of postmodernist concerns, and that since its emergence in the late 1960s postmodernist fiction has not remained formally and thematically static but has evolved. More importantly, I want to argue that close examination of Sukenick's critical writings, especially his 1967 study of Wallace Stevens and his 1985 essay collection *In Form*, can enhance our understanding of the direction of this continuing evolution, a direction predicted by Sukenick's first novel, the postmodernist metafiction *Up* (1968).

In his provocative essay, Bérubé "confesses" that although he's taught courses in postmodernist fiction for over a decade, he no longer believes that postmodernist fiction exists. To be sure, Bérubé affirms the existence of postmodernity and even of a "distinct postmodern style," although he restricts the latter to architecture and the visual arts. But "the fact remains," Bérubé argues, that "there's nothing uniquely postmodern about most of the experiments conducted in contemporary experimental fiction" (B4).[1] If we restrict our definition of postmodernist fiction solely to "stylistic terms," then Bérubé's contention seems unexceptionable. As Patricia Waugh notes, "although the term 'metafiction' might be new, the practice is as old (if not older) than the novel itself" (5).[2] Its emergence is "particularly likely," Waugh continues, "during 'crisis' periods in the literary history of the genre" (6). A primary function of reflexive fictions is to defamiliarize formal conventions that, in Shklovskian terms, have become "automatized" by "laying bare" these conventions. Because "traditional" literary forms are complicit with other cultural constructions, however, the crises signaled by outbreaks of narrative reflexivity are more than merely aesthetic. As Robert Siegle observes, "[R]eflexivity is highly charged ideologically precisely because it denaturalizes far more than merely literary codes and pertains to more than the aesthetic 'heterocosm' to which some theorists might wish to restrict it" (11). Most likely to erupt when cultural consensus is eroding, reflexive narratives suggest the possibility of new semantic systems. And "to change semantic systems," as Umberto Eco notes, "means *to change the way in which culture 'sees' the world*," such changes implying that the "world could be defined and organized (and therefore perceived and known) through other semantic (that is: conceptual) models" (274). This is what Siegle has in mind when he describes reflexive narratives as "constitutive" (9–13). As we shall see, it is also what Sukenick means when he describes his process of composition as "generative" (*In Form* 22). Viewed in this way, a primary historical function of narrative reflexivity has been to destabilize by foregrounding ("laying bare") naturalized literary effects in order to critique the cultural consensus inscribed in those effects and to suggest the possibility of alternative definitions of "reality."

But even if we agree that narrative reflexivity predates what we have come to call postmodernist fiction, it does not necessarily follow, as Bérubé concludes, that stylistic definitions of postmodernist fiction should therefore be abandoned. Although reflexive narratives are historically similar in their tendency to signal cultural ruptures and to prepare the way for new cognitive maps, possibly comprising what Sukenick dubs a "rival tradition," the respective cultural ruptures and new conceptual potentialities they signal are themselves different—an obvious enough statement but one that is frequently overlooked. The transition from a medieval world view to a more modern empirically oriented view that *Don Quixote* registers and helps inaugurate differs from the cultural shift implicit in *Tristram Shandy*. The era during which Sterne wrote is marked by the emerging dominance of Newtonian physics and the nascent realistic novel that reflects and sustains that view; postmodernist novelists revive Sterne's reflexive tactics in order to problematize the Newtonian world-picture. Even more important for definitional purposes, the particular literary conventions laid bare by contemporary metafictive devices differ markedly from the narrative processes defamiliarized in *Don Quixote* or *Tristram Shandy* or Austen's *Northanger Abbey*. Rather than outmoded Romance conventions or causal narrative sequence or the Gothic novel, postmodernist reflexive novels, as Waugh points out, "question and reject the forms that correspond to [the] ordered reality" of the "materialistic, positivisit and empiricist world-view on which realistic fiction is premised."[3] These transgressions of "realistic" codes of verisimilitude offer "extremely accurate models for understanding the contemporary experience of the world as a construction, an artifice, a web of interdependent semiotic systems" (Waugh 9), which is to say, a *postmodernist* experience of the world. Viewed from the perspective of world-making, postmodernist metafiction becomes much more than anarchistic linguistic play, its disruptive narrative techniques constituting a form of oppositional politics.[4] Our most recent outbreak of radically reflexive fiction is best understood, I think, as a part of that cultural rupture we generally refer to as "the Sixties."

The Sixties is our shorthand for the counterculture movement whose dates run, roughly, from the civil rights demonstrations of 1963 through our nation's withdrawal from Vietnam in 1973, but whose early manifestations may be traced to the underground culture of Greenwich Village bohemia which began in the 1950s and which is chronicled by Sukenick in *Down and In* (1987). In that book, Sukenick explicitly links *Up* to the social context of the 1960s, a decade during which he lived as part of the underground in New York's Lower East Side:

> When I start writing my first novel, *Up*, a book about the East Side that is a combination of autobiography and invention, I realize that that place and time is one in which we can in fact partly invent our autobiographies, in which life is not something imposed on us but a process in which we are creatively involved. The distinction between art and life in the book is reduced to a quibble of form only partly out of theoretical considerations. It's also a consequence of the kind of life that, after decades of alienation, we are finally positioned to lead. What critics don't realize when they foam, or even effervesce, about 'Postmodernism' in fiction is that it did not come out of arbitrary literary considerations but out of a kind of life. . . . If nothing else is clear about Postmodernism, it is glaringly obvious that it is impelled by a passion for reengagement with common experience, including the experience of the citizen in process of helping to create his environment though the imagination. (149–50)

Thus defined, postmodernist fiction is not only a manifestation of the revolutionary movements that erupted in the Sixties but also an attempt to relate the public events and historical processes of the postmodernist era to the lives and intellectual concerns of its characters.

Seen in this light, it is not surprising that so many definitive examples of contemporary American metafiction were published in 1968, in many respects a watershed year.[5] Not only *Up*, but also John Barth's *Lost in the Funhouse,* William H. Gass's *Willie Masters' Lonesome Wife,* Donald Barthelme's *Unspeakable Practices, Unnatural Acts,* Robert Coover's *The Universal Baseball Association, J. Alfred Waugh, Prop.,* and Steve Katz's *The Exagggerations of Peter Prince* all appeared in 1968. In one eventful year, the conventions most closely associated with postmodernist fiction are defined and, in many respects, exhausted—for if metafictional conventions continue to be an important part of the arsenal of postmodernist writers, few "pure" examples of metafiction, that is "fiction which . . . directly examines its own construction as it proceeds" (McCaffery 16), appear after the late 1960s, Sorrentino's *Mulligan Stew* (1979) and the 1970s "surfiction" of Raymond Federman being significant exceptions. But if the profuse publication of metafictions in the late Sixties directly reflects the social context of that time, not every metafiction published in 1968 is necessarily postmodernist. That is, although narrative reflexivity is a primary hallmark of postmodernist narrative (which is why I disagree with Bérubé's contention that it should be eliminated as a reliable marker), metafictional techniques do not, in and of themselves, signify postmodernist fiction, not even when they are employed by contemporary writers. Just as it is possible (paraphrasing John Barth[6]) to write turn-of-the-twentieth-century-type novels about postmodernist people and topics, so is it possible to deploy counter-realistic techniques associated with postmodernism for modernist purposes.

For example, although Gass, Barth, and Sukenick all rely on metafictional means in their 1968 publications, each uses these techniques to achieve different ends. *Willie Masters' Lonesome Wife* represents one of the last gasps of high modernism, the purpose of foregrounded artifice in the novel being to distinguish between art and "reality" (a distinction Gass insists upon in his essays of this period and in his famous debate with John Gardner). Barth's metafictive *Lost in the Funhouse*, on the other hand, is an early example of the now familiar postmodernist dictum that what we call "reality" is, like a novel, also a construct. That is, whereas classical realism tries to "mirror" an extratextual reality, metafiction in the hands of a writer like Barth insists that a more accurate model would reverse the conventional relationship between narrative and reality. In this regard, Barth differs significantly from Gass. In a famous gesture in *Willie Masters' Lonesome Wife,* Gass provides us with facing pages, one of which is a mirror image of the other. His point, of course, is that literature is not a mimetic representation of an antecedent reality but is always and only about itself. He concludes his novel with the admonition: "You have fallen into art—return to life" (n.p.). Barth, on the other hand, especially in stories such as "Frame Tale" and "Menelaiad," suggests that "reality" itself is enmeshed in layers of story and that, as Barth asserts in an essay, "the difference between the fantasy we call reality and the fantasies we call fantasy has to do with cultural consensus and with one's manner of relating to the concept-structure involved" (*Friday Book* 221). So *Willie Masters' Lonesome Wife* and *Lost in the Funhouse,* metafictions published in the same year, assume different stances vis-à-vis postmodernism. Whereas Gass's novel presents an example of what Barth, referring to the fiction of John Hawkes, calls "fine late modernism" (195), *Funhouse* exemplifies the early stage of American postmodernist fiction during which metafictional form flagrantly declares its independence from the hegemonic authority of literary and philosophical realism and from the dominant reading practices supporting that hegemony.[7]

By contrast, Sukenick's *Up* signals an altogether different direction. For if late-modernist Gass wishes to demarcate literature from life and early-postmodernist Barth wants to illustrate that life, like literature, is also a text, and if both these writers employ metafictional devices to reinforce their views, Sukenick insists, both in *Up* and in his essays and interviews of the late 1960s and early 1970s, that fiction provides us with a way to make contact with what he calls "experience beyond language" (*In Form* 112). Thus Sukenick begins to use autobiographical elements in his fiction long before most other postmodernists do, not because he wants to write about himself but, as he explains in an early essay, because "experience begins with the self" (*In Form* 26). At first glance, Sukenick's emphasis on extralinguistic selfhood and experience appears strangely retrograde, as though he were attempting to recuperate an aesthetic based in mimesis. Nothing could be further from the case. Sukenick's concept of the self, as Jerzy Kutnik points out, "has little to do with the modern idea of the individual as encapsulated ego. Personality for him is by no means stable and absolute but is indefinite, changeable, and fluid," something invented as we go along (70).[8] Moreover, Sukenick agrees with Barth that human "reality" is a construct in the sense that it requires interpretation if it is to become intelligible. He disagrees, however, with Barth's aesthetic decision to focus in his work on already existing interpretations.[9] A different direction, the one Sukenick has chosen, is to try to deal directly with "the data of experience" (*In Form* 109). Rather than acknowledging the always already interpreted nature of human experience by working self-consciously from within those constructs, as Barth and other post-modernists have done, Sukenick prefers to focus on the process of interpretation itself. The narrative becomes a record of that process, an embodiment "of the mind as it confronts and affects experience" (*In Form* 14).

Sukenick also agrees with Gass that literature, rather than being about the world, is a new thing in the world, and he applauds Gass for focusing "attention on the validity of the artifact itself" (*In Form* 39). But he rejects Gass's hermeticism. Fiction "does not refer to a reality beyond itself. Okay. But given that art is not mimetic, it does not follow that it is hermetic. When we say that creative language is nonreferential I take it we mean that it doesn't refer to other language, other concepts—it points toward the mute world beyond language, beyond history, and then itself falls silent" (38). Art's proper function, Sukenick continues, "is to connect us with the world, not separate us from it" (39). The "voodoo at the heart of mimetic theory," Sukenick maintains, is that the world is subject to human control. "The key idea is verisimilitude: one can make an image of the real thing which, though not real, is such a persuasive likeness that it can represent our control over reality" (4). Although modernist hermeticism recoils from realism and the empirical world realism promises to deliver, it does not relinquish the desire for control. On the contrary, modernist form constitutes "an imposed order" rather than "one that develops as it goes along" (21). Like realism, which replaces reality with a static model of reality, and those early postmodernist fictions that revel in their own intertextuality, modernist hermeticism valorizes product instead of process, the literary form rather than "the imaginative process that creates the form" (33). From Sukenick's standpoint, all three aesthetic modes represent a refusal of experience.

As I've already suggested, experience and form are interrelated concepts in Sukenick's aesthetic, and he uses both terms in highly specialized senses. The earliest formulation of these concepts appear in his 1962 Brandeis University doctoral dissertation on Stevens's major poems, a revised version of which was published as *Wallace Stevens: Musing the Obscure* by New York University Press in 1967. Although Sukenick's unorthodox study of Stevens's poetics was not widely accepted by academic specialists, it remained in print for almost twenty years and contains invaluable clues to Sukenick's own aesthetic. The continuing relevance of Sukenick's early thinking about literary form to his ongoing literary praxis was confirmed when he included the study's opening section, "Wallace Stevens: Theory and Practice," in his 1985 essay collection *In Form,* a collection Sukenick says comprises his "theory of composition" (ix). Only a small handful of contemporary innovative novelists—Barth, Gass, Curtis White, and possibly Federman come to mind—have provided as extensive a record of their thinking about literary form as Sukenick provides in these two books. Although more than a cursory consideration of those thoughts would exceed the scope of this essay, a brief summary is necessary before I turn finally to a reading of *Up*, the novel Sukenick wrote while he was preparing his final version of the Stevens book and one that remains perhaps the most thorough exemplification of Sukenick's postmodernist aesthetic.

Sukenick is one of those rare postmodernists who deign to use the word reality without the requisite Nabokovian quotation marks. By *reality*, however, Sukenick doesn't mean those already existing forms, social and otherwise, that realistic novelists imitate in their fiction—or, for that matter, that postmodernists such as the early Barth imitate in their self-consciously intertextual fictions. Rather, in Sukenick's specialized usage, *reality* refers to those unmediated data or phenomena (both terms recur in his critical writings) that constantly impinge upon our sensorium and that, in their unpremeditated state, present themselves as Stevens's "squirming facts" or William James's "unhumanized fringe," the yet to be conceptualized. "Reality itself," Sukenick writes, "is an entity whose chief characteristic is flux" (*In Form* 164). *Experience*, in Sukenick's critical lexicon, refers to our perception of this flux at its most inchoate state. "The artist becomes the inventor of experience from mere phenomena: that is, we're confronted with phenomena, and we want experience. Experience is phenomena taken in and made relevant to the individual psyche" (*In Form* 134). The difficulty, perhaps even the impossibility, of achieving unmediated contact with data, of stepping "barefoot into reality," to quote Stevens once more, is not lost on Sukenick. As he told Larry McCaffery: "Of course, the challenge and conscious paradox there is that no matter how hard you try to get down the data as they literally are, there are almost no literal data. They are always filtered through the creative mind, even if that mind happens to belong to the person from whom the life data has come. . . . You should always *try*, though, to capture the data of reality . . . , because it is only in making that effort to deal with those data that you finally create a legitimate fiction" (*In Form* 108–09).

Sukenick's aesthetic, then, derives from what might be seen as his theory of reality and his epistemology. The most effective literary form is that which reflects "the architecture of consciousness thinking and feeling as it processes experience" (*In Form* xviii). In *The Cantos* and

Patterson, Sukenick observes, Pound and Williams were able to achieve a "continuity of art and experience" because of their "readiness . . . to use their own unmediated experience without the intervention of predetermined form, including the experience that occurs during and because of composition, on the same level as other subject matter" (17). In other words, the act of composition itself becomes part of the experience crystallized in that act. Narrative form registers the movement of the mind in the process of organizing what Sukenick calls "the open field of the text" (13). That's why the cover of Sukenick's second book of fiction, a cover that Sukenick himself designed, reads:

RONALD
SUKENICK
Author of "UP"
WRITES
THE DEATH
OF THE
NOVEL
AND OTHER
STORIES

Sukenick's unusual use of the present tense "writes"—as opposed to the more conventional "by Ronald Sukenick"—conveys his sense of form as a spontaneous, "ongoing interchange between the mind and the page" (8), not an imitation of reality, but "an illuminating addition to its ongoing flow" (6).

Just as narrative form can vitalize the author's attachment to data, so can it assist the reader in forging a similar attachment. By interrupting the "circuit that mimesis creates in which the work gives the illusion of being a picture of the world," defamiliarizing techniques in Sukenick's fiction remind "the reader of how he himself thinks and what he is thinking, and thereby . . . activate his imagination so that he himself can look at the world, not necessarily at my version of it—in his own versions of it"(*In Form* 146). In this way, both the reader and the writer's imagination is potentially liberated from the political and economic forces that threaten to colonize it. "Because once you drop the pretense that the novel is giving an image of reality you can then begin to think about such issues as what reality is after all, how we can use our imaginations on it, what it is that controls the idea of reality. I think once you begin to talk about that stuff, once you call it into question, it becomes immediately obvious that we are not talking about reality but authority, that it is a question of who and what has the power to make authoritative statements about phenomena" (147). In undercutting "official versions of reality in favor of our individual sense of experience, now constantly threatened by the brain wash of politics and the mass market" (67), Sukenick's postmodernist metafiction serves a political function. As he tells his students, " 'If you don't use your own imagination, somebody else is going to use it for you' " (147).[10]

I do not mean to suggest that Sukenick writes out of a fully developed formal theory. What he calls "formal thinking," after Emerson, is by definition thinking that occurs "in and through the creative work" (*In Form* ix). According to Sukenick's "generative theory of composition," there "is no a priori form—form is generated by the currents of energy that interact on the page" (28). Moreover, because reality constantly changes, form that is continuous with experience will itself constantly change. "Liberation from the prison of ideas" (xvii) does not only mean freedom from official versions of reality; *any* thought, no matter how original, "once formulated, becomes an impediment to thinking" (xvii). The same is true of narrative forms. For example, Sukenick says that improvisation, which was such an important device for avoiding stale formulas and releasing the unpremeditated in his early fiction, had by the 1970s itself become a formula, prompting Sukenick to move "in the direction of formalism" in his work of the late 1970s and early 1980s (118). More recently, he has signaled a move to what he terms "not-fiction," a new rhetorical form whose "purpose is to gather data in pleasurable complexes, yield information, and argue truths" ("Not-fiction" 8). In some of its particulars, then, Sukenick's theory and practice have changed over the years; what has remained consistent from the beginning has been his commitment to the "metamorphic powers of imaginative language [as] a liberating force because it reveals the possibilities of experience" (xix).

Up exemplifies as it extends Sukenick's earliest formulations of an aesthetic theory and represents an excellent example of the novelist "at play in the fields of formal thinking"(*In Form* xvii). An improvisational interplay of present experiences, memories, fantasies, stylistic registers, and occasional typographical transgressions, all of which occasionally coalesce into a kind of stream-of-consciousness mélange (cf., 226–42), *Up* conveys a powerful sense of immediacy, as though we are witnessing narrative form in the process of working itself out. The novel records the struggle of its narrator and main character, Ron Sukenick (who, for purposes of clarity, I will refer to hereafter as Ron), to achieve a form that will "approximate the shape of experience" (*In Form* 63)—a form, that is, which approximates what in *Death of the Novel and Other Stories* Sukenick describes as "feeling keenly in harmony with my own impulses & anarchically independent of constrictions which deaden them—an experience essential to the psychology of freedom" (39).

As suggested by the recurring images of imprisonment throughout the novel, freeing oneself from deadening constrictions is no easy task. The novel's opening passage, a fantasy prompted by the lack of heat in Ron's Lower East Side apartment, introduces this motif: "Then I was led alone through a labyrinth of stairs, always descending, and corridors lit by an occasional naked bulb, to the bare stone cell with its heavy door—allowing through its tiny grill this minimum of damp light—*where I still wonder how they managed to find a place so perfect a cliché of such places*, even to the rusticated stone and a large iron ring clamped into one wall" (2, italics added).

Succeeding descriptions of fantasized prison scenes—Ron in a jail cell awaiting a firing squad (48–49), Ron tunneling his way out of a prison with a nail removed from the heel of his shoe (138), Ron as a Jewish soldier in a Nazi POW camp (148–49), Ron harassed by an anti-Semitic redneck Southern sheriff (152), Ron interrogated in a hospital operating room by a sinister surgeon (237)—are also purposely hackneyed, familiar formulas gleaned from scores of popular movies and television shows. Of course, the triteness of these descriptions is precisely Sukenick's point. By associating control with banality, Sukenick constructs an effective metaphor for the way politics, the media, and the mass market maintain power in late capitalist culture—through the manipulation of texts. "The media impose manipulative paradigms on individual experience," Sukenick writes, "so that it is almost as if people don't have any individual experience—they only have what they see being presented on television" (*In Form* 117). Mass manipulation of cultural texts also has "stylistic consequences: what is required is a language and form that is standardized so that it can be merchandised to the largest number of people, that is hypnotic and diverting, drawing attention away from ordinary experience and into an anesthetic formula that is familiar and reassuring" (*In Form* 54–55). In Althusserian terms, these familiar images "interpellate" us as an *effect* of the manipulated text, constituting our social roles and identities as though we had freely chosen them. At its most effective, that is, ideology requires few repressive measures, emanating through a system of representations that have become so naturalized they constitute our sense of the world, our sense of identity, and our sense of relations to others and to society in general. This is the kind of manufactured consent commanded by "the mild, businesslike men in quiet suits" who supervise the prison in the opening scene of *Up*: ". . . these ordinary men all about us, otherwise so bland, looked at you with expressions of such terrible implicit power that, although they never showed a weapon, not one of us dared balk" (2–3). These quotidian men, like the clichéd description of the dungeon, suggest that what Ron is struggling to free himself from is the pernicious authority of banality itself.

As his last name implies, the primary embodiment of ideological control in the novel is Strop Banally. At least one critic has argued that Banally is the "character most admired by Sukenick" (Kutnik 91), but I believe this judgment misconstrues Banally's role. The "boy genius of the communications industry" (4), Strop operates at the heart of postmodern consumer culture's boundless networks of media imagery, "his adroit finger in advertising, public relations, television, movies and publishing" (38). Less real than hyperreal, Strop is himself a walking simulacrum, the epitome of consumer images: "he looks familiar, somebody seen in a tabloid, on a screen, in a cigarette ad" (4). Kutnik views Strop's serial personalities as a positive reflection of Sukenick's veneration of discontinuity. But each of the roles Strop has played—"a cowboy, a flyer, a fashion model, a yacht captain, an actor, an undercover agent, a stockbroker, an advertising executive, and an entrepreneur" (4)—implies wealth and power, the capacity to dominate or control others. Strop, we are told, has "an incredible competitive drive for power that he seems to indulge not for the sake of conquest but simply for the pleasure of exercising it" (38). Indeed, Banally is power itself. The source and embodiment of late capitalist ideology, Strop Banally "is not outside society: he is in it; in fact he is practically on top of it" (39), functioning in the novel as a kind of Althusserian Absolute Subject in control of the representations that construct our social roles.

Like the mass produced images that have infiltrated Ron's fantasies, Banally exists inside Ron's consciousness, the warden of a prison that has been internalized. *Up* may be read as Ron's (and Sukenick's) attempt to break out of that prison, to wrest control of his imagination from the image factories of the dominant culture. Nowhere is this dominance clearer than in the ideologically enforced gender identities of the 1950s and 1960s, one of the novel's key focuses. The novel provides no physical description of Ron, but we can assume from his demeanor that he looks nothing like Strop Banally. Not surprisingly, Strop's physical appearance is a composite of images associated with idealized masculinity: "blond, tanned, well-tailored, and baritoned, football build, strength and regularity of feature" (4). Like Jay Gatsby, he resembles "the advertisement of the man"(*Gatsby* 106). But Banally, we are told, "is an infinitely more knowing Gatsby, Gatsby without illusions, Gatsby 'wised up' with the experience of the last forty years" (39). Ron, by contrast, is variously described as "feckless," "innocent," "dazzled," "unlucky," "hapless," "lovelorn," "lackluster," a bit of a schlemiel whose high school nickname is "Wrong Way Ron" (97–115). To compensate for his perceived inadequacies, Ron often casts himself as a hero in his "narcissistic fantasy meanderings" (139). But his models for those fantasy roles derive from popular representations of masculinity that reproduce the very constructions of male subjectivity that are the source of his oppression.

Popular constructions of male identity often highlight sexual prowess. Whereas Banally's priapic exploits are predictably legendary, Ron's sexual endeavors, until near the novel's end, are confused and generally unfulfilling. Not only does Ron's high school sweetheart rebuff his repeated efforts to bed her, but he is chagrined to learn years later that his rakish friend Ernie Slade had seduced Nancy while she was still dating Ron. His lone adolescent sexual experience, with the promiscuous Oola Wonderliegh, culminates in a humiliating blunder, leaving Ron unsure "whether officially speaking [he] was still a virgin or not" (146). Again, Ron compensates with fantasies (usually of violent sex with stereotypical French coquettes) or, in one instance, an out and out lie, which Ron later confesses was "pure adolescent braggadocio to assuage my delicate ego" (169–70). Although sexually active in college, Ron prefers relationships with Eastern European coeds who have escaped the conditioning of American gender construction and, "bound by a dislike for football rallies and a taste for intelligible conversation" (172), do not measure him by ideologically determined standards of American masculinity.

But if Ron chaffs under the dictates of constructed gender roles, women in the novel suffer the brunt of managed desire far more severely. Once again, Banally controls the systems of power authorizing female gender identities. Not only a communications magnate, Strop is "the Albert Einstein of the pornographic film" (4), whose representations of women as erotic objects of desire are introjected by characters such as Stewart, who spends much of his adolescence in the bathroom masturbating. Ron, too, has internalized these sexual representations, and his fantasies often associate what Strop calls "virile mastery" (190) with power and possession. Disturbing images of handcuffed women on desks or tables recur throughout Ron's imaginings, particularly in the Banally scenes. On at least two occasions, Ron fantasizes assaults on women by policemen (32, 230–31). According to Sukenick, images of sadomasochism in his early fiction emphasize "that power and sex, or violence and sex, are often confused in our culture—and . . . they shouldn't be" (*In Form* 113). Although physical violence against women in *Up* is restricted to Ron's ideologically inflected fantasies, the plight of actual women in the book—Sugar, for example, and especially Nancy—emphasizes that in the realm of erotic behavior male phallic identity often depends upon a projected female masochistic identity.

Most readers who reached puberty before the 1960s' "sexual revolution" will recognize the accuracy—and, despite the scene's hilarity, the poignancy—of the extended description of Ron's frustrated (and frustrating) attempt to seduce his girlfriend, Nancy, during their teen years in Gravesend (85–93). Dutifully submissive to "the dead weight of cultural conservatism" (*Down and In* 71) represented by her father, whose untimely appearance punctuates Ron's sexual defeat (93), teenage Nancy quite literally struggles to preserve her virtue. Years later, during her brief marriage to Slade, she becomes promiscuous and exhibitionistic to satisfy her husband's unorthodox sexual needs. Whether acting as virgin or temptress, Nancy occupies socially produced and historically conditioned subject positions inscribed by patriarchal myths of female sexuality. When Ron and Nancy are reunited after her divorce, Ron learns that she has become a nude model for men's magazines, which suggests that Nancy remains a thrall to social constructions of female sexuality and male desire.

We soon realize, however, that this is a different Nancy, one who has gained some perspective on the ideological nature of female sexual identities. "But this is all make believe," she tells Ron, referring to the photographs. "The dream trade. None of it's real" (187). Whereas before she had submissively conformed to socially constituted gender roles, Nancy now refuses to identify with the fetishized female body displayed in her pictures: ". . . it's only a photograph that people see, don't forget. The photograph isn't me. What do I care who looks at it? I don't know the difference" (185). Though necessarily complicitous with the constitutive power of male desire, Nancy has learned how to reappropriate her objectified body for subversive purposes. Not only is her nude modeling career "a lucrative business" (187), but it is also empowering, enabling Nancy to manipulate the representations of female sexuality that had previously controlled her. "Your best friends don't recognize you when they see you nude," she tells Ron. "That's one reason I like it—it's like becoming a new person. . . . I take on a new identity in response to the feelings of whoever is there" (185–86). While making love at the end of this scene, Ron senses a return of Nancy's submissiveness: ". . . it was as if she were articulating with her body over and over something . . . like, Get through to me, Help me" (189). Shortly thereafter, however, Nancy informs Ron, "That's what a woman is for. I sense what you want and I give it to you" (190). Reinforcing our suspicion that she has become adept at manipulating male desire, Nancy adds, "You deserve anything you get from me," the scene concluding wryly on that "ambiguous note" (190).

Nancy's strategy may be seen as an intervention, a subversion from within cultural constraints she can never wholly escape.[11] As such, it provides a clue to a primary formal strategy in *Up*, which may also be read as interventive.[12] The omnipresence in the novel of images from mass culture acknowledges the extent to which Ron's consciousness is relentlessly mediated by images calculated to preserve existing power structures. But the novel's unorthodox form detours these images, installing them in order to subvert them. That is, the novel's formal strangeness—conventional critiques of which Sukenick actually incorporates into the novel[13]—serves to recontextualize the dominant discourse, forcing it to signify against its own interests, implying the possibility of alternative formulations. As discussed earlier, Sukenick employs defamiliarizing techniques on behalf of his conceptions of experience and reality: "I think defamiliarization actually increases the reality quotient of phenomena. Because what happens is you get used to seeing something, let us say seeing something in a particular formulated way and it begins to lose any kind of important identity for you so that when it is defamiliarized you look at it more sharply and realize what it is again. . . . For me the whole purpose of the imagination in writing is to constantly destroy the formulations of language, to make language work against itself so that there can be an openness to data" (*In Form* 146–47). In constructing a narrative that "accommodates to the ongoing flow of experience" (*In Form* 206), Sukenick hopes to break through to the unpremeditated world, which, as we saw earlier, is Sukenick's aesthetic desideratum. The kite-flying episode represents the metaphorical fulfillment of that hope.

The episode begins inauspiciously enough: Ron dreads returning to his empty apartment, Nancy having moved out, and is described as "angry," "suspicious," and "in a bad mood" (265–67). Once he, Nancy, Otis, and Finch begin flying the kite, however, the narrative focus shifts from Ron's unsettled internal state to an extended and detailed description of the exhilarating physical activity of kite flying. No images from mass culture infringe upon this description, which seems to record, for the first and only time in the novel, something akin to Stevens's "agreement with reality." Quoting from "Notes toward a Supreme Fiction," Sukenick explains that "a true experience of reality depends not on . . . abstractions but on that sensuous relation with it during, for example, 'a walk around a lake,' when one becomes composed as the body tires and physical composure comes to be one with mental composure. At such times one is in an equilibrium, a state of 'incalculable balances,' that includes both the mind and one's surroundings. This is exactly that resolution through an 'agreement with reality' that Stevens's poetry aims to create" (*In Form* 192). It is also exactly the kind of resolution Sukenick aims to create in the kite-flying episode. The point of the scene is not that Sukenick's characters or Sukenick's description of the scene have made direct contact with empirical or, despite the flight imagery, transcendental reality.[14] On the contrary, the "particular rapport with reality" the kite-flying episode describes implies a "kind of 'truth' [that] does not depend on accurate descriptions of 'reality' but rather itself generates what we call reality, reordering our perceptions and sustaining a vital connection with the world" (*In Form* 31). As Ron informs Otis, art is about the "*invention* of reality," not its "discovery" (217, italics added).

The significance of the kite-flying episode, then, is that it signals a changed "metaphoric contact with reality, and the only way that change can occur is by breaking down the old fictions, the old constructs" (*In Form* 110). By nature, the liberating insights gained from new metaphoric configurations are fugitive, but their possibility perseveres in the new forms of reality they generate. As Sukenick explains, again with reference to Stevens's "Notes on a Supreme Fiction":

> . . . we can apprehend the substance of reality through our metaphors of it, but only for a moment; even as we make contact with the real we turn it into the imaginary, which quickly degenerates into cliché. . . . Reality is the data of the ego, but that data is transformed by the ego in the version of reality captured by the poem or the fiction. . . . The fiction, so qualified, is a credible version of reality. It is neither reality itself nor a projection of the ego, but an abstract construction of the relation between the two in which the feelings of the ego are adjusted to the fact of reality. . . . Thus a fiction is not belief in the ordinary sense but is a crystallized relation to reality that reveals reality as in some way gratifying to the ego. . . . Thus the end of belief comes down to a gratifying, sensuous experience of reality, an agreement with life rather than an idea about it. (*In Form* 187–89)

Such states of experiential flow are emancipative rather than pragmatic or utilitarian, which is why the kite-flying friends are left "happy," but with "nothing solved" (274).[15]

Because *Up*, as Bernie complains, is "a collection of disjointed fragments" (222), one hesitates to identify the kite-flying episode as the novel's climax. But the absence of conventional plot development doesn't mean, as Bernie also contends, that the narrative "doesn't go anywhere" (222). As already suggested, the kite-flying episode provides a sense of resolution, and Ron is clearly changed by the incident. This change is revealed in three successive scenes that immediately follow the episode. In the first of these scenes, Ron is canvassing for the Neighborhood Action Committee with Kenny Malcolm, who questions Ron's decision to write a novel rather than devote his time to political activism. Whereas Ron's response to previous criticisms of his fiction has been passive, he reacts assertively to Kenny's challenge, implying a developing understanding of the socially responsible role innovative fiction might play:

> "I don't see why you'd want to write a novel," said Kenny. "In the current situation. What's needed is organization. Footwork, demonstrations."
>
> "A novel is a demonstration," I said.
>
> "I mean real demonstrations."
> "A novel is real," I said. (277)

Ron's ability to act on his heightened perception is severely tested in the novel's next scene, which describes the party celebrating "Arlene's accouchement" (279–305). Although all of the novel's characters attend, the most important party-goer is Strop Banally, who appears for the first time outside of one of Ron's fantasies. "What's the matter? Didn't you think I was *real*?" Banally asks. To which Ron replies: "Yeah I knew you were real all right. In a sense I thought you were too real to show up here" (298). Strop's materialization in a "real life" scene emphasizes the extent to which, as the embodiment of ideology, he has infiltrated Ron's consciousness and, as a consequence, all of the novel's episodes Ron has written to this point. In more conventional terms, he is Ron's alter ego (they both have green eyes), come to reinforce his regulatory function. During the party scene, the hegemonic reach of Strop's control over people and events is never more evident, as we learn that most of the novel's characters—Len, Slim, Slade, even Bernie—either work for Banally or owe him favors. As if he senses the potential threat to his authority that Ron's nearly completed novel represents, Strop coaxes Ron to "spice it up" into a more commercial "property," which Banally promises to publish. "I'm in a position to know that you stand to make a lot of money sweetheart. That means you'll be famous." Ron, described as "drenched in sweat," seems to waver, like Huck vacillating over whether to send that letter to Miss Watson. Pressing his advantage, Strop taunts Ron with his intention to take both Nancy and the young Marietta Honeywell home with him, his smile "simultaneously a challenge, an insult, and a *gesture of complicity*" (300, italics added).

The incarnation of raw power, Strop has not changed. Ron, however, displaying a new self-assertiveness, cuts in on Banally while he dances with Marietta. As Ron, "doing his own step," gyrates to the music's "heavy beat," he "feels like he's shaking out of a crust. He feels like he's shaking something off" (301–02). In a rapid series of breakthroughs, he has resisted Banally's implied bribe to revise his novel, implicitly rejected Banally's construction of women as vassals, flouted Strop's dominance by usurping his dance partner, and, in improvising his dance steps, demonstrated his newfound propensity for "formal thinking," which Sukenick associates with the adversarial power of underground art (*In Form* iv). In a final gesture indicative of his release from the encrusted cultural authority Banally embodies, Ron takes Nancy and Marietta home himself.

The important party scene is immediately followed by a protracted three-part dream fantasy, which further elaborates the significance of the kite-flying episode in impelling Ron's transformation. The dream opens with Ron delivering a classroom lecture on Wordsworth. The great Romantic poet, Ron informs his students, belonged to an earlier underground movement, "whose possibilities, it seems to me, have yet to be exhausted" (306). Wordsworth's plight—"to find within the ego sources of power, harmony, affirmation, denied by the conditions of social reality" (307)—prefigures the quandary of Ron's own generation. Writing in the magazine section of what is presumably the *New York Times,* Bernie Marsh had earlier described his generation's predicament as a lack of "social context in which to experiment with . . . liberation, test it, and turn it to new forms of freedom viable both for themselves and for the life of the community" (249). Ironically, Bernie's article is flanked by ads that have appropriated his insurgent generation's rhetoric of liberation for commercial purposes (247–50), the very layout of the page reflecting the co-optative powers of the oppressive social context referred to in the essay. Imprisoned in a society "totally unresponsive to the momentous needs of the ego," Ron's generation, like Wordsworth's before it, must rely on "the synthesizing and projective powers of the imagination" to confirm "the value of the self" and then project "that self into reality to find the world suddenly responsive and fraught with value" (308–09). Drawing directly on the lesson of kite-flying, Ron shares with his students the healing equation: "Unity of experience equals reality of self" (308). Although the innovative art forms this unity generates will not themselves change society, "as a great paradigm" they can inspire social change, confirming "the importance of the imagination in confronting and even creating the world in which we live" (308).

Stirred by Ron's lecture, the students surge out of the classroom shouting "Free-DOM, Free-DOM, Free-DOM" (309), their example soon spreading worldwide, with similar demonstrations breaking out in all the major capitols before dissolving into a parodic cliché of rebellion ("Affiliated Representatives of the Unrepresented and Unaffiliated"), Sukenick's acknowledgment that all ideas, even liberating ones, eventually become sedimented impediments to original thought. Even Wordsworth, despite his early genius, was not immune to co-optation, becoming "an ex-radical, an ex-visionary, and, finally, an ex-poet. Thirty or forty years of stasis more or less, a public monument. Naturally, they made him Poet Laureate" (307). Segueing into its third part, the dream fantasy then focuses on the threat of co-optation. Banally—and banality—are back, the novel's final prison scene crackling with meaningful cliché: Ron, bound in a corner; Marietta tied to the inevitable table; Nancy drugged; Strop, a Nazi Colonel, thoroughly in command, ordering his Sergeant to "set up the camera. Our boys need dirty movies. There's a war on you know. It's the final solution" (311–12). Mock-heroic Ron gnaws through his ropes, effects a cartoon rescue of Nancy and Marietta, commandeers an old DC-3, which starts to lift off. Banally, on the runway spraying bullets from a sub-machine gun, is caught in one of the propellers and "disintegrates like watermelon in a fan" (313). The threat of co-optation has been repelled. Strop Banally is dead. Ron awakens peacefully, with Nancy and Marietta safely asleep on either side of him.

But Banally, inscribed in our consciousness, can die only in our dreams. Like the realm of ideology, Strop's eternal, though his shape may shift. He even makes a cameo appearance at Ron's party celebrating the end of *Up* (323). Interventionist fictions such as *Up* are necessarily critiques from within, tainted by an oppressive culture they can recontextualize but never fully escape. The possibility of experiences other than those manufactured by late capitalist consumer culture depends upon formal thinking, which "brings the sentient consciousness into contact with the wash of phenomena in new integrations that revitalize our sense of the world" (*In Form* xv). The kite-flying episode helps Ron/Sukenick find his form, the form embodied in *Up*, which registers the architecture of the novelist's mind as it is realized in the act of improvisation. But *Up* represents a particular crystallization of continuous experience; it is not a template for future fictions. Such "images of reality are always metaphors like kleenex that are to be used and to be thrown away and then there is the next metaphor ahead, in other words, they have an impermanent validity" (*In Form* 151). At Finch's party, Slade characterizes Nancy and Marietta as representing "being and becoming," the past and the future (296). The morning after spending the night with both women, Ron realizes that the temporal point from which his fiction must flow is the ongoing present: ". . . it's not a question he says of moments one goes along one looks both backward and forward *it's a question of being totally here* a question of response concentration the feel of things like the landscape from a car *like continual improvisation*" (314, italics added). That realization allows him to finish his novel, to finally come down, as the kite does at the end of its flight, a descent Sukenick illustrates typographically (317–20).[16]

The party that concludes the novel is a farewell party as well as a celebration. Ron invites all of his characters, from whom he realizes he is now free. "They were all part of him. He wanted nothing of them but that they exist. He was free of them" (323). In what was considered a bold aesthetic move at the time, Sukenick also "invites" real-life acquaintances to the party, including his then wife, the late Lynn Luria. Trespassing previously sacrosanct boundaries between fact and fiction, he also mentions Nora Kersh Spina and Al Amateau, who along with Lynn and Sukenick "were in the original kite flying incident a few years ago" (326). We are informed that Amateau, "with his impeccable taste," declined the invitation to the party "on grounds of aesthetic propriety" (326). Less finicky about literary conventions, the novelist Steve Katz does attend, "on a special guest appearance from his own novel" (325). Like Sukenick, Katz did not hesitate to include personal information in his early fiction. But "the use of the self," Sukenick insists, "was quite contrary to the doctrine of self-expression. We were not writing autobiography or confession—we were at times using those forms as ways of incorporating our experience into fiction at the same level as any other data" (*In Form* 24). Because the writer's data source is both internal (the writer's imagination) and external (the phenomenal world), mingling characters from both sources in the novel's grand finale emphasizes two of the novel's major characteristics: its departure from "the rather puritan conception of art as illusion, which, in a crude sense, is made necessary by mimetic fiction (if art isn't real it must be illusion)" (*In Form* 24); and its desire to record everything in the writer's mind at the moment of writing, to "Get it down. . . . Record luminous thoughts. . . . Even as it happens. Even as. Even as" (323).

Because of the novel's improvisational, discontinuous, and decidedly nonteleological form, its ending, as might be expected, is ragged, like an interminable party stragglers will not allow to end. "Stragglers" in the final episode of *Up* include the author's dedication to this book, which Ron reads at the party (325); an appeal to readers to encourage their friends to buy the book (329); an acknowledgment that not all of the seemingly autobiographical details in the novel are true (329); and even some second thoughts about concluding the novel: "Maybe I better keep it up a while longer, what am I going to do when I'm done?" (329). The playfully prolonged conclusion, a metaphor, perhaps, of endlessly deferred telos—the goal of a "poetics of experience," which doesn't propose to imitate life but to become "an illuminating addition to its ongoing flow" (*In Form* 6)—is purposeful, a final transgression of readerly expectations inculcated by mimetic texts (and an adumbration, perhaps, of Sukenick's 1986 novel *The Endless Short Story*).

The novel doesn't conclude, then, so much as it terminates, closing on a strange and evocative image. A boyish figure on a tenement roof, "among television aerials," waves a long, bare pole in a slow circle above his head. When "no signal comes," he repeats the procedure, over and over again. The boy, of course, is the artist; the pole he waves, his imaginative power, the "sentient consciousness" searching for data not yet tainted by the society of the spectacle, whose images flood the television antennas around him. His goal is to record the wash of data at the very moment of its convergence into new integrations. Such moments are rare, the integrations themselves only briefly meaningful. But such moments are all that stand between a life of calcified experience and the possibilities for meaningful experience, possibilities revealed through the unpredictable divagations of formal thinking.

As an alternative to mimetic fiction, which in 1968 was still considered normative (an attitude that three decades of innovative fiction has not totally dislodged), *Up* is one of a number of metafictions written in the late Sixties that collectively reinvigorated our thinking about narrative. Despite their common reliance on reflexivity, however, metafictions of this period veer in divergent directions, from the back-to-the-future hermeticism of Gass's *Willie Masters' Lonesome Wife* to the purposefully claustrophobic "process mimesis" of some of Barth's *Funhouse* fictions (Hutcheon 1980, 5), which represented an important early stage of postmodernist fiction. *Up*, I have argued, takes a different direction, one which, from the perspective of thirty years later, seems to have predicted the general state of postmodernist fiction in America today. From the beginning, Sukenick rejected what Chantal Mouffe describes as "apocalyptical postmodernism, which would like us to believe that we are at the threshold of a radically new epoch, characterized by drift, dissemination, and the uncontrollable play of significations" (38).

In an interventionist move, Sukenick locates the continued possibilities of experience in the radical freedom implied by postmodernist freeplay itself. If Sukenick's theory of composition, especially his recuperation of the Emersonian idea of formal thinking, is itself distinctive (the same may be said about aesthetic theories advanced by most postmodernist writers), the general implications of his fiction are wide-ranging. Insertion of the pseudo-autobiographical self into the fictional frame has become a common postmodernist tactic (e.g., Federman, Vonnegut, Barth, Auster, Maso, Curtis White, Richard Powers, Acker). By the late 1970s, most postmodernist fiction writers, including many from Sukenick's generation, were dealing explicitly in their work with public events and figures, Coover with Nixon and the Rosenbergs in *The Public Burning* (1977), Barth with CIA intrigue and abuses in *Sabbatical* (1982), and, more recently, Gass with fascism in *The Tunnel* (1995). The current generation of postmodernist writers—for example, White, Maso, Evan Dara, DeLillo, the late Kathy Acker, and especially Richard Powers—are even more socially conscious in their work, going so far as to reappropriate a theory of agency and responsibility, but from this side of the postmodernist cultural divide.[17] Sukenick's first novel is significant, then, not for its intrinsic merit alone but also for its perspicacity in predicting, as it exemplifies, the enduring importance of that still-relevant aesthetic category, postmodernist fiction.

Notes

1. Bérubé urges a global rather than a formalistic understanding of postmodernism, arguing that the potential for a true postmodernist fiction lies in English-language novels written in postcolonial countries such as India, South Africa, and Trinidad.

2. Similarly, Robert Siegle argues that "[r]eflexivity has *always* been with us and is not just a function of the modern novel's reflection of the breakdown of cultural consensus" (3, italics added). Other scholars who discuss the use of "self-conscious" literary devices in fiction written before postmodernism include Robert Alter, Michael Boyd, Steven G. Kellman, and Brian Stonehill. Key studies of "postmodernist" metafiction include works by Linda Hutcheon, Larry McCaffery, Brian McHale, and Waugh.

3. Among these forms Waugh lists "the well-made plot, chronological sequence, the authoritative omniscient author, the rational connection between what characters 'do' and what they 'are,' the causal connection between 'surface' details and the 'deep,' 'scientific laws' of existence" (7). To this list, one might add the "round" character, the preservation of a narrative frame, Modernist "distance," the distinction between "serious" and "popular" literary genres

and conventions, the distinction between fictive and "real" or historical incidents and characters, narrative continuity, and the use of conventional typography.

4. Siegle has argued that this is true of all reflexive fiction: "Reflexivity is a permanently revolutionary dimension of literature that persists in resisting the yoke of any paradigm that attempts to obscure its own self-transforming qualities" (246–47).

5. It can be argued that 1968 represents a culmination of the rebellious questioning of the grand narratives and representational schema of the Western tradition which had begun with the civil rights demonstrations of the early 1960s, as well as the inevitable coercive reaction to that rebelliousness. In rapid succession, Martin Luther King, Jr. was shot down in Memphis, university students rioted in Paris, Robert Kennedy was assassinated in Los Angeles, the Democratic convention in Chicago was disrupted by riots and police brutality, and the Czech liberation drive was stopped in its tracks when Soviet troops invaded Czechoslovakia.

6. See Barth's "The Literature of Exhaustion" (*Friday Book* 66).

7. For an excellent account of how literary realism depends upon and helps to form certain expectations in readers, see Glazener.

8. In an interview with Adrian Zupp, Sukenick says he doesn't "believe in self-expression. Something gets expressed, I suppose, but, number one, it's not the self as it is, if it's the self at all, it's the self as it's becoming, as it creates itself" ("Q&A"). Also see Sukenick's comments about identity and self-hood in *In Form*, 132–33.

9. As pointed out by Sukenick in *In Form* (108), Barth discusses this tactic at length in "The Literature of Exhaustion," describing his novels as imitations of "the form of the Novel, by an author who imitates the role of Author" (*Friday Book* 72).

10. Sukenick elaborates further upon the political function of art in his interview with McCaffery: "So I figure that one of the things that art is supposed to do is to teach people how to defend their experience and prevent it from being stolen from them by showing them how to use their own imaginations against that manipulative imagination which is not in their own interest" (*In Form* 117).

11. My analysis of the role of gender construction and interventionist strategies in *Up* has been influenced by "Chapter 6: Postmodernisms and Feminisms" in Hutcheon's *The Politics of Postmodernism* and by Hutcheon's influential discussion of postmodernist fiction's technique of installation and subversion in *Poetics of Postmodernism*.

12. In "The Rival Tradition," Sukenick describes his idea of "interventive" fiction: "The way to best understand my concept of 'interventive' is as the end of a series of things. First there was the idea of holding a mirror up to Nature, the realist tradition. Then there was the idea pushed by Surfiction that writing

could be, not an imitation of reality, but an addition to reality. The next phase is what I conceive of as interventive, meaning that writing can actually intervene in and change reality, or experience. . . . I know, as early as my first novel, *Up*, I was already writing this kind of thing" (n.p.).

13. Bernie Marsh, who misunderstands the novel as an attempt at Romantic self-expression, offers the most direct criticism (50–57, 222–26), but both Finch and Kenny Malcolm try to persuade Ron to abandon his novel (95, 277) and, in the novel's last scene, even Ron accuses Otis of being a "bad character" because he lacks "verisimilitude" (328).

14. Revelation, Sukenick says, "does not come from some source beyond ourselves, some essence that enables us to transcend our present state"; similarly, he rejects the possibility "that language makes any direct contact with reality" (*In Form* 28, 110).

15. According to Kutnik, "As a metaphor for writing, the image [of kite flying] expresses Sukenick's theory of composition as an autonomous and continuous flowing which is not so much governed by the writer as initiated by him and then imaginatively participated in. Like kite flying, writing is an activity whose meaning is the actual performance of this activity and not some goal to be reached by means of this performance and then celebrated after the fact, after the act" (97).

16. "Up really does go up," Sukenick told McCaffery; "it's a flight of the imagination. There is literally a scene in the beginning where an astronaut goes up [27–29], and then he comes down again at the end of the book. And the whole novel goes up and down in that curve in a lot ways" (LeClair 290).

17. In a series of articles on Maso, White, Powers, and the later Barth, I have tried to chart this direction. References are included in Works Cited.

Works Cited

Barth, John. *The Friday Book: Essays and Other Nonfiction*. New York: Putnam's, 1984.

Bérubé, Michael. "Teaching Postmodern Fiction Without Being Sure That the Genre Exists." *Chronicle of Higher Education* 19 May 2000: B4–B5.

Boyd, Michael. *The Reflexive Novel: Fiction as Critique*. Lewisburg, Penn.: Bucknell University Press, 1983.

Eco, Umberto. *A Theory of Semiotics*. Bloomington: Indiana University Press, 1976.

Fitzgerald, F. Scott. *The Great Gatsby*. New York: Scribner's, 1925.

Gass, William H. *Willie Masters' Lonesome Wife*. *TriQuarterly* Supplement 2 (1968). Evanston, Ill.: Northwestern University Press, 1968.

Glazener, Nancy. *Reading for Realism: The History of a U.S. Literary Institution, 1850–1910*. Durham, N.C.: Duke Univeristy Press, 1997.

Harris, Charles. B. " 'The Stereo View': Politics and the Role of the Reader in Richard Powers's *Gain*." *Review of Contemporary Fiction* (Fall 1998): 97–108.

———. " 'Blessed by Madness': Curtis White's *Memories of My Father Watching TV*." *Review of Contemporary Fiction* (Summer 1998): 101–16.

———. "The Dead Fathers: The Rejection of Modernist Distance in Carole Maso's *The Art Lover*." *Review of Contemporary Fiction* (Fall 1997): 157–74.

———. "The Age of the World View: The Critique of Realism in John Barth's Sabbatical." *Germany and German Thought in American Literature and Cultural Criticism*. Ed. Peter Freese. Essen, Germany: Die Blaue Eule, 1990. 407–32.

Hutcheon, Linda. *Narcissistic Narrative: The Metafictional Paradox*. New York: Methuen, 1980.

———. *A Poetics of Postmodernism: History, Theory, Fiction*. New York: Routledge, 1988.

———. *The Politics of Postmodernism*. New York: Routledge, 1989.

Kellman, Steven G. *The Self-Begetting Novel*. New York: Columbia University Press, 1980.

Kutnik, Jerzy. *The Novel as Performance: The Fiction of Ronald Sukenick and Raymond Federman*. Carbondale: Southern Illinois University Press, 1986.

LeClair, Tom and Larry McCaffery. *Anything Can Happen: Interviews with Contemporary American Novelists*. Urbana: University of Illinois Press, 1983.

McCaffery, Larry. *The Metafictional Muse: The Works of Robert Coover, Donald Barthleme, and William H. Gass*. Pittsburgh: University of Pittsburgh Press, 1982.

McHale, Brian. *Postmodernist Fiction*. New York: Methuen, 1987.

Mouffe, Chantal. "Radical Democracy: Modern or Postmodern?" Trans. Paul Holdengräber. *Universal Abandon? The Politics of Postmodernism*. Ed. Andrew Ross. Minneapolis: University of Minnesota Press, 1988: 31–45.

Shklovsky, Viktor. *Theory of Prose*. Normal: Dalkey Archive Press, 1990.

———. "Art as Technique." *Russian Formalist Criticism*. Ed. Lee T. Lemon and Marion J. Reis. Lincoln: University of Nebraska Press, 1993.

Siegle, Robert. *The Politics of Reflexivity: Narrative and the Constitutive Poetics of Culture*. Baltimore. Md.: Johns Hopkins University Press, 1986.

Stonehill, Brian. *The Self-Conscious Novel: Artifice in Fiction from Joyce to Pynchon*. Philadelpia: University of Pennsylvania Press, 1988.

Sukenick, Ronald. *Up*. Normal, Ill.: FC2, 1998.

———. *The Death of the Novel and Other Stories*. New York: Dial, 1969.

———. *Wallace Stevens: Musing the Obscure*. New York: New York University Press, 1967.

———. *In Form: Digressions on the Act of Fiction*. Carbondale: Southern Illinois University Press, 1985.

———. *Down and In: Life in the Underground*. New York: William Morrow, 1987.

———. "The Sarah Lawrence Orgies of 1968: An Interview with Author Ronald Sukenick." Interview with Christian Ettinger and Alexander Laurence. *The Write Stuff* (Interviews). Alt-X. <http://www.altx.com/interviews/suk.html>: n.d., n.p.

———. "The Rival Tradition." Inteview with JR Foley. *Flashpoint*. Web Issue #1. Spring 1997 <http://webdesol.com/FLASHPOINT>: n.p.

———. "Q&A: Skydiving Language: Ron Sukenick." Interview with Adrian Zupp. georgejr.com. June 1997 <http://www.georgejr.com/jun97/sukenick.html>: n.p.

———. "Not-fiction." *American Book Review* (November–December 1999): 3, 8.

Waugh, Patricia. *Metafiction: The Theory and Practice of Self-Conscious Fiction*. New York: Methuen, 1984.

What's Your Story: Narration and "A New Knowledge of Reality" in *The Death of the Novel and Other Stories*

Nancy Blake

If Wallace Stevens was right in positing that the "final belief" must be in a "fiction," then Ronald Sukenick's *The Death of the Novel and Other Stories* is an act of faith in that apprehension of reality. As they question our understanding of reality, Sukenick's fictions conscientiously perturb all standard notions surrounding ego identity. Their author's devotion to the art of Wallace Stevens is not indifferent to the elaboration of that critique of the standard Western comprehension of the self and the other that is at the center of the major productions of American modernism and upon which will depend the possibility of postmodernism. Sukenick prefers to speak of his work as belonging to postrealism, however that term is best understood as his way of underlining another aspect of the gesture. Although denying the jurisdiction of the others of reality, Sukenick's fiction poses the question of the authority of the Other. As this article will attempt to show, in the context of modernity and its descendants, the work of art sets as its goal the constitution of its own Other.

Twenty years ago, in order to write about, celebrate, or critique contemporary fiction it was necessary to insist upon the free play of language in and for itself, as opposed to any metaphysics. In the words of Roland Barthes, the "death of the author" reveals that there is "no other origin than language itself, language which ceaselessly calls into question all origins."[1] The title of William Gass's collection of essays,

The World Within the Word, sums up that aesthetic which is certainly both relevent and enlightening to the reader of postmodern American fiction, including that of Ronald Sukenick.

If claiming that the work of art constitues its own Other then is a rather jargonistic phrase, this notion may appear reactionary as it repositions the creative gesture within the structures of the psyche. In contemporary psychoanalytic theory, the Other is the term used to cover that construction which confers meaning. By depersonalizing this structural position, Jacques Lacan underlines several aspects of Freud's theory that are easily missed thanks to the preconceived notions attached to a vulgarized psychological understanding of human identity. When Lacan says that the desire of man is the desire of the Other, he insists on the fact that desire is alienating in several ways, and especially in so far as the desire of the subject is preconditioned by the desire of the Other. As such, the Other is another name for language, if language is understood in the broadest sense. The Other is clearly a personification. What does it mean to advance the proposition that the work of art, in the context of modernity, at least, intends to constitute its own Other?

It may be useful here to distinguish between the ways in which thinkers apprehend reality on the one hand, and the model they construct on the other. For a physicist, the model is an abstract representation of a part of reality, whereas for a painter (or a mathematician), the model is a part of reality, even though the work of art (or the mathematics), which has an independent existence, can sometimes, and under certain conditions, also represent reality. Another way of understanding this argument is to view the work of art not as a representation of reality, but as a screen, which, far from opening onto the world, hides any vision of the world. It is on this screen that something is given to our contemplation. This vision is then presented as fiction per se. This is a theory borrowed from the plastic arts that has become part of the foundations of modernism, at least since Cezanne. The modernist poet sees her/his production, in Wallace Stevens's words, as "part of nature, part of us."

It is well known that the crisis in intellectual history at the beginning of the twentieth century, of which modernism is one manifestation, was marked by at least two losses: that of the function of author and that of the reliance on subject matter. Marcel Duchamp and his "ready-mades" is only one symptom of a questioning of the status of the artist as author that will include an inability to maintain the category of originality as value for example. The author, and therefore the personal psychic structure of an individual as genius, will no longer be an unquestioned criteria for modernity. A second crisis for the understanding of modernist art is a corollary to the death of the author: the indifference of subject matter for the work of art. Artistic production no longer communicates to its audience only through an iconographic program relying on a cultural context and upon the consensus of a group. If self-consciousness is at the forefront of the modernist artist's mode of communication, if she/he is aware and trusts her/his audience to be aware of the history of representation accompanying the treatment of any particular theme, the thrust of the modernist artistic message is elsewhere. When William Carlos Williams, Ezra Pound, and T. S. Eliot each entitle a poem "Portrait of a Lady," as when Manet paints his "Olympia," they do so in reference to all of the works in the Western tradition that have explored those same forms; as such their work takes on the appearance of irony, but that aspect of the work is only secondary. The real impetus of the modernist work is elsewhere.

When Jacques Lacan elaborated his theory in which the place of the father in the Oedipal triangle comes to be called the Other, written A, and assumes the function of language as the "treasury of signifiers," he did so in the context of the existentialist awareness of man's condition as alienated. Lacan invites us to consider alienation as a result of the fact that man is born into language, that, as speaking beings, we do not invent the terms of our message, but rather we are spoken by the language that precedes us. This being the case, what does it mean to say that the work of art aims to constitute its own Other? If it is the Other that makes me desire as I desire, and see as I see, how can the work of art constitute an Other? Are we not born into the Other, as we are born into language? Would the Other not have to be in place in order for an expression, artistic or not, to be apprehended? It would seem that the gesture of the modernist artist is, at the very least, paradoxical. And a spiraling effect on temporality is one of modernism's characteristic gestures. It is also possible that, in the most extreme cases, the work of art places itself, from its inception, under the sign of its own impossibility.

In his preface to *In Form: Digressions on the Act of Fiction*, Ronald Sukenick refers to Wallace Stevens's splendid definition of art as a violence from within against a violence from without. One ploy Sukenick has discovered to disarm the violence of the reality principle is a simple openness to the multiplicity of possibility in the world. Sukenick is allergic to the "truth." His predilection for the term "fiction" is one indication of the phobic reaction triggered by monolithic and linear attempts to channel life into neat definitions. Thus he praises critics like Harold Bloom for being "right in characterizing Stevens's poetry as a process of progressive qualification rather than a search for absolute truth" (*In Form* xi).

Much of *The Death of the Novel and Other Stories* (1969) turns on the uneasy relationship between creative work and its derivatives: teaching, criticism, and theory. What is the "true" work of the artist? The stories were written syncronically with an academic work: *Wallace Stevens: Musing the Obscure* (1967), just as *The Endless Short Story* (1986) was written with *In Form: Digressions on the Act of Fiction* (1985). The question then is what is the relevance or the interest of metadiscourse?

"Theory is a sign of ignorance" (*In Form* 4). Knowing Sukenick's value system, however, his reader remembers to avoid crediting ignorance with a negative connotation. Ignorance is a precious option for ignorance means openness to experience. Ignorance is optimism in the face of an endless task. "As I was saying perhaps ignorance is the key. We all of course know what's going to happen next. Only artists don't know what's going to happen next a quirk of ignorance they share with history and the weather" (*The Endless Short Story* 2–3).

In his need to remain accessible to experience, Sukenick encounters a concept prized by the surrealists who developed their own world view as contemporaries of American modernism. The most striking surrealist technique to play a part in Sukenick's fiction is the "found object," and his narrator exhibits a kinship to Breton's persona in *Nadja* as he defends his passivity in the face of experience: "To continue, at that time Phoebe and I used to frequent Chinese restaurants. That was because it used to be Ero's way to plant his messages in fortune cookies and leave strictly to chance whether you received them or not—Ero favored chance because he said we must remain open to the unknown" (*Death* 169).

Exploiting the found object leads to the incorporation of heterogeneous materials in the fiction. Just as the mind is a "hall of voices," so the story is a collage: "Like improvisation, collage was also crucial as a way of making fresh contact with experience. There was a more direct relation with experience as it registers on the self without the mediation of a priori form, and a correspondingly increased importance of the presence of the self in the work. One felt the need to incorporate the vagaries of experience, its randomness, its arbitrariness, to affirm the experience of composition, and to deny the work as illusion, so that while we admitted the brokenness, the discontinuity of experience, we also swept away many of the chronic schizoid Western attitudes toward mind and experience, thought and poetry, form and chaos, and we gave to our works the only structure that seemed possible or even desirable—the structure of our own minds" (*In Form*, 19).

"The Permanent Crisis," opens *The Death of the Novel and Other Stories* in *style indirect libre*, which means that a third person narrator records the ennui of a young protagonist from the character's own point of view as he experiences the inevitability of his individual existence. In a pattern that the stories will retain as paradigmatic, the protagonist ruminates mostly in a rather Joycean interior monologue, attempting to grasp his experience by holding onto memories of past selves. He is uncomfortably aware that his mental existence threatens to preclude life in the here and now. What saves him from solipsism is the intervention of the other (small o) in the form of his wife who relativizes the province of the mind by reminding him of the prerogatives of the body. The fiction then becomes the embodiment of the need to grasp the flow of experience: ". . . all he could do was try to sense what was happening and compose it like a man as he listens to his own voice composing ceaselessly, he would have to write this down all of it, within a flood which even as he embraced that warmth wondering while he still had time if he couldn't write the whole thing down to have at least the words to repeat and understand swept him beyond his words of it" (*Death* 7). Sukenick has learned well the lesson of Stevens, "It can never be satisfied, the mind, never." So if the story ends with the self-imposed injunction to write, the protagonist makes this resolution on his way to bed with his wife.

The temptation here, as in all of the pieces which make up *The Death of the Novel and Other Stories*, is the desire to secede from life, to step outside of the self of experience, in order to somehow possess not the self so much as the moment of feeling. One of the problems is of course the fallacious impression that we all have of time as composed of discrete units regulated on a strict economy where "spending" and "wasting" are possibilities. We should know by now that time is not an entity, nor an absolute, but rather a relativity, one of the stylized conventions agreed upon to describe a multidimensional reality.

In "Momentum" the juxtaposition of two columns of notes, both seemingly private jottings not meant for a third party becomes an effort to capture the plurality of experience. The right hand column features stream of consciousness narrative, whereas the left provides a detachment of sorts, "my double view," with comments like "Crude! (But true.)" or "Real means locating the present in terms of the past locating the self in terms of the present. Wordsworth, Proust." Although the form presents itself as experimental, it is not really disconcerting because the left hand column assumes the appearance of marginalia. As such, the appearance of the piece on the page mimics the compulsive need to grasp the moment of existence: "but I knew as certainly as I ever know anything that I had hold of myself had hold of my experience no had hold of a level of experience that I mustn't ever lose sight of again . . . so I decided that in the morning I'd better get it all down as quick as I could while it was alive and I did I hope am doing it because what else is writing for" (*Death* 40).

The title story, "The Death of the Novel," although presented as straightforward first person narration, interweaves the personal history of a young literature professor, reading like a journal, with his class notes, which reflect on the form ("The didactic job of the modern novel is to teach people to invent themselves and their work—Robbe-Grillet." [*Death* 47]) with a collage-like effect. The narrative becomes, in Faulkner's term, a "hall of voices" as the I is a clearing house for the thoughts of his intellectual predecessors and the drug culture undergraduates he is attempting to teach. "Art imitates life, n'est-ce pas? But why am I always baiting my readers? That's a nasty habit. This is not *Notes from the Underground* after all. Why am I so hostile and defensive?" (*Death* 71).

The surrealists appreciated the possibilities of the "found object" because they believed, along with Freud, that the unconscious knows no accident, that what happens had to happen, it "was written" as the Arabic puts it, in a metaphor with a postmodern resonance, as long as we understand fate as another name for unconscious desire. The found object is "recognized" by the artist because it embodies the mystery he or she was destined to explore.[2]

Sukenick's decision to weld fiction to "objective chance" leads to "Roast Beef a Slice of Life," the tape recorded piece, featuring two voices, and thus posing, among other questions, the problem of authorship: who's story is this? In what sense can an author assume responsibility for the fiction? This piece takes the concept of the "death of the author" to its logical conclusion. Gertrude Stein concluded that "if it can be done why do it?" however Sukenick discovers that the doing never quite exhausts an "act of the mind." In *The Endless Short Story*, published in 1986, the dinner is duck, but, instead of the mundane chatter of "Roast Beef," the later narrator entertains his dinner companion with stories. The insistence on showcasing the pathetic fallacy is still omnipresent:

> "I didn't know you smoked."
>
> "Well I stopped, but I still like it, and in stories I can smoke without it being harmful to my health."
>
> "In that case, can I have one?"

> "Sure. In the story."
>
> "What happened next," she asked. Taking a deep drag on her cigarette. (*The Endless Short Story* 82)
>
> And she says, *Why don't you use a tape recorder, so you can get at the real truth?*
>
> And he says, *Recorders don't get at the truth, they only get at the facts, the only way you can get at the truth is to make it up. But I could make up using a tape recorder, that's not a bad idea.* (*The Endless Short Story* 85)

If the feminine companions of "Roast Beef" and "Duck Tape" are only characters in a fiction, that fact does not preclude their having a decisive influence on the piece to which they each lend a voice.

"What's Your Story" returns to first person narration and weaves in and out of dream-like pop-porno scenarios with little lip service to unities of time, place, or character. The beautiful "The Birds" is a true collage juxtaposing all levels of discourse both recognizable as that of the protagonist, interior or exterior speech, or foreign to his personality, like the words of the newspapers or of the birds.

One of the conclusions of the present study is that, in modernist poetry, and even more clearly for a postmodernist like Sukenick, the desire for self-expression on the part of a subject/artist has, on one level at least, been abandoned, not without regret, however. Or, if that judgment may seem too radical: the spiritualist error, which consists in assuming a knowledge of the self based on a subjective experience of self-consciousness, is no longer tenable. The result is whimsically nostalgic, as in John Ashbery's lines:

> . . . Lately
> I've been looking at old-fashioned plaids, fingering
> Starched white collars, wondering whether there's a way
> To get them really white again. My wife
> Thinks I'm in Oslo—Oslo, France that is. ("Worsening
> Situation," *Self-Portrait* 4)

What persists, what we have called the function of the work of art as Other, is the "use" of the work as means of rendering the world visible. The function of the poetic is to permit us to see the world. "Fiction constitutes a way of looking at the world" (*Death* 41). This is the first sentence of the title story "The Death of the Novel," a text which demonstrates the crisis of authority resulting from the demise of authorial mastery and the persistent desire to hold on to some degree of meaning. If we need fiction in order to see the world, it is because we have no unmediated access to our own experience: ". . . she had the virtue of normalizing the chaotic a charming if minor consequence of the collapse of the moral universe is this what John Ashbery means by the new spirit . . ." (*The Endless Short Story* 97).

At the distance of thirty years, which separates us from Ronald Sukenick's early collection *The Death of the Novel and Other Stories*, an intellectual kinship becomes more apparant. Serious writers in France and in the United States have been working in converging directions for some time. Sukenick and others have underlined the communality of interests of writers starting with Sarraute and Robbe-Grillet in France and finding a particularly American tone in Donald Barthelme, John Hawkes, Ishmael Reed, Jonathan Baumbach, Steve Katz, and others. It is liberating however to forget the barriers erected between fiction and poetry and to look at the work of contemporaries like Emmanuel Hocquard, Claude Royet-Journoud, and Anne-Marie Albiach in France, and Michael Palmer, Keith Waldrop, Bob Perelman, and others in the United States for writing coming to grips with philosophical concerns while pursuing them with the means furnished by the poetic.

Sukenick has stated that after D. H. Lawrence's first impact as a sexual iconoclast it should now be recognized that his real subject was the crisis of the modern psyche, and the same will come to be true of Henry Miller. Quite simply put, writing is "an act of the mind," as Stevens knew. We must avoid dismissing this in terms of solipsism or tautology; the work of art does become a funhouse of mirrors, yet the message of postmodern fiction, as of the psychoanalytic theory, elaborated during the same period, is that we have no way of coming to apprehend ourselves except through the mirror of the gaze of others. We read these books, as we read all serious books, to find out how we are to live our lives.

Notes

1. See Roland Barthes, "From Work to Text," and "The Death of the Author," in *Image-Music-Text: Essays by Barthes,* selected and trans. by Stephen Heath. London: Fontana/Collins, 1977.

2. André Breton illustrates the notion of the "found object" for Surrealism with the example of an object discovered at the flea market by Giocometti

which allows him to finish a female figure he had been working on for some time without being able to see it clearly. See *Mad Love*. Lincoln: University of Nebraska Press, 1987.

Works Cited

Ashbery, John. *Self-Portrait in a Convex Mirror*. New York: Viking Press, 1975.

Barthes, Roland. *Image-Music-Text: Essays by Barthes,* selected and trans. by Stephen Heath. London: Fontana/Collins, 1977.

Stevens, Wallace. *The Collected Poems*. New York: Alfred A. Knopf, 1978.

Sukenick, Ronald. *The Death of the Novel and Other Stories*. New York: Dial Press, 1969.

———. *The Endless Short Story*. New York: Fiction Collective, 1986.

———. *In Form: Digressions on the Act of Fiction*. Carbondale: Southern Illinois University Press, 1985.

———. *Wallace Stevens: Musing the Obscure*. New York: New York University Press, 1967.

Sukenick's Posthumans

Ursula K. Heise

Reflecting on the work of Ronald Sukenick inevitably involves a task of retrospective evaluation. Sukenick belongs to the generation of writers who crucially shaped the theory and practice of postmodern American fiction in the 1960s and 1970s, and his work up to and including *Mosaic Man* (1999) has, with some qualifications, remained committed to the poetics he helped to formulate a quarter of a century earlier. The radically anti-mimetic, anti-narrative, and highly self-referential understanding of narrative in this period has not, by and large, perpetuated itself into younger generations of writers: American fiction in the 1980s and 1990s, although it has retained an intense self-consciousness about its own linguistic, narrative, and cultural constructedness, has nevertheless returned to strategies of realist or, sometimes, magical realist narration that aim at capturing those stories and histories that mainstream cultural consciousness had previously ignored or repressed. Although a resistance to realism understood as any simple reflection of sociocultural conditions in the text remains part and parcel of this more recent variant of postmodernism, it characteristically returns to questions of historical understanding that the self-consciousness of fiction in the 1960s and 1970s had made it difficult to address. In this altered literary and cultural landscape, we must ask what relevance one should attribute to narrative projects such as Sukenick's: have they been superseded by different forms of innovation so that their chief interest today is one of literary history, and if so, what is their place in the history of the twentieth-century novel? Or do the experimental assumptions of the older postmodernists continue to matter, though possibly in quite different ways than were envisioned thirty years ago?

I will approach these questions by focusing on the issue of character construction, which stands out as one of the most striking features not only of Sukenick's experimental fictions, but also those of many other postmodernists of his generation. The antihumanism that manifests itself in Sukenick's persistent refusal to grant his fictional characters any plausible psychology or, indeed, any coherent identity that would remain recognizable over the duration of the text, has often been noted, and has either been condemned as a symptom of the degeneracy of postmodern fiction or celebrated as a welcome liberation from the musty traditions of realism, high modernism, and liberal humanism. The analysis proposed here will focus on an early text, the novel *Out* (1973), and Sukenick's latest work, *Mosaic Man*, so as to foreground the way in which the questioning of human identity in these and some of his other works is associated with a surprisingly realist conception of place and geography, on one hand, and with the exploration of how new technologies of information and communication alter the experience of space and the configuration of human identity, on the other. Even as the unstable identities of Sukenick's characters foreground their textual constructedness, they also point to broader concerns in the sociocultural perception of human identity: centrally, the question of how the human subject should be reconceptualized in its systemic relations to planet-wide nonhuman spaces, whether these be the webs of global ecology or the networks of international information technology. Seen from this perspective, Sukenick's narrative experiments as well as his theoretical statements take on a new significance; in contrast to other postmodernists of his generation who resolutely reject the notion that literature reflects reality in any way, Sukenick's accounts of his creative project remain suspended between an outspoken resistance to mimesis and the affirmation that narrative "adds to" reality. This ambiguity, I will argue, constitutes the beginnings of a conception of narrative that should be understood to aim at the articulation of a "posthuman" rather than antihuman perception of character identity.

Nomad Names

Sukenick's early work, at first sight, seems firmly rooted in the antimimetic narrative strategies that emerged between the late 1950s and the early 1970s mainly in France, Italy, and the United States. In typical "metafictional" fashion, it does not allow readers to imagine novels and short stories as alternative worlds, but reminds them persistently that what they are confronted with is text structured according to specific and highly artificial conventions of language and literature. Fragmentation of the plot, play with the typographical layout of the page, characters in stories who write stories themselves, and explicit comments from the narrative voice on its own procedures all form part of this self-referential game, and link Sukenick's fiction to that of John Barth, Donald Barthelme, Christine Brooke-Rose, Italo Calvino, William Demby, Raymond Federman, Steve Katz, Clarence Major, Ishmael Reed, Nathalie Sarraute, and Gilbert Sorrentino, as well as that of younger postmodernists such as Kathy Acker and Theresa Hak Kyung Cha. As part of the questioning of realist as well as high-modernist assumptions about narrative, fictional characters in Sukenick's novels are persistently described as textual constructs rather than representations of real-life humans. From implausible names and lack of distinctive physiological or psychological features to the absence of motivation and coherent sequences of action, Sukenick pulls all narrative registers to keep the reader from perceiving his characters as imitations of real individuals, let alone from identifying with them.

With thirty years' hindsight, this attack on the realistic character is not particularly surprising, but on the contrary forms part of a set of assumptions shared by a large number of experimental writers in the 1960s and 1970s. In 1957, French *nouveau romancier* Alain Robbe-Grillet had already declared character one of several "outdated notions" that no longer have relevance for the contemporary novel: "Le roman des personnages appartient bel et bien au passé, il caractérise une époque: celle qui marqua l'apogée de l'individu. . . . Le culte exclusif de 'l'humain' a fait place à une prise de conscience plus vaste, moins anthropocentriste. Le roman paraît chanceler, ayant perdu son meilleur soutien d'autrefois, le héros" ("Sur quelques notions périmées" 28) ["The novel of characters belongs entirely to the past, it describes a period: that which marked the apogee of the individual. . . . The exclusive cult of the 'human' has given way to a larger consciousness, one that is less anthropocentric. The novel seems to stagger, having lost what was once its best prop, the hero" ("On Several Obsolete Notions" 28–29)].[1] This rejection of plausible characters as the convention of a bygone age was shared by a large number of writers from Walter Abish and William Burroughs to Thomas Pynchon and Gilbert Sorrentino, and saw itself reinforced by the antihumanist tendency of some of the French post-structuralist theories that began to be imported into the United States during the 1960s.[2] Sukenick's own theoretical statements seem to confirm that his writing forms part of the same paradigm, for example when he declares that the contemporary experimental novel "has no plot, no story, no character, no chronological sequence, no verisimilitude, no imitation, no allegory, no symbolism, no subject matter, no 'meaning.' . . . [It] is non-representational—it represents itself" ("The New Tradition in Fiction" 43–44). In one of his short stories, he claims that "[r]ealistic fiction presupposed chronological time as the medium of a plotted narrative, an irreducible individual psyche as the subject of its characterization, and, above all, the ultimate, concrete reality of things as the object and rationale of its description. In the world of postrealism, however, all of these absolutes have become absolutely problematic" ("The Death of the Novel" 41). And in an interview, he confirms that "[i]f you drop the idea of imitation as the mainstay of fiction, then the idea that you need 'characters' drops away pretty quickly" (Interview with Larry McCaffery 295).

I will return later to the question of the extent to which Sukenick's narrative theory actually conforms to the metafictional paradigm that is typically associated with the 1960s and 1970s. First, however, I would like to explore how the dismantling of character is articulated in one his early novels, *Out*, in conjunction with a particular configuration of narrative space. *Out*, as is well known, stands out at first sight not so much by its topography as by its typography. Its eleven chapters are numbered in reverse order from 10 to 0; each page of text contains three paragraphs, but whereas the paragraphs in chapter 10 consist of ten lines each, they shrink to nine in chapter 9, eight in chapter 8, and so forth, so that the amount of blank space and the pace of reading increase until the novel reaches chapter 0, which is followed by several empty pages. This typographical entropy is accompanied by a "plot" that consists of several recurring thematic structures: first, the suggestion of a secret organization involved in an undisclosed sabotage plot, which is signalled by the persistent appearance of code-named characters carrying sticks of dynamite to secret meetings, though what their clandestine mission might be is, needless to say, never made clear; second, the journey of the protagonist(s) across the United States from New York to Los Angeles; third, the outlines of a biographical narrative that describes scenes from a childhood (we do not find out whose) in the early chapters, followed by events at a college and a counter-culture festival, an initiation at the hands of a Native American named Empty Fox, and the attainment of some form of extraordinary vision or perception by the protagonist(s) toward the end.

The fact that in all three of these "strands of plot," it is difficult to say just who conspires, travels, or is initiated and how many people are involved already points to the central problem of character in the novel: *Out* only has few characters that are identifiable as such. Instead, what action occurs is carried out by names that appear to migrate from body to body. Thus, in chapter 9, two conspirators, Rex and Ova, are mugged by a character named Jojo, whom Rex tells (falsely, the reader assumes) that they are called Carl and Velma. However, the narrative voice subsequently does indeed refer to them as Carl and Velma until Carl, somewhat later, encounters another man who calls himself Carl, and reacts by introducing himself as Donald, whereupon the narrative voice promptly begins to call him "Donald." The new Carl takes Rex-Carl-Donald home to meet his wife, Ova, who is apparently not identical with the woman previously associated with Rex. Chapter 8, instead of following "Donald's" further adventures, returns to two figures who had appeared in chapter 10: Harrold, a male, and President Nixon, "Nixie" for short, a female, except that Nixie now appears to have transformed into Trixie: whether this is the same or a different woman is not spelled out. In chapter 7, a character named Nick (perhaps a male version of Nixie?) driving a camper picks up a couple called Scott and Ova, makes love to Ova, then leaves the camper and hitches a ride himself with a man who calls him Carl and claims he himself is Nick until the newly minted Carl exposes him as "Tommy the Tourist," which effectively turns Nick into Tommy—but only until some college students a little later (mis)take Carl for Tommy the Tourist, which makes him Tommy for the next few pages. And so on, and so forth: Sukenick's nomad names attach themselves to whatever human "body" happens to appear, and it soon becomes impossible for the reader to remember the series of transformations that each character has undergone (which include, sometimes, transformations of age and gender) and consequently, to distinguish individuals from each other. This is even true of a character named Sukenick, who appears in chapter 5 but subsequently turns into Roland Sycamore and then into R. Arr and finally R ("Roland Sycamore you don't know this yet peeled off from the Sukenick character . . . and the latter is no longer a character at all but the real me if that's possible I'm getting out of this novel," the narrator slyly comments [164]). The difficulty in distinguishing the characters is heightened by incidents that occur several times over, but that involve—or seem to involve—different persons; secret meetings, robberies, seductions, coded messages, stays at "New Vacancy" chain motels, hitchhikers on the road, and confrontations with the police recur in almost identical form. This replacement of well-defined figures by an inventory of proper names, incidents, and tag phrases that are frequently recirculated has led one critic to speak of a "stream of character" in the novel (Bergmann 9).

Startling though this procedure may be, it is not wholly unparalleled in postmodern fiction: late Beckett and Robbe-Grillet novels, though they differ in other aspects of narrative technique, play with recirculated names and incidents in similar ways. Accordingly, Sukenick's strategy has been interpreted as a means of derealizing character and foregrounding that human identity is a fluid process of constant becoming rather than a fixed entity.[3] This abstract though not inaccurate interpretation, however, does not take into account how the perpetual displacements of unreal human identities in the novel line up with spatial displacements that are mapped out in terms of real geography. The journey the novel describes progresses from New York City to the vicinity of Niagara in upstate New York (53, 64), Indiana (86), across the Mississippi to Rochester (92–93) and Blue Earth, in Minnesota (95), to the Corn Palace in Mitchell, South Dakota (106–07, 115), Kadoka and Rapid City in the same state (132, 134), the Black Hills (140), Harney Peak (147, 155) and Mount Rushmore (139, 149), Red Desert in southern Wyoming (164–65), crosses the Continental Divide (180), and moves on to Dinosaur and Panguitch, Utah (200, 208–09), Bryce Canyon National Park (217–21), Las Vegas (221–23), Santa Anita, in the Los Angeles area (224–25), Balboa (238) and Laguna Beach, south of Los Angeles (236), and finally out into the Pacific Ocean in the last chapter. "Part of the message is get a road map all these places are real even the more unlikely ones I've traveled among them slept in their campsites their motels form is when you look back and see your footprints in the sand," the narrator claims in one of the novel's most self-referential chapters (164).[4] It is true that the places named in the novel are all locatable on maps of the United States and allow the reader to trace the geographical if not the logical progression of the plot precisely; what is more surprising, however, is that a narrator who usually does his best to remind the readers of the text's fictionality ("Hi. Everything up to here has been a novel" [162]) would suddenly foreground its referential accuracy to insist that at least in terms of space, the novel does have a firm hold on reality. Why would a novel that so ostentatiously thwarts all expectations of narrative logic, normal chronology, and plausible character identities nevertheless retain a realistically mapped-out space?

Interpretations that focus only on Sukenick's play with textuality and narrative conventions cannot, I believe, adequately account for this dimension of *Out*. This is not to deny that the text foregrounds the narrative constructedness of the protagonists (early on, one of them remarks, "I have something to confess to you Carl isn't my real name. That's because I'm not real. I'm only trying to be real. Like a character in a novel" [26]), but to emphasize that these metafictional games have a point besides pure self-referentiality. I will argue that the combination of changing, shifting, and blending characters with the gradual progression through American landscapes implies that *character is defined as an experience of space.*

Indeed, the foregrounding of characters' textuality is precisely the mechanism whereby Sukenick connects humans with nonhuman species and environments—that are evidently also textual. Textual self-referentiality, in other words, serves to link spheres that could not normally communicate directly. This is suggested by a scene toward the beginning of the novel that at first sight seems oddly out of place in a text that up to this point had focused on social conflict, repression, resistance, and counter-resistance. The protagonist, named Carl at this stage, has just escaped a violent demonstration tear-gassed by police and is on his way to a secret meeting—he has forgotten with whom—near a tiger cage at the zoo. But his co-conspirator has not shown up: "He wants to leave. If he doesn't leave something terrible is going to happen to him but his body won't move. His body likes that other bigger body behind the bars likes its bigness likes its gravity it's a more serious body than his own it draws him he wants to merge with it embrace it be consumed destroyed he doesn't he begins to shake and sweat" (20). Suddenly, instead of his partner, an unknown man appears, fearlessly approaches the cage and begins to speak to the tigress, who clearly understands and obeys his words. Carl asks him how he manages to communicate with the animal but gets only vague answers, and the unknown man turns to leave. "Just then the tiger roars. The world ends. Then it begins again. When Carl looks the man in khaki is gone another man is there instead" (22)—this time the person he was originally supposed to meet, and who introduces himself as Carl, while the earlier Carl turns into Donald. The sudden disappearance and substitution of the man in khaki foreground, as so often in Sukenick's novels, the author's power to alter the realities of the text at will; but in the brief fictional scene that precedes, the textual character that had suddenly turned up is able to communicate with a (paper) tiger, accomplishing verbally the communion with the non-human other that Carl had desired physically.[5]

The full significance of this odd scene emerges only much later in the novel, when the protagonist "Ron Sukenick," narrating his story in the first person, encounters a Native American with the telling name Empty Fox in the Black Hills of South Dakota, who initiates him into a new way of relating to landscape (and who is, incidentally, also able to make visions of other people appear and disappear in front of Sukenick's eyes, in an echo of what the narrator did for Carl in the zoo scene). Empty Fox makes Sukenick pick out a rock that he feels a special connection with, and as Sukenick explores the shape of this stone, his perception changes:

> . . . its idiosyncracies make it shine in the light this way and that I look up. Something is different dark green of pines more intense
>
> blue of sky deeper granite rocks sharper denser the picture postcard lake more convincing the ground more solid I love this place I'm flooded with love for it. I lie down and put my cheek against the earth breathing deeply slowly then a strange thing happens. I feel heavier warmer my
>
> body flows tingles quivers glows I feel the gravity that connects me with the earth passing through me like a current like a responding love the sun hugs me the sun is in love with me I get up breathe deep I can't understand this. Then the words come into my mind I don't know
>
> where they come from the secret is that there is no secret. (148–49)

The desire to merge with the nonhuman is temporarily fulfilled in this scene, and the somewhat naïve ecomysticism of the protagonist's experience is at least partly compensated by the final line, which precludes the kind of transcendence or metaphysical insight that typically accompanies such encounters with nature. Furthermore, in the following sentence, Ron is brutally awakened from his meditation by a family of tourists whose consumerist attitude toward the landscape stands in sharp contrast with the perspective that has just opened up to him. Nevertheless, his experience realizes what Carl, during the earlier incident at the zoo, had only been able to imagine: the fusion of the human with the nonhuman.

Shortly afterwards, during a marijuana high, Sukenick imagines that he is swimming in the ocean among whales, and indeed seems to have become one of them, in yet another moment of fusion with the natural world.[6] As a consequence of his encounter with Empty Fox and these experiences, the protagonist, now transmuted into Roland Sycamore, develops perceptions and abilities that appear supernatural but do not add up to any coherent alternative vision or mission. After he meets Arnold, whose name is not only an anagram of his own but also of the author's, he asks him, one by one, about the other conspirators that had appeared earlier, but all of them are either dead, in prison, drug-addicted, or have defected to the other side; in other words, as the protagonist's relationship to the nonhuman environment changes, many of the past identities he has drifted through disappear from the text, and his own identity seems to focus, shrink, and fold in upon itself as he successively turns into R. Arr and then simply R, the figure whom the Sailor takes out to the Pacific in the last two chapters. It is unclear whether the final vision of an airplane over the ocean writing figures in the sky—figures that assume, among other things, the shape of a whale (290)—is in the end a dream or not; little does it matter, given the uncertainties of the text as a whole. What is clear is that the protagonist, at the very end, seems to have found a way out of shape-shifting identities and out of text altogether into a merger with the ocean that is not articulated through any words or meanings, but simply through the reader's confrontation with a set of blank pages—a particular experience of natural space translated back into the spatial expanse of the book.[7]

It is worth emphasizing, however, that this ending does not amount to any kind of nature mysticism; nowhere does the text suggest that the protagonist's entropic dissolution has any redemptive qualities, or any definable meaning at all. Rather, what *Out* aims at capturing especially in its final pages is the simple experience of space, of a nonhuman environment that cannot be made more human or more experienceable through language. In the course of the novel, what confirms this reading is that nature itself seems to be subject to entropic processes that threaten its existence as much as that of the protagonist. Already in the middle of the transcontinental journey, when the characters Rex and Alma approach the Mississippi, they notice miles and miles of dying corn fields (91). On the other side of the Mississippi, "[t]he dying corn is the same only there's more of it and more of it is dying. And there are these long uncooperative stretches of pure distance naked to the eye and to the wind rising across their widths ripping through occasional islands of cottonwoods far off" (93): a first hint that the deterioration of nature goes along with an exposure to pure space.

In the second half, references to ecological disaster appear more and more often: "Roland turns on the radio flash an A-bomb blast at the testing grounds has leaked an atom cloud into the atmosphere Vegas on evacuation alert oil spills on the coast earthquakes reported near Los Angles avalanches in the Sierra Nevada flooding mudslides in the hills in the south brush fires burn out of control the seals facing extinction from DDT pelicans seabirds whales dying out fish poisoned" (223–24), one passage runs, subsequently combining the natural with a series of social catastrophes. The same occurs again later on: "Oil. Last major Pacific Coast nesting colony of the great blue heron. Seal rookeries thousands of volunteers struggled. Pick up birds and clean their feathers. 'Maybe three per cent. All this may be completely hopeless.'

WHALES STILL MAKE GOOD PET FOOD. More than 600,000 harpooned and cut up. Blue whale largest creature ever probably over the brink. MOBY DICK WAS A SPERM—IS FACING EXTINCTION" (261).[8] That the extinction of whales is repeatedly foregrounded in these passages is no coincidence, not only because Melville's *Moby Dick* functions as one of Sukenick's models as a chase after nothingness, but also because the whale had earlier appeared in "Ron Sukenick's" dream. Not only does the protagonist's own identity shrink into nothingness, then, but the creature with whom he seeks to identify symbolically disappears at the same time. Whatever natural space the (post)human protagonist merges with at the end can therefore clearly not be understood as a redemptive alternative to the cultural sphere.

A brief look at the novel that followed *Out*, *98.6* (1975), may serve to confirm some aspects of this analysis. As Jerzy Kutnik has pointed out, *98.6* foregrounds ecological issues and the conflicts between scientific and artistic activity quite explicitly (118–19). Especially the long middle section of this novel, entitled "The Children of Frankenstein," focuses on a group of men and women who attempt to build a commune that is integrated into nature. Even though these characters initially have much more recognizable identities than those of *Out*, they too change their names (some of them several times) in the course of the chapter and finally end up with names that designate places and phenomena of nature (Hornung, "Absent Presence" 19): Bud, Branch, Blossom, Eucalyptus, Dawn, Cloud, and Wind. Even more unequivocally than in *Out*, the effect of the name-shifting is the blending of human identity with the nonhuman environment, since it soon becomes difficult for the reader to keep track of what the original name and gender of each character was. And if the protagonist(s) of the earlier novel occasionally experienced moments of identification with animals and their mode of being, the members of this commune have such insights frequently and attempt to re-orient their lifestyles accordingly (two of them rename themselves initially "Goose" and "Feather"). Play on the textual nature of these transformations once again facilitates the amalgamation of the human with the nonhuman: one of the characters, Ron, later renamed Cloud, begins to write a novel about the commune, but decides to let actual events constitute the writing rather than any of his words on paper, though of course the reader only learns about these events through written words.[9] Ultimately, however, this attempt to return to nature through a social collective fails through internal personal tensions, pressure from other social groups, and possibly also from the community's failure adequately to confront the otherness of the nonhuman and prehuman as well as its sameness.[10] As many (though not all) of the characters revert to their original names at the end of the chapter, the experiment in a collective identity that would not oppose human to nonhuman modes of being comes to a close. In both *Out* and *98.6*, then, the dissolution of recognizable character identities is associated with the experience of space and an altered perception of the natural, nonhuman sphere. So, far from being merely an exercise in narrative self-referentiality, it points to a different conception of human identity; its instability in both texts suggests the possibility of an integration of the human into a nonhuman space that also includes other kinds of life and modes of existence, without, however, presenting this fusion as a form of transcendence or redemption.

Character and the Resistance to Mimesis

Although Sukenick's handling of character in *Out* and *98.6* counteracts the illusion of fully rounded, psychologically plausible human figures, it does not, as the foregoing analysis indicates, reject referentiality on all counts. A brief look at the author's theoretical statements about his own work confirms this ambiguity in his approach to narrative mimesis: although Sukenick considers mimesis an outdated concept, he in fact repeatedly justifies his representation of the human by arguing that it reflects tendencies in contemporary society. In addition, Sukenick draws a clear line between his own novelistic endeavor and that of other contemporary writers who aim at detaching literary expression as much as possible from any representation of reality. His complex poetics rejects literature as a means of reflecting or imitating reality, but casts it instead as an addition to or supplementation of the real—the novel as a particular form of experience. In light of these statements, Sukenick's experiments with character construction can be understood as one in an interdisciplinary range of attempts to move beyond the anthropocentric perspectives of traditional humanism to reenvision human identity, at the turn of the millennium, in relation to natural as well as technological spaces and modes of being—in other words, to develop a "posthumanism" rather than the "antihumanism" that has typically been associated with postmodern theories and practices of writing in the 1960s and 1970s.

"Reality doesn't exist, time doesn't exist, personality doesn't exist," Sukenick states categorically in the essay/short story "The Death of the Novel" (41)—a claim that seems to lead logically to just the focus on pure textuality that is the hallmark of much postmodern fiction. Yet when he explains just why he has considered it necessary to abandon conventional strategies of character construction, Sukenick does quite often invoke contemporary sociocultural conditions as the model and motive for his experiments. In an interview with Larry McCaffery, for example, Sukenick argues that, on one hand, characters are simply conceptual and semiotic entities that have nothing specifically human about them ("What goes on beneath the ordinary idea of characterization . . . is really not very unlike the ordinary process of the mind in any inquiry about anything. In this case, instead of the entities being concepts, ideas, symbols, points of view, they are called Frank, Mary, and Larry" [295]); but on the other hand, he claims that the notion of "character" as a distinctive individual no longer adequately reflects contemporary social realities:

> The other side of this . . . is the sense I have that individuals' personalities are becoming less and less important and less defined. . . . It seems that people now, for better or for worse and for good reasons usually, are less defined—more "laid back," as they say, "going with the flow" and all that. I'm using these clichés on purpose to show that people think about personality, even their own, in this way. I also like to believe that you can have a more flattened out, flowing, less rigidly defined personality that is still not necessarily uninvolved on its own terms . . . this idea of pursuing a job or career, with the individual succeeding through conflict and struggle; the idea that character . . . was the thing that saw you through that process and was its driving force, man's most essential untouchable element—all that has been eroded by the sense of collectivity, by the sense that people's character traits can be drastically changed by drugs, by brainwashing, by the interchangeability of people in corporate slots, by the rate at which information comes at us. It's just very difficult to absorb and respond to so much information while having a hardened, brittle personality circumference, as opposed to one that is porous.
>
> (295–96)

The idea articulated in the first paragraph seems loosely derived from David Riesman's hypothesis of a transition from "inner-directed" to "other-directed" character in late modern societies, a claim he first made in 1950 in *The Lonely Crowd*, but that achieved wide public prominence and influence in the 1960s.[11] In another interview, Sukenick similarly declares, "Maybe there aren't real characters. . . . Maybe people are much more fluid and amorphous than the realistic novel would have us believe," and he adds: ". . . my drive is to dissolve character. I think that that's not only a need on my part, but I presume to think that that's also a cultural need for a lot of people, for the culture in general perhaps. And I think that it is *happening* that modes of character are breaking down, as a matter of fact. They're becoming inadequate" (Interview with Joe David Bellamy 62, 64; original emphasis). In these and similar statements, Sukenick justifies his experimentation with character in the novel by arguing that it reflects one dimension of really occurring cultural processes—the erosion of "character" as a mark of personal strength and individual distinction; in other words, he claims implicitly that his character construction is at least partially mimetic.

This sense of a basic tension in Sukenick's attitude toward fictional mimesis emerges even more clearly in other, more general statements. In response to Joe David Bellamy's suggestion that people always make up their own characters to some extent, he remarks, "Oh, yes, of course. I just think what I'm doing in that respect is an *imitation* of how we perceive things" (Interview with Joe David Bellamy 62; italics added). More generally but even more pointedly, he claims in another interview: "My feeling is that you have always to move in the direction of the data of experience in 'reality,' whatever the chances you can't do this" (Interview with Larry McCaffery 282), and a theoretical essay again clearly posits the attempt to capture a dimension of reality as the root motive for formal innovation: "I presume that the movement of fiction should always be in the direction of what we sense as real. Its forms are expendable. The novelist accommodates to the ongoing flow of experience, smashing anything that impedes his sense of it, even if it happens to be the novel. Especially if it happens to be the novel" ("The New Tradition in Fiction" 40). Obviously, this kind of statement is incompatible with a straightforwardly antimimetic poetics that would see fiction primarily as a means of investigating the functioning of language. Sukenick, then, must be understood to argue against a specific, historically conditioned form of representing reality that has come to be called literary "realism" rather than against the more general project of representing reality as such. And even though he concedes that narrative language may resist this project to some degree ("whatever the chances you can't do this"), he clearly does not consider the representation of reality or experience in narrative impossible or meaningless as a matter of principle.

Despite occasional negations of the real—no doubt meant to provoke more than to persuade—Sukenick's poetics therefore does rest on a broadly understood mimetic foundation, however anti-mimetic his narrative practice may appear at first sight. When he speaks of a breakdown of mimesis in his theoretical writings, he usually refers to the obsolescence of a particular mode of representing the real—that of the nineteenth-century novel. In response to this breakdown, he argues in one interview, one possible reaction was what he calls the "retreat into literature" (Interview with Larry McCaffery 281–82), which he sees as the strategy chosen by such writers as John Barth, William Gass, and Robert Coover. His own route, as he defines it, is not the one into pure textuality, but the reinvention of form under the imperative not only to render experience more authentically, but indeed to add to it. More than *imitation*, *supplementation* of experience is the basic concept that informs his poetics: ". . . the kind of book I most want to write is the kind of book that *fails* back into the experience which it is about. It emerges—and re-emerges—with this experience, having added itself to it. . . . My work has to cancel itself out to do what it is trying to do. It isn't trying to transcend experience, but is trying to add to experience" (ibid. 293; original emphasis). How this somewhat cryptic program might translate into narrative practice is perhaps most clearly visible in *Out*, where the story of the dissolution of character into a variety of urban and natural spaces lapses out of language and into the experience of the space of the blank page, which both refers to the experience of space described in the novel and constitutes its own experience of textual space apart from any referential function. This combination of a fundamental mimetic impulse and the relentless destruction of established mimetic forms—whether they derive from the nineteenth-century or the high-modernist novel—is the hallmark of Sukenick's brand of postmodernism. His most recent novel shows how this complex treatment of mimesis operates in his partly autobiographical, partly fictional approach to the question of Jewish identity.

The Posthuman Mosaic

Mosaic Man, through its title pun, combines Sukenick's interest in human identity put together from a multitude of fragments with that in human identity shaped by Jewish law and culture. On the surface, this novel seems to have a more coherent protagonist than *Out* in that it appears to be structured as an autobiography. The early chapters revolve around the fantasized cartoon identities of a young boy and the sexual adventures of a college-age male American in Paris, whereas the later ones focus on journeys in search of identity and history undertaken by a gradually aging Jewish-American writer: the character Sukenick travels to Poland, the country of his family's origin as well as of Auschwitz; to Jerusalem, the place where Jewish identity can (perhaps) come into its own; to Venice, site of the oldest Jewish ghetto, where the aging writer encounters his own younger ego; to Mainz, where he reads to a German audience along with two other Jewish writers; and back to the United States at the time of the Gulf War. However, like many of Sukenick's earlier fictions, *Mosaic Man* mixes autobiographical elements with free-wheeling invention, and the protagonist is prone to shifts of name, age, and gender. *Mosaic Man* plays with a profusion of characters whose names resemble or are identical to that of the author—Ronnie, Ron, Ronda, Ron Sukenick, Ronald Martin, RaMSCaN, RamSCaM, Ramsey Shade, Rona, Ronda Fry—and especially in the last chapter, the protagonist changes gender and names so often that it is difficult for the reader to know how many different characters are involved. Some of these characters appear in sections of the novel that echo other texts and authors, from Thomas Mann and Henry Miller to Vladimir Nabokov, Ishmael Reed, Thomas Pynchon, and Sukenick's own previous novels.[12] Like *Out*, then, *Mosaic Man* combines a protagonist whose identities shift frequently with spatial settings that are configured in realistic terms.

But the experience of *physical space*, whereas it remains an important concern in *Mosaic Man*, is not as overriding an issue as it was in *Out*. The changing locales certainly contribute to the instability of the protagonist's identity, but more centrally, the novel explores how identity is shaped, refracted, and distorted through the *virtual space* of communication and information media. Scripture is the most obvious of these: one of the two sections that subdivide the novel is entitled "Writing," and the titles of individual chapters, "Genes," "Ex/Ode," "Umbilicus," "Autonomy," "Profits," and "Hand Writing on Wall" allude to books of the Hebrew Bible or to events described in them. The first few paragraphs of the first chapter, "Genes," reflect explicitly on the word and its relation to the picture, a dimension that is even more emphatically foregrounded by the introduction of five hand-drawn icons in the second chapter. However, much of the bulk of the novel reflects on more recent communication technologies and their role in shaping memory and identity. Thus, the chapter "Ex/Ode" consists in large part of transcripts of tape recordings of family conversations that make up part of the protagonist's memories of his parents and older relatives. However, because the tapes are not completely preserved, the resulting text is a jigsaw puzzle of fragments and unfinished sentences alternating with blank spaces that sometimes assumes an almost lyrical quality in its incompleteness.

More modern technologies appear through a character—if that is indeed what he is—of Elvis (Presley), who surfaces in the novel by way of multiple alleged sightings, media images and imitations. Elvis, whose name the novel reinterprets as an anagram of "Levi," becomes the quintessentially mediatized, simulated and ubiquitous character whose presence is dispersed all over the globe. Even more pointedly, the last chapter of *Mosaic Man* features characters that appear to be incarnations of new communication technologies: Shadrak, a character offshoot of the hard-boiled detective figure Ram Shade, communicates exclusively via FAX, and another avatar of the protagonist, Rona Fray, is threatened by two characters named Rom and Ram, whose calling card displays their names as "ROM/RAM" (245).[13] These acronyms, which literally stand for Read Only Memory and Random Access Memory, terms that have specific technical meanings in computer architecture, here point more broadly to questions of access to history and memory that much of the text is concerned with.

It is not only human identity that is shaped and reshaped by different communication technologies, however. *Mosaic Man* also includes extended newspaper quotations on current events (not unlike the quotations from media that had already appeared in such earlier texts as *Up*, *The Death of the Novel,* and *98.6*) so as to foreground the channels through which the protagonist relates to world events, as well as to create a counterpoint to the narrative voice. Sometimes these media clips highlight the fact that human wars and military conflicts such as the Gulf War do not only have human victims, for example when the narrator quotes from a *New York Times* article on the starvation of animals in the Kuwait City Zoo (259), or when he considers the televised consequences of war-related oil spills for the environment:

> SCREEN ON. We watch long enough to see that the monster has run amok, storming through the desert, perfecting its own technology. Whatever noble motives may have gotten involved.
>
>> Pure love of humanity justified the creation of the dreadful, and sanctified the terrible. (Chayim Bloch, *The Golem*)
>
> It is written.
>
> Also we see that the Iraqis are releasing oil into the Red Sea, creating an ecological disaster dwarfing the Alaska oil spill. Once again pictures of oil mucked critters dying their slow deaths. Painted in oil, art brute. Totalling our totems.

> Why is it that it's the exceptional animal that isn't beautiful, especially among the wild ones? SCREEN OFF.
>
> +
>
> Later it turns out that that image of the doomed cormorant trying to escape a pool of oil, played over and over again, is from stock footage. So that even the imagery of truth is deceptive. And what about the images we aren't shown?"
>
> (252–53)

This passage, echoing the reflections on a California oil spill in *Out,* written twenty-six years earlier, highlights the central questions that many of the media scenarios in *Mosaic Man* are concerned with: the connection of Operation Desert Storm with the legend of the Golem suggests a world of technology in which human intentions are side effects rather than basic causes, and the bird covered with oil as a stereotypical image of ecological disaster points to a world of media in which the relationship between representations and reality has become uncertain to the point where even a highly mimetic image can be untruthful, whereas disruptions of the mimetic mode (such as the blanks on tape recordings) can foreground realities that were not previously visible.[14]

The protagonist's reflections on the fate of animals in human warfare also points to another set of concerns in *Mosaic Man* that relate to the very definition of what is "human" at the turn of the millennium, concerns that are here alluded to by his reference to man as an "exceptional animal." On one hand, these concerns surface through the protagonist's sense that after the horrors of war and holocaust in the twentieth century, the humanist tradition has lost its credibility, and that cultures have become "posthuman" in that the value of human life has diminished. In a reflection that echoes in some ways Horkheimer and Adorno's consideration of the obsolescence of the Enlightenment, he comments on the waning of humanism: " 'Fifty million people have been slaughtered within six years. The great tradition of Humanism wasn't worth shit in a chateau, a fox hole, a death camp, a stately state palace. Never mind post modern, we're all post humous as Europeans, including the Europeans themselves. Post human' " (197).

But the idea that the value of human life needs to be reconsidered also surfaces in a more affirmative context. The exploration of issues surrounding Jewish identity had occasionally appeared in Sukenick's earlier fictions (for example, in his first novel *Up*), but was much less central to the play with experimental and semi-autobiographical characters than it is in *Mosaic Man*: not only the protagonist's shifting identities, but also a myriad of perhaps real and perhaps imagined plots, counterplots, mini- and macro-conspiracies of overwhelming complexity that reach back to the beginnings of Judeo-Christian history here frame the investigation of Jewishness. Although this inquiry is undoubtedly paramount in the novel, Sukenick gradually turns Jewish selfhood into a trope for the dispersed and uncertain identities that the narrator considers typical of what it means to be human at the turn of the millennium. Pointedly, he translates the issue of the Jew living in non-Jewish societies into the question of human identity in the midst of multiple nonhuman forms of life: "Personally, being Jewish is just an advanced case of being human, and being human may be a terminal disease that's run its course. Personally, maybe we're just beings, forget human, beings among other beings, some hairy, some furry, some feathery, some leathery, and some who possibly will soon arrive from other sectors of the universe" (16). The semantic tension between the emphasis on the personal (repeated twice) and statements that place humanity not only among other life forms on Earth, but indeed in the universe, circumscribe what I take to be one of the novel's underlying concerns: the question of how cultural definitions of human identity in terms of ethnicity, religion, race, or nationality relate to the understanding of humans as one biological species among others. The reference to aliens arriving from outer space in this passage is not entirely random, either, because such aliens do in fact visit the protagonist's apartment on the novel's last page, apparently forming part of one of the multiple conspiracies. Interestingly enough, their bodies in some respects resemble earthly animals, because they wear "helmets with gas masks and horns," have webbed feet and "red pincers for hands" (261), even as they look down on humans as stupid but beautiful creatures (ibid.). A send-up of science fiction as a genre, to be sure—just as *Mosaic Man* parodies autobiography, the hard-boiled detective novel, the *Bildungsroman*, and quite a few others—but as in so many other instances, the text mixes fun and seriousness.

Mosaic Man, then, reflects on "posthuman" identity in a variety of ways. Not only does it consider how the weakening of the Western humanist tradition might affect valuations of human life, it also, sometimes playfully and sometimes earnestly, addresses the question of how human identity must be rethought through the new information and communication media that have arisen in the second half of the twentieth century, on one hand, and on the other, in relation to the threat it poses to nonhuman species whose claims to life the humanist tradition did not take into account. The experimentation with fictional character is crucial to the exploration of these issues and therefore again functions on more levels than the one of narrative self-reference. If Sukenick's early novel *Out* uses the dispersal of character as a means of defining an alternative experience of physical space that puts humans in more immediate contact with their surroundings, *Mosaic Man*, which deploys decentered and fragmented characters in the context of Jewish diasporic identities, uses them at the same time to raise complex question about the nature of human identity in an age of rapidly changing communication technologies and the accelerating extermination of nonhuman species. Sukenick's experimentation with narrative representations of the human links his work to more theoretical explorations of "posthuman" identities that have recently been undertaken both by scholars who study new technologies and their consequences, and by those whose primary concern is humans' relationship to the natural environment and other species.[15] Although his basic literary technique has not changed fundamentally since the 1960s and 1970s, Sukenick's most recent novel shows how the resistance to conventional constructions of character, which arose in a context of heightened emphasis on narrative self-referentiality, assumes new functions in altered social, cultural, and technological conditions several decades later. The ambiguous status of Sukenick's posthumans, between narrative constructs and individuals whose uncertain identities point to the ecological and technological destabilization of the human at the turn of the millennium, allows them to function in literary and cultural frameworks substantially different from those that prevailed a quarter of a century ago. Sukenick's experimentation with character, "threatening to humanists with its humanness" (*In Form* 33), is attaining new relevance in the interdisciplinary search for articulations of a posthuman identity, both individual and collective.

Notes

1. The translation is Richard Howard's.

2. For a more detailed discussion, see Brooke-Rose, "The Dissolution of Character in the Novel," Currie, "The Eccentric Self" (60–69) and McHale, *Postmodernist Fiction* (121–24).

3. See the discussion in Kutnik (99–115) and Currie (61–64).

4. Sukenick repeats the last part of this sentence in slightly altered phrasing in his essay, "The New Tradition in Fiction": "Form is your footprints in the sand when you look back" (35).

5. This scene is echoed in a later chapter when a character is torn between sympathy and disgust for a severely ill cat that regularly comes to visit his apartment.

6. "Soon I'm on the wing I'm in the ocean sky sunny whales are spouting their heads break water they slide slowly to the surface spout their long backs glide roll under with a slow sweep of the flukes one especially surfacing next to me a great dappled grey whale very old his immense back mossy and barnacled I can see the bristly folds of his blow hole a naval [sic] connects him with his mother the air his flukes as he sounds waving high over me like a gesture goodbye follow me" (157).

7. That this is tantamount to a mimetic interpretation of the blank pages is a paradox about which I will have more to say below.

8. The omission of the word "whale" from this sentence translates species extinction into syntactic elision even as the ensuing juxtaposition of "sperm" and "extinction" reinforces the sense of a confrontation between life and death.

9. For a detailed analyis of the metafictional implications of this scene, see Kutnik (121–23).

10. The settlement repeatedly suffers mysterious destructions of property that one of the inhabitants finally attributes to the presence of a "Sasquatch," a being that according to Native American legend pre-existed humans, but could not speak. This hypothesis is rejected and ridiculed by other members of the commune until several of them perceive a very large and unidentifiable creature fly over their heads in the forest. Unlike other animals the group encounters, this being remains incomprehensible to the humans.

11. Riesman's *The Lonely Crowd: A Study of the Changing American Character* was originally published in 1950, but attained great popularity in the 1960s and was twice republished (in 1961 and 1969) in a slightly abridged version.

12. The autobiographical dimensions of Sukenick's fiction have frequently been discussed, as well as Sukenick's own rejection of the term "autobiography": in keeping with his more general statements on narrative mimesis, he is not interested in autobiography as a rendering of a past life, but at best as an re-creation and addition to this life (Interview with Larry McCaffery 281). On Sukenick's use of autobiographical elements, see Timothy Dow Adams, "Obscuring the Muse," Alfred Hornung, "Absent Presence" and "Autobiography," and Peter Currie, "The Eccentric Self."

13. There are also characters that already appeared in earlier Sukenick novels, like Strop Banally from *Up*, or Mr. Huge a.k.a. Howard Hughes, and Dr. Frank Stein from *Out*.

14. The oil-covered bird as a stock image of ecology in the media as well as the question of ecological disaster as a consequence of the Gulf War have been analyzed by Andrew Ross (*The Chicago Gangster Theory of Life* 159–201, esp. 171–72).

15. For human identity in relation to emerging technologies, see Donna Haraway, "A Cyborg Manifesto" and N. Katherine Hayles, *How We Became Posthuman*; in environmentalism, the work that most explicitly questions anthropocentric perspectives is so-called "deep ecology": see Arne Naess, *Ecology, Community and Lifestyle*, and Bill Devall and George Sessions, *Deep Ecology*.

Works Cited

Adams, Timothy Dow. "Obscuring the Muse: The Mock-Autobiographies of Ronald Sukenick." *Critique: Studies in Modern Fiction* 20.1 (1978): 27–39.

Bergmann, Linda S. "*Out*: A Novel by Ronald Sukenick." *Chicago Review* 25.3 (1973): 9–12.

Brooke-Rose, Christine. "The Dissolution of Character in the Novel." *Reconstructing Individualism: Autonomy, Individuality, and the Self in Western Thought*. Eds. Thomas C. Heller, Morton Sosna, and David E. Wellbery. Stanford, Calif.: Stanford University Press, 1986. 184–96.

Currie, Peter. "The Eccentric Self: Anti-Characterization and the Problem of the Subject in American Postmodernist Fiction." *Contemporary American Fiction*. Eds. Malcolm Bradbury and Sigmund Ro. London: Edward Arnold, 1987. 53–69.

Devall, Bill, and George Sessions. *Deep Ecology: Living As If Nature Mattered*. Salt Lake City, Utah: Gibbs Smith, 1985.

Haraway, Donna. "A Cyborg Manifesto: Science, Technology, and Socialist-Feminism in the Late Twentieth Century." *Simians, Cyborgs, and Women: The Reinvention of Nature*. New York: Routledge, 1991. 149–81.

Hayles, N. Katherine. *How We Became Posthuman: Virtual Bodies in Cybernetics, Literature, and Informatics*. Chicago: University of Chicago Press, 1999.

Hornung, Alfred. "Absent Presence: The Fictions of Raymond Federman and Ronald Sukenick." *Indian Journal of American Studies* 14.1 (1984): 17–31.

———. "Autobiography." *International Postmodernism: Theory and Literary Practice*. Eds. Hans Bertens and Douwe Fokkema. Amsterdam: John Benjamins, 1997. 221–33.

Kutnik, Jerzy. *The Novel as Performance: The Fiction of Ronald Sukenick and Raymond Federman*. Carbondale: Southern Illinois University Press, 1986.

McHale, Brian. *Postmodernist Fiction*. New York: Methuen, 1987.

Naess, Arne. *Ecology, Community, and Lifestyle*. Trans. David Rothenberg. Cambridge: Cambridge University Press, 1989.

Riesman, David, with Nathan Glazer and Reuel Dennehy. *The Lonely Crowd: A Study of the Changing American Character*. Abridged edition with a 1969 preface. New Haven, Conn.: Yale University Press, 1969.

Robbe-Grillet, Alain. "On Several Obsolete Notions." *For a New Novel*. Trans. Richard Howard. Evanston, Ill.: Northwestern University Press, 1989. 25–47.

———. "Sur quelques notions périmées." *Pour un nouveau roman*. Paris: Minuit, 1963. 25–44.

Ross, Andrew. *The Chicago Gangster Theory of Life: Nature's Debt to Society*. London: Verso, 1994.

Sukenick, Ronald. *98.6*. New York: Fiction Collective, 1975.

———. "From *Out*." *Massachusetts Review* 14 (Spring 1973): 93.

———. *In Form: Digressions on the Act of Fiction*. Carbondale: Southern Illinois University Press, 1985.

———. Interview. With Joe David Bellamy. *The New Fiction: Interviews with Innovative American Writers*. Ed. Joe David Bellamy. Urbana: University of Illinois Press, 1974. 55–74.

———. Interview. With Larry McCaffery. *Anything Can Happen: Interviews with Contemporary American Novelists*. Eds. Tom LeClair and Larry McCaffery. Urbana: University of Illinois Press, 1983. 279–97.

———. *Out*. Chicago: Swallow Press, 1973.

———. "The Death of the Novel." *The Death of the Novel and Other Stories*. New York: Dial, 1969.

———. "The New Tradition in Fiction." *Surfiction: Fiction Now . . . and Tomorrow*. Ed. Raymond Federman. Chicago: Swallow Press, 1975.

Interruption Discontinuity Imperfection It Can't Be Helped

Campbell Tatham

Never interpret.

Gilles Deleuze and Claire Parnet, *Dialogues*

The professor had taught *98.6* often over the years, and the notorious "blond" sections had always proved the most controversial. Students, men and women, reacting with hostility ("he's like a . . . a jerk, a pig, yuk!), contempt ("cheap shots, y'know, the guy's like straining to be, uh, provocative"), and/or disbelief ("is he for real?"). Yet Ron has always defended this sequence, insisting that it too is part of the reality he wants us to experience. In an interview with Larry McCaffery, the question of the writer's "seeking a truth 'beyond literature' " came up.

"What is the nature of such a truth?" Larry asked.

"There is experience beyond language," Ron replied. And went on to talk about "feeling" (using pain as an example) that may be "prelinguistic—and also postlinguistic" as an example of such experience.

"And sex," suggested Larry.

"Yes," said Ron. "In a way, sex most of all. . . . The reason sex is so powerful is because it's where the feeling turns into feelings more easily."

Turning more specifically to *98.6*, Larry wondered, "Is this one of the reasons why so many of your characters—especially in *98.6*—seem to relate to each other, both sexually and personally, through violence or other means of heightening their reactions?"

Ron deferred somewhat: "In *98.6* I was very unsympathetic to these tendencies. I diagnosed the culture as lapsing into sado-masochism and suggested this was a kind of sickness" (*In Form* 112–113).

❖ ❖ ❖

"Sickness or not," muses the professor to his class on postmodern fictions, "the scene generates a certain *energy* that is its own experience. The blond of the second part plays into the narrator's fantasies: 'I don't care do whatever you want to me she wants to be destroyed. She wants to be torn apart and completely helpless and at the mercy of. That's the way he thinks of it' " (*98.6* 33). "Irresponsible!" cry his students. "That's an attitude that would justify violence to our sisters!" shout the women in his classes. "Hopeless," they conclude. Of the novel or of himself, he's not sure.

❖ ❖ ❖

Sukenick is nowadays fond of referring to "Reader Liberation": "Teaching the reader to read in ways that are not dictated but which in fact are calculated to release the reader's own thought processes and make the reader think for him or herself. . . . One of the ways of doing it is to write in different ways so that readers can get out of the molds that are prepared for them" ("Word Bombs").

It's not a new idea for him. In fact, in *Wallace Stevens: Musing the Obscure*, more or less his doctoral dissertation, he emphasizes the importance of the imagination mediating experience in the world: "At the heart of this interchange between the ego and reality is the effect of the imagination in bringing the two into vital relation" (14). Moreover, Sukenick insists that, at least for Stevens, "this was not merely a point of theory . . . but rather an intensely real experience upon which the theory was constructed." That "vital relation," however, is inevitably produced by the disruption of ordinary, routine perception, and the deliberate cultivation of a willingness to see—and *experience*—the world anew. Thus: the extraordinary.

Carlos Castaneda's sorcerer guide, don Juan, speaks of "stopping the world," by which he means the suspension of that inner voice of logic and reason that holds our world together, a voice influenced by cultural injunctions, dreams, unconscious urges, public and private pathologies, history and so on. Our own and not our own. To break its hold on us, we must disrupt it—don Juan manipulates his apprentice through hallucinogenics, altered states, bizarre drama, absurd demands, and impossible tasks.

The fictionist, also therefore a "shaman," as Sukenick nowadays is fond of insisting, manipulates the reader through what Deleuze calls "deterritorializing," a term which partakes of "defamiliarizing" and "deconstructing" (*Dialogues* 18). The goal is production through multiplication, and not interpretation, which is always reduction. "This is the good way to read," Deleuze explains: "all mistranslations are good—always provided that they do not consist in interpretations, but relate to the use of the book, that they multiply its use, that they create another language inside its language" (*Dialogues* 5).

Referring to Castaneda's "fictions," Sukenick writes in *Down and In*: "art, which exercises the imagination on experience, cannot be judged true or false. It applies, among other faculties, the power of feeling to the world. Feeling is neglected not only as a response in our culture but as a way of knowing and an efficacious force. For Castaneda's don Juan, 'the world is a feeling,' so you can say that the power of a sorcerer is the power of feeling he can, through the imagination, bring to bear on our sense of the world. . . . The sorcerer applies the full force of the imagination to experience and in making this manifest, Castaneda creates a dialogue between the rational and the nonrational, between the modern and the socalled primitive, between the literal and the metaphorical" (254–55).

❖ ❖ ❖

The professor realizes, more or less, how deeply he is implicated in what he is saying. And, hopefully or despairingly, performing. He typically reminded himself, as he put it up-front to his seminar on postmodern fiction: he virtually "grew up," came into something approaching intellectual maturity (if not emotional, certainly not emotional, which is also part of the point) with these writers. Something in him resonated instantly to the possibilities they seemed to open. *98.6* was one of those life-changing experiences, becoming over all the years virtually a sacred text. Given, like postmodernism itself, to self-reflection/reflexivity, he always wondered why—why this particular book? Given, as a teacher, to articulation, promotion, dissemination, he always hoped to express to various groups of students, his changing and shifting versions of why, really, no shit, postmodernism, whatever it means, still has something to say that is important, a matter of life and death. And so on.

He wondered, too, what drew others to this strange landscape. And became fascinated, too and maybe most of all, by those writers who struggled so nakedly with that issue, like Federman, or in such intricate and devious ways, like Sukenick.

He thought he understood parts of it, at least in his own story. Put simply: a powerful attraction to multiplicity, an attraction which itself had dark and light aspects. In its more benign manifestations it emphasized openness to complexity, appreciation of difference and otherness, a certain intellectual rigor, promotion of change. In its darker undercurrents, it encouraged over-intellectualizing and accompanying loss of affect, failure to take responsibility, inability to make decisions or to commit, afraid of depending on stability.

He *was* a schizoid, his life a flux. Why?

[Real Time Window[1]: From some e-mail postings to the professor's on-line forum for his course on postmodern fictions, in which *98.6* is being discussed:

Subject: the blond

Posted by: Ron Sukenick on 19:23:39 2/27/2000:

what's interesting is that 98.6's blond is still a bombshell. But one thing nobody seems to notice—what do you think all that stuff about not being dead, about the war atrocities, about the Hells Angels murder, is doing there? sexual relations are like a very sensitive magnet for the filings of the zeitgeist. Sadomasochism is part of the subject of the book, not part of the form that contains it.

Subject: sociology or literature
Posted by: Ray Federman on 23:23:57 2/27/2000:

I am puzzled by the discussion concerning ron's writing—you guys make it sound more like he's written sociology than literature

I cannot resist pointing out that
a novel is less
the writing of an adventure
than the adventure of writing]

❖ ❖ ❖

"No, no," the professor pleads, "you're missing the point. To stop or pull back there is to fail to allow yourself the larger, far more interesting *experience*. The narrator imagines, note, that the blond (second part) 'wants to go all the way back to animals and past animals to things. She wants to go back to her thing nature and be part of the rest of the world for once in her thingness a thing among things. She wants to die what a relief it's a special kind of death it feels like shitting in reverse no more fighting off all the deadness in the world letting it in' (*98.6* 33). **[Who inserts page numbers? I ask.]**

"Now there are a number of ways to read this. Yes, one way is to see it as an example of sadomasochism projected on to the blond in order to justify the narrator's own sickness. He goes on to tell us, 'he wants to destroy her secret her innerness he wants to turn her inside out he wants to depersonalize her it's the claim of her personality he can't bear that make him furious. It won't work' (33). Of course, that he realizes and implicitly judges this urge within himself complicates the situation. But okay, let's accept that, in this reading, the point is a criticism of the phallic need to affirm itself through the subjugation of the other, a tendency toward which Ron feels obviously 'unsympathetic.' "

The professor doubts they'll let him get away with something this transparently simplistic. He's right. "But, but," protests a student, "doesn't Sukenick in that, you know, online AltX interview admit his, I mean, incredibly perverse pursuit of a 13 year old high school student? Yuk, really—he's like saying, uh, I've got it right here: 'I met her the day my first novel was accepted. I went to see these underground films in the Village and started talking to this girl in line next to me for a ticket. It was very dark in there and we started making out during the movie. When we got out I was astonished to see this girl was actually a kid. We started going out. I liked going around with her in public because everyone would look shocked. Making out in public and people would look appalled'(AltX). Seems to me that he's like actually turned on by that stuff."

Are you turned on, too? the professor imagines himself saying to the student, who just happens to be a shapely blond herself. But he knows better. Instead: "Still, another reading would be simply that Ron is exploring feelings that people do in fact have, no matter how disturbing. After all, the narrator noted earlier, 'All men are rapists at heart just like all women love a fascist right. Right' (19). Right? Apologies to Sylvia Plath, of course." Blur the issue with inflammatory, if not merely obscure, textual references.

"So more to the point," he continues, "is to notice that the passage about the blond is part of a network of evocations of the darker undercurrents of the collective (and individual) psyche, all of which must be acknowledged lest they assault us in other forms." (The professor happened to be teaching *Beloved* that semester, you see.) **[Whose**

voice is this? this?] Reflex gestures on the professor's part, reflecting his deepest implication in what he was saying? Or performing? Whatever.

❖ ❖ ❖

That night his mother woke him up, whimpering to the verge of hysteria—"Let me sleep in your room, oh please, keep him away from me." Hearing his angry father stumbling around downstairs, deconstructing furniture, stammering in a drunken tongue. The boy found himself crouching hunched, his back against the locked door, staring up with his father, looming darkly over him.

"What the fuck do you think you're doing, huh? This has absolutely nothing to do with you, get your ass out of here!"

The boy looked down, but didn't move.

They stood there for long minutes, silent and somehow working out a new assemblage of relationship. Then the father lurched off, muttering, while the boy continued motionless, feeling virtually nothing, a jingle running endlessly through his head, "Pepsi-Cola hits the spot. . . ."

The next morning, when his mother, leaving, asked if he would join her or stay with *him*, while his father stood on the side, frozen in fury and frustration, the boy again looked down, motionless, his mind hearing only the jingle. The mother left, the boy stayed. And stayed, while his father proceeded down the alcoholic road to his death, some time later. Leaving an inheritance of anger, bafflement with the turnings of the world, deep distrust of revealed emotion. One defense against an all too threatening world was the cultivation of an aloofness, supported by a high-altitude philosophy itself remarkably cool, impenetrable. Talk of deconstructing.

For Ron, he realized much later, it was the opposite: "An absence inside the family, leaving us to our mother. So there was nothing to keep the mother at bay, no ally. In the absence of the father it's hard for the son to be born" (*Mosaic Man* 239–40). But for both, judging from their adult constructs, mixed feelings toward women were inevitable.

No wonder Sukenick's fictions felt so familiar to him.

❖ ❖ ❖

The novel explores various theories to combat The Problem.

For Cloud, "in Frankenstein the old programs are inadequate this is what he calls The Problem" (*98.6* 124). The old programs are based on dualisms, always this or that, and promote what he calls "skimming" (131). The Problem reflects the extent to which we are out of touch with "enchantment" as well as with ourselves (11–12).

How do we escape the old programs? We must apparently move out of "The Phase of Cruelty" (e.g., the blond), through "The Phase of Imagination" (e.g., the idealism of the children), and into "The Phase of Illumination" (e.g., the making of the novel into a new experience by the reader). There are always dangers along the way.

❖ ❖ ❖

The professor is given to pontificating. "Sukenick realizes the problem: 'Many people catch the disease you have to be as hard as whatever it is that hurt you. You have to become what hurt you. Or else. Or else it may hurt you again' "(*98.6* 179). This is always a difficult point for the professor to convey to any class, much less believe with confidence himself. Nevertheless, he continues.

"And though Sukenick himself insists that 'the sadistic culture,' in which the blond exists, 'is not endorsed by the book' ("Love Conks Us All," page unnumbered [**he says this?**]), the novel also insists that 'if you can't go around it go through it. That's how you do it' " (12).

"But, but," the blond in the first row waves her hand again. "But Sukenick also says on the very first page, right here, 'You intuit. That's how you do it.' Doesn't that mean something different?"

"Precisely the point. You have to go through it, all of it, and how you do it is to intuit, whatever that might mean. Well, maybe it means that what you try to avoid will inevitably reappear in some monstrous form—which is what happens to the children of Frankenstein. So what do you do when you intuit? You let go of 'ordinary' or 'rational' or 'linear' modes of consciousness. You open yourself to other levels of experience, including those you may most fear.

"Or, as he puts it later in the novel: 'We deny nothing. We incorporate the negation in the affirmation'—this is on page 180—'You have to incorporate the negation in the affirmation. . . . You have to ponder cruelty. You have to meditate on despair. You have to remember the exile and that we're all in exile. . . . And it's not enough to think about all this you have to imagine it. You have to live it. You have to get down on your knees and roll your head in the dust and if you have to scream then you scream.' "

"So you're saying," this from the smart-ass bearded guy with a perpetual sneer, "that this justifies the sadomasochism of the blond section? Man, that's bullshit." What's his name? Rodia? No.

"Well, first of all, it's not me, it's the novel." Cheap avoidance, the professor has to admit to himself. Still.

"Still, isn't it maybe worth considering that without a willingness to confront, even, okay, ponder cruelty, we run the risk of denying it and thereby allowing its manifestation in all sorts of ways? Like whatever it is that attacks the commune?"

But, the professor wonders privately, how do you ponder cruelty without perpetuating it, justifying it through sophistic wordplays? Has he caught the disease? Is he always already part of the Problem?

❖ ❖ ❖

His first marriage, for example. That night he realized for certain he would leave. They sat cross-legged near each other in front of the fake fireplace in their shabby flat, neither looking at the other. She sobbed, "Why? Why can't you let go of this? It didn't mean anything, *he* didn't mean anything, you know that, you knew all along it would happen, you *let* it happy, Jesus Christ, sometimes I think you *wanted* it to happen, you *made* it happen, why?"

He ran the back of his hand up and down along the edge of the bricks, up and down, deepening the rough cut. The sight of his blood was somehow reassuring. So he could look at her, blankly, coldly, showing her how far away he was, wanting her to feel finally his total lack of caring. Whatever she said could not matter now. Through his head went a kind of chant, "fuck you fuck you fuck you fuck you."

"I don't want you to leave, please don't leave, please." He stood up and stared down at her, cradling one injured hand in another. "I have to fix this," he said and turned away. Watching himself from a distance, he was somewhat surprised by how little he felt, other than a dull anger. An anger he let wash over her, diffuse and impossible to deflect, so that she cringed. And whimpered, pathetically. "Please." Ah.

> **[Real Time Window: Lance Olsen comments on certain aspects of socalled 'critifiction' in an e-mail that distracts the professor from the anxieties these speculations dredge up:**
> **"Of course critifiction is a ludic act.**
> **But it is also a serious variety of reminding.**
> **A serious variety of reminding that doesn't simply talk about its subject in predictable Newtonian forms, but enacts it, performs it, riffs on it, over and over again, often in Heisenbergian manifestations, driving home the point one of my favorite critifictionists, Roland Barthes, made so beautifully almost a quarter of a century ago: 'that a text is not a line of words releasing a single "theological" meaning (the**

"message" of the Author-God) but a multidimensional space in which a variety of writings, none of them original, blend and clash.' And one of those varieties of writing is me. One of them is you. Is the reader, that is. The text having always already been permeable."

The professor put aside the impossible performance he was working on and posted back to Lance: " 'Never interpret,' advises Deleuze (in *Dialogues*), and I've been searching for a critical method which incorporates storytelling, refuses the illusion of objective truth-searching (interpretation), and which employs the fiction under examination as a jumping-off point, a site on which to extend the narrative(s). In so doing, I have invented a surrogate character, a certain professor, whose own story weaves in and through and around the multiple fictions that interest me. And so, insofar as there are 'sides' to this process, for me, critifiction begins as a response to others' stories, blurs boundaries and borders, and projects itself into new stories. It is a kind of critical gesture that refuses its own interpretive impulses and insists on its final fictional status. Or that's my hope."

He knew that Lance would call him on the potentially stultifying dualism between 'fiction' and 'criticism,' but he figured to counter it with yet another appeal to his personal literary shaman, Deleuze: "We must pass through dualisms because they are in language, it's not a question of getting rid of them, but we must fight against language, invent stammering . . . which will make language flow between these dualisms" (*Dialogues* 34).]

❖ ❖ ❖

Each book in this genre contains its ex- or im-plicit counterbook. Its own self-deconstruction, such is its distrust of the solidification of structures. A certain escapism there. Evelyn presents the most compelling opposing position in *98.6*: "She feels the whole bit is based on some kind of evasion and she thinks it's loathsome. Already Ron is moving out of contact. Turning hard" (87). Just as later she observes the difference between "those who are committed to an idea" and those who are, presumably, "realworld" "gardeners [. . .] who are committed to gardens" (114).

On the other hand, it's Evelyn/Eucalyptus who gives up on Ron and gets it on with Buck, who in turn introduces her to cocaine ("she likes it" [152]) and who's on what she admits and accepts as "a death trip" ("she digs it" [153]). Or, perhaps, her fate is "arranged" by Ron, who compulsively undermines the legitimacy of her earlier critique. He's the one writing the story and who therefore controls it. Doesn't he?

No single "position" is simply affirmed or rejected by the larger assemblage of the novel; each is encouraged to resonate "against" the others, generating a disruptive energy, to be in turn picked up—experienced—by the reader. The novel, then, "equals" the sum of all its interior smaller assemblages.

Similarly, the criti(fictional) act becomes a performance of pluralization, multiplying the text by emphasizing discontinuities, misreadings, appropriations, playgiarisms—as well as its own reactions, emphasizing fictionalized personal memories, myth, cultural borrowings, virtually whatever comes into the mind of the (criti)fictive reader. That reader, too, becomes a producer of new experience.

Or, as Deleuze puts it: "Substitute the AND for IS. A *and* B" (*Dialogues* 57). AND = □ .

One risk: the whole thing turns into what Barth, long ago, condemned as "technical circus tricks" ("John Barth" 6). Postures that constitute an evasion. Loathsome. "Oh God comma I abhor self-consciousness," intoned Barth in one of his endless narrative incarnations (Barth 113). Precisely a failure to incorporate the felt dimensions of experience—in Ron's terms, "art . . . applies the power of feeling to the world" (*Down and In* 254).

Of course, some feelings more than others, which becomes The Problem.

❖ ❖ ❖

Just as Federman had his closet, so the professor had his own escape routes and hiding places and evasions. Whenever accused of "lying," as he often was, part of him wanted to answer, "Of course I lie—so does everyone—it's a matter of life and death!" Other parts wisely evaded such confrontational outbursts, realizing the frequent falsity of such postures. For he always knew when his lies were also dishonest (not all lies are, of course).

"There's something missing in you," she still said after many years of marriage. Because there was something missing in him, he didn't know how to respond. So he would retreat to the one feeling he did understand: anger. For finally he knew that he could go further into his anger with its hints at total loss of control and violence, than she could. So long as he could use his anger to promote her fear, he would be . . . safe. Of course, it's a strategy that cannot be overused, lest it create a kind of numbed immunity. So variation and uncertainty become crucial components. Terrorized himself, at least in his own story, he determined to terrorize.

Which, he knew too well, is The Problem.

❖ ❖ ❖

This performance is intended to waver along two axes. One that's horizontal, inescapably linear now matter how the mosaic of fragments is juggled. The "real" axis, there/here, the page I'm producing and you're reading (a notion which is quite oddly made problematic by the electronic nature of the actual production, but still). Along this axis, there is a beginning and an ending, a point at which you stop turning pages. Struggling against the force of this axis is always already futile, and failure is assured. Often the struggle is all the more celebrated, insisted on, as is the failure ("another failure," the last words of *98.6*).

The other axis has qualities associated with verticality: possibility, diving deep and surfacing, return and ritornello, repetition and difference. It too reflects certain realworld activities of the reader, who never simply reads in straight lines: there are detours, pauses, speeds, abandonments, an entire array of feelings. Finding words for this axis is always already futile and failure is assured ("another failure," the last words of *98.6*).

Whatever "meaning" the novel might have, then, is always relational, a matter of multiplying intersections. A web site always under (de)construction: http://www.uwm.edu/~ctatham.

❖ ❖ ❖

The professor felt increasingly confident that he could get them to understand, to feel, to . . . to, yes, *experience* if only for a moment, that shift in perception Sukenick meant his fictions to promote.

"Uh, excuse me!"

Always sits in the last row, sprawling, one of them in every class, often more than one when the subject is postmodernism, what's his name? Waldo, yes, that's it.

"Yes, Waldo?"

"Well, I mean, really, like, how does reading something like this, this *98.6*, do whatever it is you say it, like, does—I mean, whatever it is you think it does? I mean, come on, no one reads like that."

"Can we agree that such an experience would be worthwhile?"

"Well, I don't know, maybe, but let's like assume its value—so what then?"

"Okay. Then the . . . *experience* of reading the novel and having to keep in mind—to juggle all *at the same time*, as it were—the three levels, none of which has any necessary priority, stretches a kind of consciousness that Sukenick is willing to call, okay, 'imagination.' Which in turn 'stretches'—it's hard not to stammer when talking like this—our ordinary (routine) perceptions and understandings, stretches them and creates cracks, uncertainties. An uneasiness and a need to reconsider. Something like that."

"Sounds kinda vague to me."

"Ron refers to it, nowadays, as 'deprogramming.' "

"Isn't that a little paranoid?"

"Once we begin to wonder, to interrogate what's present to us, then other possibilities present themselves, and our worlds expand. As in what he says—in your handouts—from *Down and In*: 'a kind of consciousness for which social values are, to begin with, problematic, always to be questioned. . . . The underground is a form of resistance to conventional wisdom, constantly testing the status quo that mainstream art basically accepts in its acquiescence to conventional forms of discourse, even when it expresses dissenting opinions' " (240).

Would he read the page number? What is going on here? And what does this have to do with *98.6*? **[Who's asking?]**

❖ ❖ ❖

Early on, Sukenick insisted that "the movement of fiction should always be in the direction of what we sense is real" ("New Tradition" 40). But what we sense is real is not a dimension or construct with fixed coordinates; it is first and last an "experience," one of Sukenick's favorite value-words: "novels are experiences to respond to, not problems to figure out, and it would be interesting if criticism could begin to expand its stock of responses to the experience of fiction" (40)—better yet, if criticism could recognize its own experiential value.

For Sukenick, perhaps, "experience" captures much of what Deleuze and Guattari call "event," that which is beyond or before interpretation. Lacking both the purity of the Sartrean in-itself and the self-reflexivity of the for-itself. And the immersion in "the truth of experience" can get us, in Sukenick's terms, "beyond our fossilizing formulas of discourse, to get at a new and more inclusive 'reality,' if you will" ("Autogyro" 294).

[Real Time Window: the professor receives Sukenick's latest, *Narralogues*, in the mail and realizes instantly that it has to be inserted into the assemblage this was becoming. It seems to confirm much of what he sensed, a direction Sukenick had been moving in from his first meditations on Stevens to his latest hyperfictions: what he finally allows himself to call "a spiritual unconsciousness that Sukenick seems to insist on" (*Narralogues* 66) finding himself attracted to, of all predecessors (yet how inevitable), Emerson, who proposes "a state beyond the normal level of consciousness that bypasses the individual ego and taps the extrapersonal, the universal. Why, it's practically shamanistic!" (67). Of course. Predictable, too, that he would hedge a little: "Sukenick doesn't get mystical about this, he's not talking about a direct line to heaven or some sort of spirit world. He's talking about, for example, the voices of the dead as preserved in books, the polyglot babble of community, the abyss of history, the wisdom of babyspeak, the instincts of the body, the realm of the senses, the insight indispensable to research, the influence of place and the weather, the information of animals, the impact of light, the complexities of chance, the gravity of love, the power of eros, the erosions of time, the contortions of pain, the pervasive sadness of death" (85). Oh. Okay.

Yes, the very events that permeate Sukenick's own fictions. Note to Matt: mark my words, dissertations on Sukenick and the ethics of postmodernism will use this passage as an epigraph and organizing set of concerns. Add that to the Mosaic Musings.]

❖ ❖ ❖

"So consider then," the professor finally seemed to be getting to some kind of point, the blond sighed forward, Waldo shifted slightly in his seat and picked up the novel, "what Sukenick calls in *Narralogues* 'the gravity of love' and 'the power of eros.' He presents us with three distinct perspectives in each part of the novel. There's the notorious blond that we've already discussed, right? Dark impulses but nonetheless real. Felt. Maybe for most of us this gets pushed too far with the girl who's sodomized and the grotesque pretense that she somehow even enjoys it. Certainly he—whoever 'he' is at this point, let's not assume too easily that 'he' equals the author—'took advantage of it and it was really terrific. He loved it. He hated it. He stayed for a second time' (42).

"So okay, we react with moral outrage—our response is predictable enough—maybe even . . . 'programmed'? At any rate, in Frankenstein the sado-masochistic routines are seemingly entrenched. So the children drop out and try to open themselves to alternatives. For a while it seems to work, and there's 'the sudden access of erotic energy' (83). They want to believe that they have avoided infection by the overcoded patterns of Frankenstein. And in that wanting, perhaps they fall into an equally dangerous mode of dishonesty, even bad faith."

"Uh, excuse me?" Waldo again. "Isn't all this sadomasochistic stuff really just coming from some attempt to like shock us, and, you know, it just isn't all that shocking any more, not to me anyway and I don't think to any of us here. I think, maybe, Sukenick's like being way too melodramatic, and he's so self-conscious about it that it keeps us from really, you know, feeling what he's talking about."

"Okay, now connect those scenes with those in the second part where love is again in some sense divided by power. For example, some of the moments between Cloud and Eucalyptus, say pages 147 to 148, where Cloud's bad faith and avoidance cause him to attempt to manipulate (abuse?) Eucalyptus and her insistence on the legitimacy of her feelings: 'it's crazy,' he says; 'that's the way I feel,' she responds. And of course, that must be linked to an earlier moment (page 119) in which 'Eucalyptus is angry about his making love with Dawn at the potlatch' and justifies her own sex with Wind as 'just friendly passion.' The Eucalyptus/Dawn/Cloud triangle in turn returns in the Eve/Rebekah/Ron event of the third part. Except that this time, or on this level, the tripart assemblage evolves into the third phase, The Phase of Illumination, manifested through the Luminous Orgasm." The professor paused, losing track of his point.

"But," the blond, "it seems pretty obvious to me that when he like invests all these characteristics in women, he's going back to some pretty tired stereotypes: like the masochist who wants to be kicked, the bitch who tells it like it is, the wise woman who sees the fundamental truth the man blunders away from, the funny but, uh, mysteriously powerful old lady—I mean, come on, we've seen all this before, right?"

"Sure, these are stereotypes, but also powerful codings within all of us, certainly in those of us who are men. So having to pay attention to these various linkages, then having to think and feel our way through our assessments of them, creates that tension that Sukenick claims stretches, maybe even liberates consciousness, which in turn might underlie concrete social and political changes in the world."

Waldo: "Hey, man, sounds kinda thin to me. A-and so you end up like all the rest, staking the legitimacy of your approach on the same old realism and social responsibility trip that I thought you were saying this guy challenges. Or whatever."

❖ ❖ ❖

Typically, the professor was awash with internal dialogue, tiresomely segmented refrains that locked him into routines—routines that were familiar and therefore comforting, but also limiting. He found he could disrupt those codes by intense bodily activity—jogging, racquetball, sex of course—but also by a certain kind of reading.

He had, let's be honest, always liked straightforward storytelling, Barthes' "readerly" texts, but he'd also been deeply dawn to "writerly" texts as well, those odd books that constantly kept him just slightly off balance, unable to hold on to any certainties about plot or character or intent. Books that, whenever he tried to say something about them, led him to stammer through endless digressions. Somehow, learning the discipline required to maintain that stammering, to avoid premature closure, that experience deeply felt countered his frequent feelings of helplessness elsewhere in his worlds. The sense of so much happening "at the same time" within a text was restorative, whereas that same sense in other areas of his life was paralyzing.

Was, then, his attraction to Sukenick and similar fictionists simply indicative of a failure to live fully in nontextual way? Or was his experience of textual multiplicity as valid as any other sort of experience?

❖ ❖ ❖

In an unlikely conversation between Matt Roberson and Ronald Sukenick, conducted no doubt through the medium of e-mail, the latter insists yet again that writing is "an impt actvty it gets us alng hlps us re cr8 r lives. It hlps us in2 an hnst pstn a plc whr we cn say smthng abt r own xperiences whr we cn say smthng directly."

"Directly," Matt says. "I don't know if anyone can say anything directly."

"Wll the challng & cnscious paradx is that no matter how hrd u try 2 gt dwn the literal data thr r almost to litrl dta they r alwys filtrd throo the cr8ive mind. But u shld alwys TRY to captr th dta of reali t u have alwys 2 move in the direction of the dta of xperience in reality whatvr th chances u can't do this u have 2 try u have 2 try bcause it is only in mking tht ef4t 2 cr8 a legtmate fiction. U don't cr8 a legtmate fiction mrly dealing with othr fictions u need 2 get beyond them 2 get 2 wht lies beynd constrcts."

"Which is?" Matt asks.

"It hlps us get byond formulated emtns back 2 an undeniabl source of emtn. Ths may b th same sense we get in lnguag or ficshnl forms whn u psh it 2 gt byond yr conceptual control our cultrl cntrl our conventional cntrl. Tht 4 exmpl is xprience b yond lnguag as far as I am cncrnd."

❖ ❖ ❖

"So is your point," this from another guy, short and dark, usually sits in the back, first time he's opened his mouth the entire semester, what's going on here? "that you have to 'go through' all this wordplay and games and so on, in order to access the ancien caja—whatever that is—and that such experience is supposedly beyond language?"

What's his name? Matt, that's it. "Yes, I know it sounds kinda strange—can't we call it a paradox?—but we need to go through language to get beyond language. Or maybe: an experience in one part is transferable to other parts."

"Well, but," Matt insists, "doesn't this sound exactly like what he refers to, right here on page 174, as 'philosophical abstractions an option today reserved for puerile theorists.' I bet if he were right here, he'd laugh at us for just that reason."

"Yes, of course," the professor is tired now, probably unclear, the class is coming to an end, surely, hopefully. "Of course. But folding into the text the most telling self-critique is essential to keep the multiplicity of the whole assemblage in motion—a motion that generates energy, and, if it all actually works, an energy that is . . . like, sustaining."

"Sure," sneers Waldo, "but does it 'actually work'?"

Probably not, he has to admit, to himself if not to them. The blond is stacking her books, impatient to leave. The construct collapses. Again. Another failure.

Note

1. A playful device used by Sukenick in *Mosaic Man* that speaks in a present tense "outside" the time frame of the narrative but which inevitably remains folded into the text and thereby calls into question our assumptions

about time linearly conceived. To "work" it must be accepted as real, actual, nonfiction—impossible? **[Yes, certainly.]**

Works Cited

Barth, John. *Lost in the Funhouse.* Garden City, N.Y.: Doubleday, 1968, 113.

Deleuze, Gilles, and Claire Parnet. *Dialogues.* New York: Columbia University Press, 1987.

"John Barth: An Interview," *Wisconsin Studies in Contemporary Literature* VI (Winter-Spring) 1965.

Sukenick, Ronald. "An Interview." <http://www.altx.com/int2/suk.html>.

———. "Autogyro: My Life in Fiction." *Contemporary Authors Autobiography Series*, Vol. 8. Ed. Mark Zadrozny. Detroit, Mich.: Gale, 1989.

———. *Down and In: Life in the Underground.* New York: Beech Tree Books, 1987.

———. *98.6*, 2d edition. Boulder, Colo.: Fiction Collective Two, 1994.

———. *In Form: Digressions on the Act of Fiction.* Carbondale: Southern Illinois University Press, 1985.

———. *Narralogues: Truth in Fiction.* Albany: State University of New York Press, 2000.

———. "The New Tradition in Fiction," *Surfiction: Fiction Now and Tomorrow.* Ed. Raymond Federman. Chicago: Swallow Press, 1975.

———. *Wallace Stevens: Musing the Obscure.* New York: New York University Press, 1967.

———. "Word Bombs." <http://www.altx.com/wordbombs/suk.html>.

Explorations of Postmodern Time, Space, and Image: Considering the Works of Ronald Sukenick and David Salle

Charles Russell

> The collapse of illusory time in realistic fiction parallels the collapse of illusory space in perspectival painting and serves a parallel function: the assertion of the validity of the work of art in its own right rather than as an imitation of something else.
>
> Ronald Sukenick, "Twelve Digressions Toward a Study of Composition" (*In Form* 9)

More than most contemporary writers, Ronald Sukenick has been keenly aware of the strains of artistic developments across all the arts of our era. He has recognized, in particular, the affinities between his work as an innovative fiction writer and the struggles of painters to develop visual languages appropriate to their experience of our times and culture. Sukenick came of age during the height of abstract expressionism and the early emergence of the pop sensibility. His first novel, *Up* (1968), appeared after the first flowering of pop art, yet was clearly consistent with the spirit of the art's popular cultural enthusiasm. His early writings recall, in particular, James Rosenquist's fascination with the high gloss of culture, its fragmentary, surface imagery, presented through striking, unexpected combinations, and his general celebratory spirit.

Sukenick also suggests, however, a disturbing undertone to his subject not found in most of the pop artists. And, perhaps because Sukenick earlier responded to the passionate struggles of abstract expressionists to affirm an individualist vision, we sense in his works a more personal involvement with himself and his subject than that which Rosenquist and other first generation pop artists allowed themselves to display. Sukenick's fiction reveals a greater investment of self, a more extensive engagement of creator and subject, or at least an exploration of the ambiguities of self, world, and work than they.

In many ways, Sukenick's work foreshadows the later aesthetic strategies explored by young neo-expressionist visual artists of the 1980s, who, while deeply entrenched in a post-pop ironic attitude toward art and culture, also look back toward the example of the expressionists to present painting itself as, in the words of David Salle, an explicit act of "making meaning" (Tuten 79). Indeed, a comparative analysis of the writings of Sukenick and the painting of younger artists such as Salle would illuminate many of the core aesthetic issues of this period known as the postmodern.

Digressions on Time, Space, and Image

Comparisons between the literary and visual arts, however, are always somewhat difficult. Often, critics speak only in broad terms about parallels, analogies, or homologies and restrict themselves to the literature and art of a single historical moment and culture. Yet although the various art forms may emerge from a shared cultural context, they are also deeply grounded in their separate art historical traditions. Furthermore, the "content" of music, painting, or literature has different meaning in each of these cases. Specific cultural referents enter into the artworks in significantly different ways across the art forms. To be productive, a comparative methodology needs to account for the real differences among the media while identifying the affinities that justify the comparison.

One means of comparing literature and art—fiction and painting specifically—is to focus on the principles and strategies of the art work's formal structure within a given historical period. What does form mean and how does the work claim to assert meaning in the various arts of an era? What, especially, is the function of innovation within the art form's aesthetic strategies? How do challenges to a given formal convention break with fundamental premises and to what extent do they ultimately affirm traditional practices? Certainly, these are issues at the heart of the broad historical movements of modernism and postmodernism. For the past century, artists in all media have made the investigation of the principles of composition and the problematic bases of meaning explicit aspects of the aesthetic experience.

This is a direction particularly evident in the critical and theoretical writings of Ronald Sukenick. Although he broadly invokes "parallelisms" between painting and art in the passage above, he identifies the specific importance of analyzing the meaning and function of changes in the formal premises of the artwork. He argues, in the essay from which the passage is taken, for an analysis of the principles of composition—how the work emerges as a self-evident structure of meaning. Here, he articulates a basic premise of all the arts of postmodernism. In literature and art, in particular, the contemporary artwork makes its existence as a self-reflexive agent of meaning a core component of the work. Both literature and art present themselves as explicit semiotic systems for which the possibilities and limits of meaning-making are the central challenge of the work. Thus, for Sukenick, the "validity of the work of art in its own right" is more important than its referential capacity to "imitate" aspects of the world.

What is especially significant about this passage, however, is Sukenick's identification of the issues of the use of space and time in painting and fiction, respectively, for here he points to specific grounds of comparison between postmodern art and writing. Broadly speaking, the core of the work of fiction—narration—is a structuring of time; the organization of a painting is a structuring of space. The analysis of a visual or literary work's composition necessarily will encompass the configuration of spatial and temporal dimensions. And ultimately, as space and time comprise two basic dimensions to our experience, the structural principles of the artwork constitute essential statements about the nature of experience.

Implicit in Sukenick's reference to the imitative, or mimetic, function of art is the question of the role of the image as the locus of the aesthetic structuring of time and space. The "subject matter" suggested by the image, "is just one element of the composition" (*In Form* 10). Rather than what the image means, how it means—how it is used as a structural unit—is Sukenick's concern. Indeed, in all literature and art, image is a core component of the organization of time and space. Where and how the image is placed within the artifice, how it relates to, changes, and is changed by its immediate context and the total artwork are key to understanding the work as a whole.

Nonetheless, we must also confront the dissimilarities of the art forms. Image can have entirely distinct meanings for painting and fiction, even though both have long traditions in which the image serves representational intentions. In contemporary painting, the image may continue this function, referring to the "real" world, or it may refer to—or appropriate—existing images from art history or another medium. The postmodern image may also be a self-reflexive sign of a painting method, such as a highlighted brush stroke or evident references to the planar ground of the painting. In fiction, the image may describe an object, a scene, an event, a character, or it may act as a component of the self-referential textuality of the work. However, within both postmodern literature and art we observe similar approaches to the interplay of image and meaning system. In these arts, the image serves as a semiotic element which derives its meaning from its original discourse and also in relationship to discrete, but simultaneous discourses that envelop it. Common aesthetic tactics entail engaging the play of interpenetrating discourses and appropriating images from separate discourses to shape a self-reflexive text that serves as a primary terrain of competing meaning systems. These methods are especially evident in the works of Ronald Sukenick and David Salle.

Sukenick and Salle

For three decades, Sukenick's fiction—as well as his theoretical and critical writings—have illuminated many of these postmodern concerns. His writing has made the act of creation a central subject of each literary work by developing highly self-conscious formal and thematic strategies that explore the processes and challenges of meaning-making. In the process, his works contest many of our assumptions about the literary text. Correspondingly, the painter David Salle is representative of a postmodernist approach to painting which enacts similar challenges to the process and assumptions of visual art. Although they are of different generations, Sukenick and Salle signal characteristic postmodernist premises concerning three traditional aesthetic issues: formalist structure; subject and theme; self-consciousness, identity, and the creative presence. Their generational differences, however, are manifest in a fourth aesthetic area of contention: the sense of authorial tone and attitude.

Issues of Formal Structure

Postmodern works, in Sukenick's terms, operate in "the absence of wholes," the apparent lack of coherence to both external reality and personal experience upon which the aesthetic artifice can be based. Fundamentally, the writer and artist seek to justify the structure of the work, that is, the rationale for the artwork's structure, without relying on the presumed authority of any external meaning. They attempt to validate the organization of narrative time in the novel and compositional space in the visual arts in self-revealing terms. One option Sukenick suggests is self-reflexive synthesis (psychosynthesis), or what he calls "The Mosaic Law." In *98.6*, one of the characters offers a coda: "life is a lot like a novel you have to make it up. That's the point of psychosynthesis . . . to pick up the pieces and make something of them. Psychosynthesis is based on The Mosaic Law. The Mosaic Law is the law of mosaics a way of dealing with parts in the absence of wholes" (122).

Rather than art imitating life, here, it is life that can learn a lesson from art. Presumably, both are indefinitely mutable. Denied totality, and in the presence of so many fragments, the character or writer chooses and composes. The resulting structure, or mosaic, betrays its composite identity in the interstices of the fragments, the visible mortar or the abrupt linkages between the segments. This vision may be grounded ultimately in the modernist strategy of collage, the creation of new wholes from fragments of disparate discourses. But unlike the modernists who assumed the individual writer's subjective power to substitute the overarching authority of art for debased or rejected cultural codes that provided the fragments for their collages, the postmodernist has little faith in the transcendent, or totalizing power of the artwork (or, for that matter, even the authority of the creative subject). Postmodern mosaic is also unlike traditional metaphors for there is little suggestion of a coalescence of meanings into a third term. The interplay of semiotic elements rather calls attention to the interstices of discourses, the gaps within meaning systems, as well as the competition of invading discourses that intrude on and subvert other meaning systems. One result of this is the undermining of all hierarchies of meaning. The image ripped free of immediate context enters into ambiguous relationships with other discrete and deracinated images. One discourse seems no more essential than any other. As a consequence, we are constantly made aware of the precariousness of the narrative structure, the fragility of the artwork.

In the work of fiction, this sense of fragility is felt most in the experience of time, the temporal organization of the text. In Sukenick's works, self-reflexive process replaces stable structure; improvisational flow defines narrative time and the shape of text as reading experience. In *98.6*, writer and reader are brought together in the ever-unfolding present moment of the text: "Interruption. Discontinuity. Imperfection.

It can't be helped. This very instant as I write as you read a hundred things. A hundred things to tangle with resolve ignore before you are together. Together for an instant and then smash it's all gone still it's worth it. I feel. This composition grown out of ongoing decomposition. So far there are fifty-eight words in this composition" (167).

Sukenick's fictions compose themselves and submit to their necessary decomposition as a way of illuminating the central truth of all narratives that the narratives themselves attempt to deny. All narration is based in time, thus based on change, on the constant transformation from one state of being to another. As such, it always involves the notion of lack, of inadequacy, of incompleteness, either as a primary condition that is recognized or discovered, thus generating the desire to overcome it, or as a condition into which one is thrust which one then attempts to surmount. Traditionally, narration seeks closure, a righting of imbalance, a mastering of the conditions of time. The text acts for the reader. We seem to need narration; we constantly turn to stories; we desire the sense of meaning that only fiction can provide. The imaginary space of the artwork presents a world like our world, but ultimately different from it. It exists to assuage the felt inadequacy of the reader. But except in romance, this inadequacy is never fully overcome. At best a compromise with reality is negotiated in which a lesson takes place—the learning of limits. Yet even this satisfaction, this sense of perspective and understanding, usually achieved by the fictional character and manifest through the presumed pleasures of the text, is illusory, is delusory. Time is not mastered; all lessons are ephemeral.

Sukenick's fictions work from this understanding and thus, on one level, are deeply unsatisfying. They deny closure; they do not end in resolution, but in silence (as in *Out*), in the blunt self-assessment of "Another failure" (*98.6*), or in the shaggy-dog situation of a character in *Long Talking Bad Conditions Blues*: ". . . wishing they hadn't demolished the old public toilets because he had to piss a fact more fundamental than a fund of epiphanies but reflecting that all things come to an end at the same time recognizing that there was no point imposing a sense of tragedy on old public toilets and that things didn't have beginnings and endings in that sense they just start and then they stop" (114). They stop, but there is no final punctuation, no end stop. They will just start again. There is no stopping, indeed, no punctuation in *Long Talking Bad Conditions Blues*. And there are no epiphanies; there are, however, a series of recognitions that emerge and dissipate within the flow of narrative time. Sukenick's works teach a lesson appropriate to all fiction. One way to analyze a novel is to focus on limits: the limits of narration; the limits of meaning; the lesson learned that returns us to the temporal condition of a provisional order and its consequent vulnerability to further narrative disruption.

Yet if there is a sense of necessary failure in Sukenick's works, that failure comes not only from the instability of experience, the ever-emerging "lack," but also from the overwhelming sense of plenitude. Life and time ceaselessly thrust new experiences, new data at the individual, the writer. Art cannot keep up with life. No formal structure can contain the fullness of experience. But it can suggest that fullness, and celebrate it. For Sukenick recognizes that the closure sought in the traditional text also symbolizes a closing off of experience, a death of possibility, a false sense of mastery of life. Hence the fragments in his works, at once signs of incompletion, act as well as suggestions, as markers of a rich, complex world. "One cannot have control 'over' that of which one is a part, or even to formulate it completely—one can only participate more deeply in it" ("Twelve Digressions Toward a Study of Composition," *In Form* 4).

In the works of David Salle, as well as other postmodern painters, such as Julian Schnabel, George Condo, and Sigmar Polke (who had a formative influence on many artists of the eighties), the simultaneous organization and disruption of the artwork play out within the spatial principles of its composition. In their paintings, we note often the absence of a central image, the undermining of a hierarchy of plane or ground, and an inconsistency of medium. Their paintings present depth without perspective through the suggestion of multiple planes and discrete, fragmentary images, all unified to a minimal degree within patently obvious, but traditionally defined two-dimensional compositional terms. Frequently, the works are organized by a formalist composition perilously arbitrary and off-balance. Traditional terms of structural unity are held in seemingly fragile suspension, self-consciously suggesting arbitrary juxtapositions and imminent dissipation. Like Sukenick's fictions, these works announce themselves as performances, at once displaying and attending their own creation, their dance above the void, and they intimate their threatened dissolution into the flow of time.

David Salle's work *Colony* (1986), for example, presents at least eight disparate images and possibly separate planes to create a work of significant mystery and tension. The painting is dominated by an image of a reclining woman, seen from above. Her eyes are closed, her breasts bared, her left arm jutting forward toward the viewer, possibly in defense. Perspectivally, the arm is disproportionally large and almost dominates the foreground of the work. However, a thin loosely drawn blue line is superimposed on the arm and extends across most of the painting, linking two separate images, both drawn in the same blue paint—a small biomorphic abstract form to the left and a sketchily

Figure 1. David Salle, *Colony,* 1986. Acrylic and oil on canvas, 94 x 136 inches, David Salle/VAGA, New York, NY. Photograph courtesy of Gagosian Gallery, New York.

drawn scene (suggestive of 1930s prints) of workers playing musical instruments and relaxing. Also superimposed over the woman at various spots are a rectangle containing a Venetian canal scene, a loosely spread green wash, brown figures suggestive of the African sculptures beloved of early modernists, a small golden drawing of a male head with its eyes closed, and an image of a single eye staring out from the work at the viewer. This eye, drawn in a stark, graphic poster style, has become a repeating image in Salle's paintings, further upsetting the confused planes into which the viewer is drawn by presenting an image that moves from the painting's planes outward in the opposite direction of the viewer's positioning—to catch the viewer viewing.

In this and other works, Salle offers what he calls "simultaneity and also . . . a new kind of sequencing" within a spatial composition (Tuten 80). His simultaneity suggests different moments of art history, but it also connotes a dislocation in time and space of artist's and viewer's frames of reference. In *Tiny in the Air* (1989), for example, Salle establishes a primary image as a mannerist, art-historical referential ground, but then incorporates a plethora of free floating images and emblematic painterly marks to present a range of competing aesthetic languages from distinct art-historical moments and contexts (geometric abstraction, representationalism, abstract expressionism, photographic images, and mixed media). Here he apparently recreates—or "quotes" from—a tapestry copy of an "old-master" painting, to suggest an already second order work of art. On top of his mundane and indifferently painted, hence further distanced, reproduction, he layers modernist art-historical references (Giacommeti's drawings, an abstract expressionist painterly swath, pop cartoonish sketches) and his signature style images of harshly drawn nude women fondling strange anatomical objects. All art moments, he implies, exist simultaneously, yet none assumes a primacy, including the contemporary instant, which limits itself primarily to referring to other art historical moments. The past is undermined, but the present acknowledges itself contained within the terms established by that past.

Furthermore, if Salle's self-reflexive art works do not contest or imagine an alternative to the art historical context, this particular work also betrays a reliance on familiar formalist devices. The contradictions of plane, of imagistic context, and aesthetic styles do not extend beyond their inherent visual dynamism to challenge the formal tradition of the frame. Although we may have varying degrees of difficulty identifying the primary plane and see the authority of plane undermined by competing floating grids, the work as a whole is essentially balanced—composed—in fairly conventional terms. It assumes a type of stability

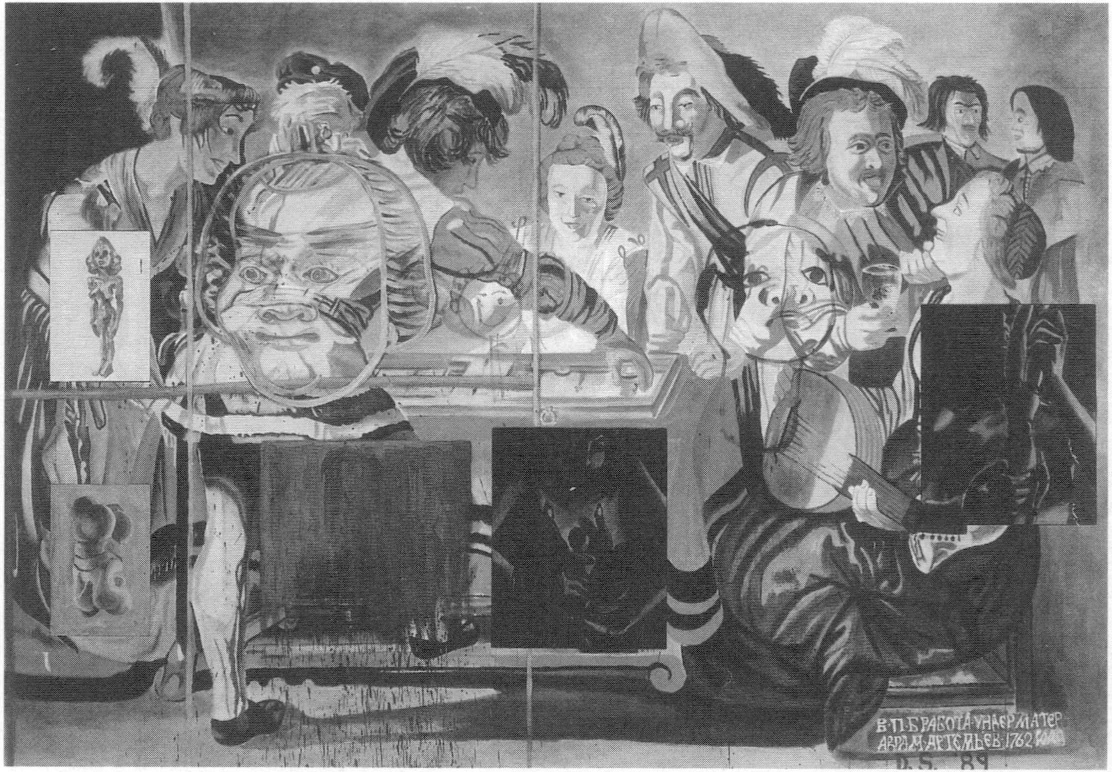

Figure 2. David Salle, *Tiny in the Air,* 1989. Oil and acrylic on canvas, 94 x 136 inches, David Salle/ VAGA, New York, NY. Photograph courtesy of Gagosian Gallery, New York.

emphasized by the internal repetition of geometric, rectangular blocks, themselves replicating the structures of a Mondrian-like or constructivist composition.

In part, this reveals an underlying conservatism in recent postmodernist works. Salle and many of the artists of the eighties and nineties came after the more radical challenges to the frames of art, art history, and the art market posed by the minimalist and conceptual artists who were Sukenick's contemporaries in the sixties. The artists of Salle's generation observed the absorption of those challenges by the art world and they exemplify an academicism of the avant-garde assault on convention through the acceptance of the art historical frame. Salle has remarked, in fact, that "painting essentially comes out of painting . . . there's a problem now in that there is less to react to, less painting that feels central. . . . Of course the history of painting is sufficient—but it begins to feel, well, historical rather than of the moment" (Tuten 78). The limits of this strain of postmodern thought lie in its self-enclosure within a primary discourse—art. Although it makes use of simultaneous meaning systems, and casts a reflexive doubt upon the authority of art, ultimately, contemporary art only brings other texts and languages into play to enact the internal conflicts of the still privileged realm of high art. No contemporary artist, including Salle, dares to make anything that is not art, anything not contained within the world that goes through the motions of questioning itself via the now-enshrined strategies of self-conscious disruption.

We can observe much the same phenomenon in postmodern writing, especially in the "literature of exhaustion" that envisions a literature that can only refer to other literature. Sukenick, in contrast, has consistently argued against the belief that art can only come from art, or that literature must deny its relation to life. But the life he invokes is the life beyond language, even if language is our only means of attaining it. "Creative language . . . points toward the mute world beyond language, beyond history, and then itself falls silent. Art is an escape from language and abstraction—and verbal art is the most conclusive escape into our birthright in the world beyond language from which language above all separates us, and which, therefore, it has the power to restore" ("Fiction in the Seventies: Ten Digressions on Ten Digressions," *In Form* 38). Sukenick defies the tradition of "serious" fiction (a.k.a. literature) by responding to the diverse and disruptive forms of mass culture and challenges the privileged languages of literature. As a result, he produces works which lie on the margins of art and take the gamble that they will be unrecognizable as literature.

Subject and Theme

Sukenick's fictions do inhabit the edges of literature. They seem to owe more to the spirit of popular culture than high art. Although as a critic and scholar Sukenick is extremely well versed in literary history, there is little trace of, and certainly few references to past literary works in his texts. Temperamentally, his literary forebearers are writers most open to the constant influx of the energies, richness, and chaos of unconstrained life—Rabelais, Sterne, Henry Miller—and like them his subject matter arises from the web of daily and vernacular experience. In Sukenick's fictions, however, we are constantly made aware that contemporary culture is highly mediated culture. The realm of the "real" toward which the novelist traditionally turns is known increasingly through the frameworks and imagery of mass media.

The world presented in Sukenick's fiction, like that displayed in the pop art of the sixties, the innovative writing of the sixties and seventies, and many of the "neo-expressionist" and "appropriationist" works of the 1980s and 1990s, is heavily inflected with images from pop culture and the mass media. It is as if the so-called real world that has traditionally been the subject of mimetic art has withdrawn from view and been replaced by an omnipresent web of constructed images purporting to speak for the real. To this extent, fiction refers to fiction, painting to pre-existing visual languages. The stuff of art is often the fluff of simulacra.

Sukenick and Salle are emblematic in their response to this mediated world. They exhibit similar approaches to a shared imagery. Both mine readily available contemporary cultural, political, and literary or visual glossaries for their iconography. These are often pop-media images, dislocated from our encompassing social texts and cultural codes. Sukenick is particularly attuned to pop narratives originating from the radio programs of his youth and from movies, as well as mass culture adventure stories, pornographic books, and glib journalist psycho-social babble. Salle turns more to the visual vocabularies of advertising, men's sex magazines, and television-land, in addition to his constant references to low and high art seen through the lens of college-level art history texts.

Sukenick's fictions and Salle's paintings approach this subject matter in a like manner. Adopting a comic, sometimes ironic, but always critical posture toward these pop-culture discourses, they cut images loose from their originating context. Appropriated, fragmented, and distorted, the images are then rearranged and juxtaposed with images from other high and low cultural contexts to suggest a social satire, a cultural critique via postmodern simulacra. The critique, however, indicates the ambiguous power of both image and originating discourse. Each image has its own integrity and bears evidence to the residue of the meaning system from which it was sundered. In the process the image appears alternatively to have overarching power and yet to be seen as deflected, deracinated, and weakened.

In the mosaic works of Sukenick and Salle, specific images, torn from their original cultural contexts, assume uncanny preeminence seemingly out of proportion to their residual meaning. They dominate a visual space or narrative moment, looming without apparent roots, cross-fertilizing other, similarly orphaned, but transgressive images. The art work and literary text display constantly emerging and dissolving terms and signs of transitory meaning. Formerly discrete realms of reference compete via incomplete yet potent signs within the ambiguous semiotic terrain of the artwork. The fractured images imply an omnipresent, if not a threateningly omniscient web of culturally encoded meanings, yet their arbitrary and tentative suspension in an aesthetic solution creates a sense of the ultimate inconsequence of any particular image. Singular images carry disproportionate weight, yet they also undermine their own particular significance in the flux of competing vocabularies.

The short stories in Sukenick's *Doggy Bag*, for example, mobilize appropriations from horror movies of the 1930s—vampires, mummies, zombies, werewolves—into comic pastiches of contemporary media and cultural manipulation. The child, Ronnie, in *Mosaic Man* moves in and out of Captain Midnight stories, merging fictional, autobiographical, and historical narratives of radio adventures, childhood in Brooklyn, World War II and the holocaust, creating a web of interpenetrating tales at once surreally comic and frightening. Similarly, in Sukenick's early novels, *Up*, *Out*, and *98.6*, the narrative glides among pop cultural narratives, contemporary allusions to political and historical stories cropped from the news media, autobiographical references, and pure fictive invention. Indeed, re-reading Sukenick's first works after thirty years, one is struck by how embedded in topical history they are, even as they announce narrative strategies that foreshadow aesthetic struggles of the decades to come.

Similarly, Salle, some of whose work recalls—as does Sukenick's—Rosenquist's glossy pop-cultural pastiches, manipulates the social texts latent in televison commercials and magazine advertisements, appropriating clichéd media images of suburbia, pop-psychology anomie, art historical iconography, and pedestrian pornography. Many of his paintings present cold and crudely drawn images of women in degrading sexual positions. These harsh scenes, seemingly lifted from vulgar men's magazines are juxtaposed with images of 1950s' decorative objects, diffident artist notebook sketches, or flatly drawn images suggestive of other artist's works. Rendered in grisaille fashion, the women suggest a disturbing undertext over which colored image fragments of art historical references or commodity objects float rootlessly. In Salle's art, pornography, commercialism, and art history are interdependent. Personal fantasy and mass cultural iconography merge. The material world and sexual desire are equated with the so-called high culture realm of art.

Strikingly, the works of both Sukenick and Salle frequently focus on sexual fantasies. Their works engage blatant reworkings of pop pornographic images, suggesting at once the power of these images over the readily receptive male mind and their pervasive cultural presence. Their banal eroticism always connotes a male presence, though whether it is that of the artist or solely the dominant culture is ambiguous. In Salle's works, the recurring use of fixed, socially constructed images of women in denigrating postures suggests more personal fixation than cultural critique. Sukenick frequently makes his narrator's fascination with sexual fantasy and the pornographic adventures of his alter-ego, Strop Banally, an obsessive point of contestation between the personal and the social workings of the imagination. In *Doggy Bag*, he invites the reader to engage in the bad faith delights of filling in the blank spaces he leaves in his pornographic story, "The Burial of Count Orgasm." This text recalls Robbe-Grillet's recurring use of fragmentary or unconsummated pornographic images, putatively in the name of cultural critique, but more evidently a personal fascination with clichéd eroticism.

This ambiguous status of sexual imagery in both Salle and Sukenick highlights a further tension with postmodernism: the conflict between cultural codes and individual subjectivity.

Self-Consciousness, Identity, and the Creative Presence

The works of Sukenick and Salle image the embattled status of the individual subject in a world seemingly dominated by cultural codes. Both raise the most basic questions about art as depiction of experience and art *as* experience. Their postmodern works indicate the ceaseless creation and loss of personal identity within competing codes of meaning. The individual self is presented as image; the self is posited as the creation, or extension of varied and numerous cultural discourses. The key point of contestation—for the artist, the writer, and the audience—

is the degree of the individual's ability to engage, manipulate, or alter those codes. The fragmented images and structures within their works suggest that no coherence to self or experience is possible, or alternatively that disruption, re-arrangement, and improvisational play may be effective creative tools of the resistant subject. Like many postmodernists, they question whether the subject is free to play, to manipulate the rules of discourse through disruption and recombination of social and aesthetic codes, or if the self is at best trapped in a cultural game not of one's own making, a contest in which control over structure and identity are limited, if not delusive, options.

Sukenick's characters are presented as fragmentary, barely self-conscious creatures subject to constantly changing conditions. Integral identity is unsupportable and is willfully abandoned. Instead, his characters appear as epistemological processes in flux. They seem transitory loci of shifting, incompatible, and incompletely known desires, fears, events, external forces, and cultural codes over which they have little control and scarcely more knowledge, but to which they attempt to give temporary, self-consciously improvisational order. The self is known as a function of temporality. The past ideal of stable character is displaced by a self-conscious mutability of identity. There is no control " 'over' that of which one is a part."

In these self-reflexive fictions, the situation of the mutating character stands as well for the situation of the author engaging the unstable and essentially fictive discourses of the culture—literature included. Like the fictional self, the writer is known as a mutable locus of shifting consciousness and experience. Author and character embrace and live within the flow of events, creating their identities and asserting a degree of freedom from external control by improvising with the fragments of self and the stimuli constantly thrust at them from the chaotic, overdetermined environment.

Sukenick's primary referents are elements from his autobiography. His texts explore identity in reference to his "real" life and his imagined life, as well as to the ever-self-present experience of writing the self. This act of creating the self testifies to the ambiguities of self-knowledge and creation. Incidents from life ground the fiction in a distinct realm of supposed truth, but entering the world of the fictive artifice, they become just "any other data" ("Thirteen Digressions," *In Form* 24). It is frequently unclear, however, whether the autobiographical elements are "truthful" or embellished, "real" or imagined, whether, in fact, one can ever tell between real and imaginary. This is at once an expression of an ideal of freedom and self-creation and an intimation that the self is itself but an imagined and delusive concept. On the one hand, Sukenick offers that "the main didactic job of the contemporary novel is to teach the reader now to imagine his own life. Art is not imitation; it is example" ("Thirteen Digressions," *In Form* 25). On the other hand, this formulation is asserted in explicit opposition to its troubling opposite—the notion that we might have control over neither our identities, the formulations of the world around us, nor our imaginations.

> We are not talking about reality at all but authority . . . it is a question of who and what has the power to make authoritative statements about phenomena . . . we are dealing with our fate in a much more direct way, we are talking about who controls our imaginations, what has the authority to do so, whether it is proper authority, whether we want it in control of our imagination. Maybe something other than what we want controlling our imaginations is controlling them. Then we can really begin to talk about the way our lives go from day to day, whether it is being just, for example, manipulated by politics, the media or the mass market in the United States. ("Cross Examination," *In Form* 147)

Such a problematic and ultimately paranoid struggle between the individual and a threatening cultural environment characterizes much postmodern fiction. A fairly traditional, no matter how inventive, approach is to construct imaginary, fictive worlds, as does Pynchon, and to set in play absurd interpenetrations and transfigurations of characters and their ambiguous and competing worlds. But unlike the notoriously absent Pynchon, Sukenick is hyper-present, as writer and character, as constructor and construct. Because he is his primary subject, the interplay between self and outside world—known mostly as pop cultural narratives and images—is extremely problematic. Sukenick's fictions speak more directly to the struggles to be or to invent a self and simultaneously to leave oneself open to chance and external configurations, even as that openness entails vulnerability and, perhaps, paranoia.

Yet although Sukenick draws our attention to the mutability of self, the constant shifting of identities and mutation of reality, he is also constantly concerned with the residue of his past, especially his childhood experiences. If at one point in *98.6*, his characters are described as "creatures of biology and chance" (123), they, and all of Sukenick's characters—most especially Sukenick the writer/character, himself—enact as well the ceaseless contention between their past identities and their present openness to their unknown and hopefully imagined selves. In contrast to the ideal of constant flow and flux (writing a novel that changes as it goes; experiencing a self mutating), Sukenick also offers the idea of Mosaic Man, the self built up of discrete and relatively unchanging parts. Some of those parts are fragments of the past, memories of events and people, as well as past imaginings of self. Others are imaginative self-projections. No matter how focused in the present the text and subject are, the past constantly returns. In a mosaic, narrative time becomes composed space. The past incident is experienced as a fixed fragment, even as it may provide the basis for an imaginary variation of that past or fictive future selves. It intimates the limits of self-invention, even as it also suggests the limits of the external world to change or obliterate that past self.

Significantly, Sukenick's recent novel, *Mosaic Man*, presents the most sustained portrait of the writer/character Sukenick. It seems his most traditionally autobiographical work, a novel seeking a sense of the constancy of identity, including the persistence of his desire to be free of a consistent identity. The work oscillates between autobiographical and imaginative fragments of a life in time and text. More than any of his previous works, the mosaic of *Mosaic Man* is structured by a primary and sustained "external" reference: Judaism. Although all elements of the text are in constant flux—past and present self, autobiographical and fictional identity, sociocultural references, even the ever-debated nature of "the" Jewish experience—all fragments in this mosaic relate to the dominant question of being Jewish. The work explores the degree that the individual, particular self may be shaped by cultural, historical identity. But even if this book achieves a coherence that no other Sukenick fiction allows, ultimately, there is still little cohesion to the life he presents. For the essential reality Sukenick recognizes is that consistency escapes us. Neither identity, experience, nor art can provide a sense of totality; nor should they, he would maintain. For however seductive a sense of complete vision might be, Sukenick also knows it would be false. "The only thing he can't imagine yet is himself. That cheers him up" (*98.6* 124).

Salle's works also figure the ambivalent play of subjective freedom and submission to external, cultural codes. But unlike Sukenick, the painter's investment of self in these conflicts is muted. In Salle's paintings, we are often struck by the detached gaze, the sense of a somewhat removed artist. Given the artist's distance and minimal affect, the viewer is also set back from the work, viewing it with a withdrawn response. The distance that Salle evokes allows for a suggestion of mystery, or at least of ambiguity that is a bit unsettling. We wonder how personal the paintings are and what the intersections of individual concern, even obsession, and cultural commentary imply.

Certainly, Salle's early works, which dramatically figure naked or partially clothed women in awkwardly submissive, oddly sexual poses, raise the questions of personal identity and cultural formation, individual obsession and social cliché. *Midday* (1984), for example, contains two panels. The right third of the composition, a minimalist abstraction, is juxtaposed against the left panel image of a supine woman, wearing only a bra and high heels, arms and legs raised in a manner suggesting both sexual exposure and defense. (Comparisons have been made to Caravaggio's *Conversion of St. Paul*, setting in motion both an appropriationist self-consciousness and a perverse contrast between the sexual and spiritual contexts.) The room the woman is in contains furniture similar to that in Salle's home. Superimposed on this scene are sketches of a steam engine and a portrait of a man who looks vaguely like Salle. The scene offers a sexually charged but ambiguous narrative. The enigmatic image and the personal reference to the painter's home suggest a number of interpretations, none mutually exclusive. Similar to the adolescent and coyingly perverse narratives of Eric Fischl, this painting implicates viewer, artist, and culture. We wonder what is occurring, and not knowing, are forced to imagine a pertinent narrative. And what is the source of that imagined narrative? The scene may imply a drama in Salle's home, in Salle's life. The woman may be just a model, similar to the female figures so frequently seen in his other paintings and the working photographs he took for these works and then presented independently in gallery exhibitions. But why these poses? Other than unusual artist's figure studies, they also allude to the cheap pornography of men's magazines, hence may be a cultural commentary on Salle's part. But the fact that Salle was employed as a layout man for one such magazine, *Stag*, returns us to the ambiguous position of the artist within his culture. Our inability to settle these questions leaves us in the uneasy position of complicity in the scene and our imaginative creations of its meaning(s).

Less problematic are Salle's later works, in which he seems to withdraw further from the scene. Having been castigated for his use of pornography, his subsequent retreat from personally charged imagery deflated the tension of the individual-social conflict, leaving us with works at once formally dramatic and emotionally vapid. His "Product Paintings," for example, collage images taken from magazine advertisements into decorative mosaics of commercial referents. Though some, like *Picture Builder* (1993) and *Big Letter Rack* (1993), seem especially derivative of Rosenquist's billboard style paintings of the 1960s, their prominent references to familiar commercial products suggest more evident efforts at social commentary. *Gilbey's* (1993), which essentially

Figure 3. David Salle, *Midday,* 1984. Oil, acrylic, and wood on canvas, 114 x 150 inches, David Salle/VAGA, New York, NY. Photograph courtesy of Gagosian Gallery, New York.

juxtaposes in three panels three distinct advertisements (with only the slightest superimposition of a few painterly marks), provides a simple allegory of a nuclear family of the 1950s or 1960s: mom (the plastic work gloves), the "youngster" (at the center enthusiastically downing his chocolate milk), and dad (represented by the bottle of gin). This may be a 1990s' reworking of pop art, but in Salle's hands, we recognize both a postmodern appropriation of an earlier aesthetic and a haunting suggestion of an ambiguously placed subjective presence. In these and his works of 1999, which prominently figure scenes of a suburban household, one catches glimpses of autobiography and yet may also be looking at only a removed commentary on commercial, cultural ideals represented by media images of the "good" life of middle America. The vapid quality of the works suggests either a cooly disdainful regard of the lives others lead, an intimation that one's own identity is so much a function of mass culture discourse, or an emotionally neutral withholding from one's own experience. The fragmentary compositions present themselves as performances, alternately implying a controlling

Figure 4. David Salle, *Gilbey's,* 1993. Oil and acrylic on canvas, 82 x 92 inches, David Salle/VAGA, New York, NY. Photograph courtesy of Gagosian Gallery, New York.

artistic self and an essentially irrelevant, if not absent, functionary, who merely coordinates the appropriated images. Thus, once Salle moves away from his emotionally charged, if ambiguously complicitous soft-core pornography, his works suggest either well-played performances of a confident choreographer of fragments or diffident reworkings of formulaic compositions.

Authorial Tone and Attitude

Although Sukenick and Salle underscore the formal, thematic, and subjective challenges of postmodern fiction and painting, temperamentally their responses to those challenges differ significantly. They both accept the postmodern given—that all meaning systems, including art, can be seen as artifice, ultimately groundless and fictive, if nonetheless controlling and inescapable. As postmodern artists, they position themselves self-consciously within the webs of discourse, but while necessarily submitting to the various codes, they also seek to identify and inhabit the subjective space of creative freedom. In doing so, they offer two distinct visions of creativity particularly evident in their differences of authorial tone and attitude toward their works. Similar to many postmodern writers and artists, Salle adopts a critical, self-conscious distance from his subject, himself, and his art by constructing an ironic, self-protective attitude that encompasses all he sees and presents. Sukenick plunges in and attempts to disrupt and reformulate the cultural codes, to establish a temporary, ever-mutable space of relative, if doomed freedom in the improvisational moment. These two options reflect the subtle differences between the metaphors of game and play evident across postmodern culture.

Game signals an ironic negotiation with the prefigured conventions of social and aesthetic meaning systems and is most evident in what we can call the academicism of the avant-garde. There, the ceaseless promulgation of new styles and aesthetic strategies operates within the established expectations of formalist innovation. Unlike an earlier avant-garde belief that the new language of art could presage new modes of perceiving, thinking, and acting, indeed would effect a change in human life, contemporary aesthetic innovation speaks more to the premises of—and the promise of—an investment oriented art market. The academy is not a traditional structure against which the artists rebel, but rather the oxymoronic tradition of conventional rebellion. The *ism* that defines contemporary art, it's been suggested, is *commercial*ism. However ambivalent an artist's participation within this academy, the artworld seems essentially to be a game. Hence certified quality is often determined by skillful or dramatic performance, and the artist observes the performing self at a remove, always within the context of the established game.

Play may also accept the metaphor of art or writing as performance, but its characteristic mode is improvisation. Free play thrives in the self-present moment, focusing more on the engaged performer than the defining game. In play, the self is more at risk and engaged as process and subject. It announces a self-conscious engagement with the processes of disruption and recuperation of the codes of the game, testing the limits and constraints of the rules, displaying the ever-shifting emergence and disappearance of self. Postmodern play and irony differ in spirit and tone. In doing so, they delineate the realm of freedom and its—and our—limits.

Clearly, the dominant postmodern tone is ironic, the putatively self-protective, detached attitude of the artist too cool and self-aware to risk any strong or individual statement that inevitably will be challenged and found to be but one more fictive construct. All ironic texts and art works hold themselves at a distance, aesthetic baubles suspended over a deconstructive void. Salle's works are exemplary of this mode. His tone is diffident, detached, decidedly ironic.

Salle's paintings indicate a sensibility trapped—and quite plausibly content—within cultural constructs that deny subjective presence. Their diffidence is challenged only by an implicit distaste for their subject matter, whether it be the objectified women or pop commodity culture. Salle once stated: "I loathe popular culture. I have no use for it whatsoever. I'm only interested in elite culture" (Tuten 81). On one level this makes no sense. For Salle has great *use* for popular culture; in fact he is almost entirely dependent on it as subject and discourse, even if only to function within the so-called elite culture of the dominant art market. Yet on another level, that loathing is apparent throughout his paintings. There certainly seems to be a complete absence of humor in Salle's works. There's no delight in the subject of his works, nor, it seems, in the act of painting. They are definitely not pretty; there's little apparent effort to render with any degree of interest in the subject. He's clearly not a colorist; nor does he communicate a significant, personal mark. Rather, the paintings and drawings hold our interest primarily by the notion of their subject matter and the coolly detached performance that manipulates that subject matter. In his clinical, and implicitly cruel, regard for a commodified culture he simultaneously critiques and indulges, he is perhaps much closer to his generation of writers than Sukenick. Brett Easton Ellis comes foremost to mind.

In contrast, Sukenick's works constantly invoke the spirit of imaginative play. They affirm an openness to chance, both as unexpected opportunity and inevitable disruption of self and world. If he recognizes that no matter how much he seeks not to write a novel, he's part of the ever-shifting, but recognizable tradition of the novel—the new—he also asserts that the essence of that tradition is to challenge the form in order to allow the imagination to confront the texture of life beyond art. "The whole purpose of the imagination in writing is to constantly destroy the formulations of language, to make language work against itself so that there can be an openness to data" ("Cross Examination," *In Form* 146). His fictions enact the ceaseless confrontation of meaning and nonmeaning, of language and "data." And rather than confining themselves to an artful, if ironic, presentation of discrete and incomplete fragments of parallel discourses within a carefully composed artifice,

Sukenick's texts playfully unmake themselves. They seek the void, the silence, if only to find stimulus and occasion to speak again.

In this Sukenick is closest, perhaps, to the spirit of John Cage. For like Cage, Sukenick welcomes silence, improvisation, and chance. Instead of trying to control something of which one is but a part, or even to give form to it, Sukenick encourages us to "participate more deeply in it." Rather than seeking a self-protective distance from the darker aspects of the world through irony, in Sukenick's playfulness, the serious becomes comic; the comic turns serious through a constant glissando of literary invention and play.

Works Cited

Sukenick, Ronald. *In Form: Digressions on the Act of Fiction.* Carbondale: Southern Illinois University Press, 1985.

———. *Long Talking Bad Conditions Blues.* New York: Fiction Collective, 1979.

———. *98.6.* New York: Fiction Collective, 1975.

Tuten, Frederic. "David Salle: At the Edges." *Art in America* 85.9 (September, 1997): 78–83.

Sukenick in Space, or, The Other Truth of the Page*

Brian McHale

The Fiction Collective is not now, and never has been, an aesthetic school or movement on the model of the historical avant-gardes of the first half of this century. It was founded, rather, to serve as an alternative network of distribution and promotion, and so has more in common with current online discussion lists and linked Web-pages than it does with more recognizably school-like phenomena such as Language poetry or 1980s cyberpunk. Fiction Collective writers possess little in the way of a shared poetics. Nevertheless, if we restrict our focus to the first wave of Fiction Collectivists—writers like George Chambers, Steve Katz, Raymond Federman, Clarence Major, and Ronald Sukenick, the subject of this essay—then I suppose there is one aesthetic principle that many of them would have been willing to endorse, and that is the principle articulated by Sukenick under the rubric of "the truth of the page." I want here to complicate this notion of "the truth of the page," and to show that in Sukenick's theory and practice there are in fact two "truths," each entailing a different range of narrative options. The two "truths of the page" are not irreconcilable or incompatible, but they do exert pressure in different directions, and the cross-currents they generate make for a richer, stranger, more chaotic, less predictable poetics.

"The truth of the page," Sukenick told an interviewer some five years before the founding of the Fiction Collective, "The truth of the page is that there's a writer sitting there writing the page. There's a dictum of Burroughs which goes something like 'the writer shouldn't be writing anything except what's in his mind at the moment of writing,' which means to me the same thing as 'the truth of the page' " (*In Form* 25).

We have heard this truth before, and the citation from Burroughs reminds us where, in case we have forgotten. This is the Beat aesthetics of improvisation, such as we find it not only in Burroughs but, classically, in Jack Kerouac's "Essentials of Spontaneous Prose" (1953), a text that Sukenick cites frequently in his manifestos and interviews of the 1970s and 1980s. Or, to be more accurate, this is the aesthetics of an entire "culture of spontaneity," to quote the title of a useful recent book by Daniel Belgrad (1998), that arose in the United States immediately after World War II as a "third-stream" alternative both to a timid and reactionary high culture and to the onrushing juggernaut of mass culture. Sukenick has documented episodes from the history of this culture of spontaneity in his memoir/oral history, *Down and In: Life in the Underground* (1987). This is the culture from which Sukenick himself emerged, along with the other Fiction Collectivists of his generation, and it embraced a range of cultural practices, from abstract-expressionism, collage, and assemblage in the visual arts, through Beat and Black Mountain writing, to bebop and free jazz. Sukenick mentions all these practices in connection with the truth of the page.

Jazz improvisation, in particular, serves as a model for Sukenick, as it did for Kerouac and the Beats. "In improvisation," Sukenick writes in a manifesto from the mid-1980s, "the mind's language solos like speech without sound, like an ongoing sentence that forgets how it began. . . . Not writing like speaking [but] writing as the written extension of all that mental jazz, recording the mind's ongoing music, like taping a saxophone solo" (Charters, *Portable* 87). Sukenick's language here echoes Kerouac's instructions for "sketching from memory" in spontaneous prose: "sketching language is undisturbed flow from the mind of personal secret idea-words, *blowing* (as per jazz musician) on subject of image" (Charters, *Portable* 484). One recalls that Raymond Federman, whose poetics approaches Sukenick's as closely as anyone's, was a jazz saxophonist before he was a writer.

"The truth of the page," then, implies writing that preserves the trace of the writer's actual activity in real time and real space, writing that registers the process by which the page itself was inscribed.[1] A commitment to "the truth of the page" appears throughout Sukenick's fiction, but nowhere more plainly than in the closing pages of his novella, "The Death of the Novel" (1969). On page 90, Sukenick sets himself a deadline: "Here begins the last hour that I allow myself to finish this performance. Go." In the ensuing twelve pages, disjointed episodes tumble out at a frenetic tempo, interrupted at intervals by the writer urging himself on as, presumably, the time ticks away: page 91, "Go on./I can't./Keep going"; page 92, "Faster," then "Keep going," then "Go on. Faster"; page 93, "Keep it up. Faster"; page 96, and again on page 97, "Keep going"; and so on, until the story's last words, "End of story." The allusion here is obviously to Beckett's *The Unnamable*, though a more relevant Beckett text, both for "The Death of the Novel" in particular and for the notion of "the truth of the page" more generally, is *Texts for Nothing*, in which Beckett has left the record of nightly "sessions" at his writing-desk.

Elsewhere in Sukenick's fiction, the principle of "the truth of the page" gives rise to texts such as "This Is the Part" (*The Endless Short Story*). Once again composed under a time constraint (Andrei Codrescu needs the text "right away"), "This Is the Part" is also governed by certain "rules," including "write fast," "totla [sic] improvisation and . . . most important don't correct typing" (60). The precursor here seems to be William Carlos Williams, a foundational figure for the postwar culture of spontaneity, who famously wrote in a passage from *Patterson*, Book Three (1949), "Only one answer: write carelessly so that nothing that is not green will survive" (Williams 129). Sukenick quotes this line in his 1975 manifesto, "The New Tradition"(212).

Commitment to "the truth of the page" also underwrites Sukenick's use of tape-recording transcripts in texts like "Momentum," "The Death of the Novel," "Roast Beef: A Slice of Life" (*The Death of the Novel and Other Stories*) and "Duck Tape" (*The Endless Short Story*).[2] Transcribing taped speech is something like the verbal equivalent of hyperrealism in painting; Sukenick in an interview (*In Form* 131) calls it "doing imprints of reality." In Sukenick's use of tape transcripts, the orality that (according to Daniel Belgrad) is a feature of the culture of spontaneity converges with the improvisatory aesthetic of jazz. Think of that characteristic Sukenick book-title, *Long Talking Bad Conditions Blues* (1979).

One consequence of "the truth of the page"is the lifting of all constraints on subject-matter (*In Form* 25); presumably, one can write about anything at all while adhering to "the truth of the page." Nevertheless, like any writing practice, this one has a special affinity (let's call it) for certain types or ranges of narrative content. One catches a glimpse of this characteristic narrative content in (of all places) the poet Frank O'Hara's "Personism" manifesto (1974), which Sukenick cites (*In Form* 43). O'Hara here is parodying Charles Olson's manifesto, "Projective Verse" (1951), one of the touchstone texts of the culture of spontaneity, but its parodic purpose does not make O'Hara's any less of a document of spontaneity itself. He writes: ". . . I don't . . . like rhythm, assonance, all that stuff. You just go on your nerve. If someone's chasing you down the street with a knife you just run, you don't turn around and shout, 'Give it up! I was a track star for Mineola Prep' " (O'Hara, *Selected Poems* xiii). "You just go on your nerve": this is another way of asserting spontaneity, improvisation, "the truth of the page." But when you *do* go on your nerve, what sort of stories do you end up telling? O'Hara's campy little vignette suggests an answer: you end up writing about being on the run, being in motion. Think of the restless motion, the one-thing-after-another urban flâneur's experience of O'Hara's own characteristic "lunch poems."

Writing about being on the run—or, better, writing about being on the *road*: here, once again, Kerouac is the great exemplar. In his practice, spontaneous prose is revealed to be the ideal vehicle (in every sense) for narratives of cross-country travel, restless shifts of locale, casual or accidental encounters along the road. This correlation between spontaneous prose and (post)modern picaresque, having achieved its classic expression in Kerouac, persists down to the first-generation Fiction Collectivists and beyond; what is Federman's *Take It or Leave It* (1976) if not a rewrite of *On the Road* in a metafictional mode?[3]

Practice of "the truth of the page" has a special affinity, in other words, for what Bakhtin ("Forms of Time" 243–45) called the chronotope of the open road. This special affinity is confirmed throughout Sukenick's fiction, but especially in his 1973 novel of the open road, *Out*, whose very title captures its projective, or projectile, narrative motion.[4] The continent-spanning itinerary and picaresque structure of *Out* represents one version of the chronotope of the open road; another version manifests itself in the restless, hyperkinetic circulation, changing partners, and fluid identities of texts like "Boxes" (*The Endless Short Story*), or, on a larger scale, *Long Talking Bad Conditions Blues*. These texts reflect what the title of a Wallace Steven poem calls "The Pleasures of Merely Circulating"; and Sukenick, himself a Stevens scholar of course, knows exactly what these pleasures are.[5]

Elsewhere in Sukenick's fiction the open road changes key, taking on aspects of Henry James's "international theme" in the Americans-abroad narratives of *Doggy Bag* (1994) and *Mosaic Man* (1998). There is even a parodic version in the jet-set adventures of Sukenick's pop-culture alter-ego, the secret agent Strop Banally of *Up* (1968) and *Mosaic Man*, an "international man of mystery" who anticipates Mike Myers's Austin Powers by some thirty years. All of these variants of the chronotope of the open road seem to be recapitulated in the "After the Fact" section of *Mosaic Man*, which narrates Sukenick's travels in Germany with Raymond Federman (himself an "international man of mystery"), and does so in a way that remains faithful to "the truth of the page" in an era when the "page" has become a laptop's screen, and registering real-world interruptions (like the phone-calls that interrupt the last hour of composing "The Death of the Novel") has become a matter of opening "real time windows."

But there is an alternative "truth of the page." In an early manifesto, the "Thirteen Digressions" of 1973, Sukenick speaks of "the two realities behind literature: the reality of the spoken word and the reality of the written word" (*In Form* 30). The first of these corresponds, obviously, to the underlying orality of spontaneous prose that is brought to light by practices such as tape transcription; it corresponds, in other words, to "the truth of the page" in the sense of real-time improvisation, the writer "sitting there writing the page." The second of these "realities," that of the written word, has different consequences. For the poet, full recognition of the reality of writing might entail concrete poetry, or the replacement of traditional metrics by "arrangement on the page," whereas for the novelist it means "no longer leaving one of the most important elements of composition in the hands of the typesetter: the placement of print on the page becomes an expressive resource of the novel" (ibid.).

Only a few years later, in a piece from 1977, Sukenick will sound less even-handed, aligning himself, perhaps surprisingly, with a print-based and spatial, as opposed to voice-based and musical, poetics of fiction: "Fiction, finally," he writes, "involves print on a page, and that is not an incidental convenience of production and distribution, but an essential of the medium" (*In Form* 46). Even tape-recorder practices come in for reinterpretation from this alternative perspective: "Only on the page does electronically recorded speech of any kind acquire the power of writing . . . only on the pages does [it] become . . . a way of saying that however much the word may resound with associative and etymological resonances it is still fundamentally a mark on a page, an image on a surface, a visually concrete manifestation whose power of abstraction comes from the fact that it is a real object . . ." (*In Form* 94–95). Nor is this strictly a retrospective interpretation, imposed on texts that were originally unproblematically oral in their orientation; for in fact, several of Sukenick's earliest tape-recorder transcripts (e.g., "Momentum," "Roast Beef") used a double-column presentation that exploited "the placement of print on the page." In other words, the two orientations, the two "realities," coexisted in Sukenick's practice from the very beginning; the truth of the page as oral improvisation coincided with a different truth.

This other "truth of the page" is the truth of writing's *materiality*, its existence as a structure of real objects: the white space of the page, the shapes that typography makes, the concrete "technological reality" of the book (Sukenick, *In Form* 206). "A novel," Sukenick writes, "is both a concrete structure and an imaginative structure—pages, print, binding containing a record of the movement of a mind" (205). The difference between the two "truths" is the difference, let's say, between the closing pages of "The Death of the Novel" ("Here begins the last hour that I allow myself to finish this performance") and the closing pages of *Blown Away* (1986), which are punctuated by the phrase, "In the book you're reading"—as in, "In the book you're reading it all turns out the way Crab predicts" (165); "Meanwhile in the book you're reading the Sheriff investigates the origin of the fires" (168); "In the book you're reading Drackenstein winds slowly down the canyon in the yellow Stingray" (170); and even this, on page 166: "In the book you're reading a xerox of part of a page of the *Los Angeles Times* for [Tuesday, October 24, 1978] is included on page 167." And sure enough, on the facing page one finds a (barely legible) photocopy from the *Los Angeles Times*.

Or, to speak in terms of another Fiction Collectivist's practice, the difference between the two "truths" is the difference between Federman's improvised novel of the open road in the Kerouac manner, *Take It or Leave It*, and his "shaped" texts, such as *Double or Nothing* (1971, 1992) or *The Voice in the Closet* (1979). Or think in terms of Sukenick's book-titles—*Long Talking Bad Conditions Blues*, *Out:* as we have seen, these seem to connote orality, improvisation, motion, the truth of the page-as-process. But now consider his titles in the context of the alternative truth of the page-as-material, the page-as-object, even the page-as-*place*. In this context Sukenick's "directional" titles—*Up*, *Out*, *Down and In*—seem to acquire a different connotation; they come to sound like directional arrows on a keyboard, allowing us to maneuver around the two-dimensional space of the (virtual) page—*up* toward the top of the page, *down* toward the bottom, *in* toward the center, *out* toward the margins.

If Sukenick's poetics calls attention to "the truth of the page" in the sense of the writer's activity in real time and space, it also calls attention to "the truth of the page" in the sense of the materiality of writing. Sukenick's strategies for foregrounding the materiality of writing vary ingeniously from book to book. Non-alphabetic signs interrupt the prose of his most recent books: strings of punctuation-marks in *Doggy Bag*, hand-scrawled symbols (Star of David, dollar sign, etc.) in *Mosaic Man*. Earlier in his career, Sukenick's principle resource for foregrounding writing's materiality had been spacing. I have already remarked on his use of double-column layout to present tape transcripts; elsewhere, his layouts mimic newspaper columns (as in "Fourteen," "This Is the Part," and passages of "The Death of the Novel"), or even scrapbooks of newspapers clippings, as in the "Frankenstein" section of *98.6*. Sukenick uses spacing in lieu of punctuation in a number of texts, including *Long Talking Bad Conditions Blues* and "Bush Fever," and, with a particularly witty twist, in "The Burial of Count Orgasm" (from *Doggy Bag*), where the blank spaces open gaps in a narrative of sexual activity, forcing the reader literally to fill the gaps himself or herself, and so become an accomplice in pornography. It is only a short step from such "spaced-out" pages to pages of "shaped" typography, whether geometrical, as in a text like "Boxes," or free-form, as in certain passages from "The Birds," "Dong Wang," "Bush Fever," or, spectacularly, in certain pages from *Up* (1968) that recall Mallarmé's *Un coup de dès* or the Mouse's Tale from *Alice's Adventures in Wonderland*.

Indeed, some of Sukenick's texts are entirely structured by spacing. The prime example is *Out*, whose first chapter is arranged on the page in units nine lines long, separated by one line of blank space; the second chapter reduces the units to eight lines of print, separated by two lines of blank space; the third chapter reduces the units still further, to seven lines of print separated by three blank lines, and so on, the white space progressively expanding and the print shrinking from chapter to chapter, until the last, when single lines of type are separated by ten blank lines—after which (what else?) the text disappears into the blankness of the empty page. Another example is *Long Talking Bad Conditions Blues,* which begins as a solid block of unpunctuated prose, followed by a prose block in which "gaping holes" have been introduced in lieu of punctuation, followed by pages in which blocks of prose and rectangles of white space alternate, followed by pages arranged as long, newspaper-style columns on the right-hand side of the page, blank space on the left. At the exact center of the text, page 57 is entirely blank; then the whole sequence is recapitulated in reverse—newspaper-style columns (but on the left-hand side of the page this time instead of the right), then alternating prose and white space, then prose punctuated by gaping holes, then a solid prose block to the end. Each of these configurations of type and spacing serves some particular function in context; the progressively expanding white spaces of *Out*, for instance, mirror the narrative's advance into the "wide open spaces" of the American West, until it loses itself in the void of the Pacific Ocean. But each configuration also performs a secondary function, that of exposing to view the material basis of writing: shapes inked onto pages bound into a book.

Just as there are two "truths of the page," the truth of the page-as-process and the truth of the page-as-material, so there are two correlative types of narrative content. Improvisatory, process-oriented writing, as we have seen, favors narratives of picaresque adventure, restless circulation, the open road. "Materialist" writing, by contrast, tends to favor fixed sites, bounded spaces, fictions of *place*; think of the writer's *room* in Federman's *Double or Nothing*, or the *closet* of *The Voice in the Closet*. To revert to the coded discourse of Stevens's poetry (a discourse in which Sukenick is fluent), if the page-as-process evokes "The Pleasures of Merely Circulating," the "materialist" page evokes something like the "Anecdote of the Jar": a virtual space over which the imagination "takes dominion." The space of the page becomes a figure for this virtual space of fiction, and vice-versa, the fictional space mirrors the space of the page.

Hence the fixation on *places* and *spaces* in so much of Sukenick's fiction. Hence, for instance, the liminal space of the Continental Divide in "Divide" (*The Endless Short Story*); hence the utopian spaces—hippie commune, imaginary Palestine—of *98.6*; hence the concentric circles of island and city that bound, constrain and intensify the hectic, back-and-forth motion of the characters in *Long Talking Bad Conditions Blues*; hence, especially, the Los Angeles of *Blown Away*, which Sukenick evokes by parodying another memorable place in fiction, the London of Dickens's *Bleak House*:

> Smog. Smog over Hollywood. Smog over Beverly Hills. Smog over Bel Air and Griffith Park. Smog over Pasadena and Santa Monica. Smog over Watts and Torrance, Encino and Van Nuys. Smog over Long Beach and Huntington Beach and Redondo Beach and El Segundo. Smog over Palos Verdes. Smog over the Valley. Smog over San Berdoo. Smog over the San Gabriel Mountains and the Santa Ana Mountains. Smog over Palm Springs and Palm Desert. Smog over Marina del Rey. Smog over the Miracle Mile and the Sunset Strip. Smog over the chic office buildings of Century City. Smog through their revolving doors and up their elevators. Smog through their air conditioning vents and into their offices. And the thickest smog in the offices of Universal International Productions. . . . (*The Endless Short Story* 75)

Los Angeles has often been caricatured as the quintessentially *placeless* postmodern space—space without center, structure, or landmark, "all-over" space, resistant to "cognitive mapping." However true this may be of the real Los Angeles, it is not true of Sukenick's fictional reconstruction of it. Like the architectural historian Reyner Banham, in his pathbreaking 1971 book on Los Angeles, Sukenick orients his Los Angeles relative to a definite center, transforming mere space into place. For Sukenick, as for Banham, that center is Simon Rodia's Watts Towers, which figure conspicuously in *Blown Away* (102), and to which Sukenick had earlier devoted a separate short story, "What's Watts" (*The Endless Short Story*).[6]

It is, finally, entirely characteristic that Sukenick's history and memoir of American "underground" culture, *Down and In,* should focus so fixedly on the *places* of the underground. The book's endpapers feature a map of Greenwich Village, East and West, and marked on it one finds the various gathering-places and watering-holes—coffeehouses, bars, and clubs—that at different periods housed and hosted the underground scene: the San Remo and the White Horse, the Cedar Tavern and St. Mark's Church, the Electric Circus and the Mudd Club. But even beyond the places of the underground, Sukenick is interested in its *spaces*, the *interiors* through which underground people passed, and in which they enacted their scenes. All this culminates in a tour-de-force mapping of what Sukenick calls the "geography of Max's [Kansas City]":

> Like New York, Max's Kansas City was a city with five boroughs, not one bar but five bars in one, each room having its distinct tone, rhythms, and clientele. The geography of Max's dictated the action. There was the arabesque-shaped bar on the left as you came in, leading into the middle room, which was the most anonymous area, often filled with a miscellany of photographers and models, nobodies and celebrities. The red alcove off the bar in the front room was where the artists hung out—John Chamberlain, Robert Smithson; Larry Zox, Poons, and Rivers; Clement Greenberg's crew, others. The back room was the home of the Warhol bunch and assorted rock musicians. And upstairs was the music scene, the first rock disco, the beginnings of Glitter and Punk, the room that helped launch the careers of various rock and country musicians: Bruce Springsteen, Alice Cooper, Waylon Jennings, Willie Nelson, Billy Joel, Bob Marley and the Wailers, among others. (*Down and In* 204)

For Sukenick, history is geography, and that includes the geography of the interior.

Michael Davidson (1997), writing of contemporary spatially-oriented poetry, distinguishes between, on the one hand, spacing that functions as a notation for performance—which tends to be the case with Charles Olson, for instance (Mackey, "That Words" 1993)—and, on the other hand, the use of the page as an arena for engaging in the *work* of writing, where the traces of that work are preserved. Davidson refers us to the notebooks of George Oppen (housed at University of California, San Diego), and to the published poetry of Susan Howe for examples. He calls this latter type of spatially oriented poetry *palimtext*, and associates it with archaeology ("the gradual accretion and sedimentation of textual materials," "Palimtexts" 69) and with the (post)modern ruin ("a kind of ruin that emerges in an era when ruins no longer signify lost plenitude," 68). Sukenick's spaced-out prose seems to me, in most cases, to belong to Davidson's category of palimtext, rather than to the category of performance-notation; it is more like a ruin than it is like a page of music.

For confirmation, we might turn to Sukenick's most recent fictions, which take an interesting archaeological turn. In *Doggy Bag* and *Mosaic Man*, he seems to literalize the metaphor in the subtitle of *Down and In: Life in the Underground*. The underground here is no longer a metaphor for a cultural movement, but literal subterranean spaces into which Sukenick's protagonists venture: caves in the *Doggy Bag* stories, for instance, and the Tunnel of Hezekiah under the Old City of Jerusalem in *Mosaic Man*. But if his newest narratives expand his repertoire of virtual spaces—expand it *downward* and *inward*—they also introduce a new motif, that of writing itself as "A form of archaeology" (*Mosaic Man* 206). For the buried and ruined surfaces of *Doggy Bag* and *Mosaic Man* are also *written* surfaces. Thus, when "Ron," the protagonist of *Mosaic Man* acquires a graffiti-daubed fragment of the Berlin Wall—a characteristic (post)modern ruin, if ever there was one—he recognizes it as a form of "concrete poetry," literally "the writing on the wall" (*Mosaic Man* 184). We can safely assume that the same reciprocity holds here as in Sukenick's earlier fiction, so that if the archeological surfaces in these stories are textual, then, reciprocally, their textual surfaces are archaeological: palimtexts.

Nowhere does this appear more clearly than in the story "50,010,008" from *Doggy Bag*. The writing on the subterranean wall here seems not to be man-made, but it hardly matters, for Sukenick plants a clue that allows us to read this site as a version, in fact a kind of scale-model or *mise-en-abyme*—literally *en abyme*!—of his poetics of the material, palimtextual page. For he identifies the subterranean space of this story as *l'Aven d'Armand:*

> But the great earth opus in the Midi, rivalling the visual odes of Lascaux, is the inhuman iconography of little known l'Aven

> d'Armand, the work of millions of years of millions of sulphurous dribbles scribbling a vast subterranean epic. . . . With the tremendous size of its single chamber, into which you could fit a fleet of Colosseums, all of it structured like some immense Piranese ruin made of gargantuan vaults and stalactic columns, and embellished with extravagant colors and runic elaborations taking on different forms and degrees of complication depending on whether you're observing them close up or from the vast heights and distances possible in the cavern, you have the impression when you first see it of an involuted and barbaric articulation shaped like the inside of your brain. (Sukenick, *Doggy Bag* 92)

L'Aven d'Armand, Sukenick assures me, really does exist; but that hardly prevents it from functioning here (intentionally or otherwise) as a literary allusion.

"Buried" in Sukenick's *l'Aven d'Armand* is an allusion to Armand Schwerner (1927–1999), author of *The Tablets*, a long poem masquerading as a translation of ancient cuneiform inscriptions. Left uncompleted at Schwerner's death, the twenty-seven extant *The Tablets* have appeared in a posthumous edition from the National Poetry Foundation (1999). Archeologies of knowledge, *The Tablets* mimic the conventions of scholarly editions, using strings of non-alphabetic symbols (ellipses, plus signs, square, and round brackets) to indicate where passages are missing because of the deteriorated condition of the original clay tablets, or where they are untranslatable because of gaps in our knowledge of their original language, or where the scholar-translator has supplied speculative reconstructions. Neither the tablets themselves, nor the language in which they where purportedly written, actually exist, of course. The result is something like a benign hoax, and something like a concrete poem; but most of all it is like a palimtext in Michael Davidson's sense—a poetry of traces overlying other, half-obscured traces, poetry as archeological ruin (McHale, "Archaeologies" 1999). By burying Armand Schwerner's palimtext deep inside his own story-space, Sukenick seems to be announcing that his text, too, is palimtextual.[7]

A final note: in view of the "concrete," materialist, palimtextual character of his poetry, one might not have expected Armand Schwerner to be a performance-oriented poet. Intriguingly enough, however, he was; the posthumous edition of his *The Tablets* even includes a CD of Schwerner performing selections from the poem. Schwerner's poetry readings were not only histrionic, they were also literally musical: he often interrupted his readings of the text to play on a collection of flutes and other primitive wind instruments. Perhaps we should not be too surprised at this; Schwerner, after all, emerged from the same underground "culture of spontaneity" as Sukenick and his fellow Fiction Collectivists, the culture of abstract expressionism, spontaneous prose, and projective verse. And jazz, of course: like Raymond Federman, Armand Schwerner played jazz saxophone; he even studied jazz improvisation with Lennie Tristano. Here, once again, the two "truths of the page" coincide.

Notes

* A version of this paper was presented on the panel, "Dangerous Aesthetics: The Twenty-Fifth Anniversary of the Fiction Collective" at the 115th Modern Language Association Annual Convention, Chicago, 28 December 1999. I am grateful to Jeffrey DeShell for organizing the panel, and to my fellow panelists, Gayle Fornataro, Ralph Berry, and especially our respondent, Stephen Davenport, for valuable feedback.

1. Steve Davenport reminds me that, as far as Kerouac was concerned, the theory of spontaneous improvisation sometimes diverged markedly from his actual writing practice. *On the Road*, for instance, though it may well have been composed spontaneously on the legendary continuous roll of teletype paper, subsequently underwent several rounds of editing and rewriting (see Charters, *Kerovac* 133–34, 146–48). As Davenport puts it, in his response to the MLA panel at which the present paper was delivered, Kerouac was "practicing Sukenick's truth, but on an earlier page."

2. Here again, Sukenick's precursor in tape recorder experimentation, as a means of capturing spontaneous oral performance in prose, is Kerouac; see Charters, *Kerovac* 154–55. William Burroughs's tape recorder experiments come a decade later, and serve a different aesthetic purpose, that of disjunction and cut-up.

3. Think also, in this connection, of Frank Zappa's much-underrated metafictional film, *200 Motels* (1971), subtitled *Life on the Road*.

4. Not incidentally, perhaps, it also seems to echo the spatial themes and projective poetics of the Black Mountain poets, for whom the word had special connotations; Olson, for instance, dubbed Robert Creeley "the Figure of Outward," whereas Ed Dorn dedicated a poem to Olson with the title, "From Gloucester Out."

5. See *Wallace Stevens: Musing the Obscure* (1967), and "Wallace Stevens: Theory and Practice" (*In Form* 157–198). These are "the pleasures of merely circulating,"according to Stevens: "The garden flew round with the angel,/The angel flew round with the clouds,/And the clouds flew round and the clouds flew round/And the clouds flew round with the clouds." Compare Sukenick,

from *Out*: "I want to write a book like a cloud that changes as it goes" (*Out* 136). Surely it's no coincidence that the character "Ron" in the "Children of Frankenstein" section of *98.6* changes his name to Cloud (*98.6* 98); "Cloud feels that life is a lot like a novel you have to make it up" (122).

6. Banham, though he declines to say much about Rodia's Towers (presumably because so much had already been said by others), marks their locations on all of the half-dozen or so maps in his book, including maps of the water-distribution system, the original Spanish and Mexican ranchos of the area, and so on. In other words, the Towers serve as Banham's reference point, no matter what aspect of the city might be under consideration. The Watts Towers serve a similar orientational function in, for example, Thomas Pynchon's "A Journey into the Mind of Watts" (1966) and, more recently, Don DeLillo's *Underworld* (276).

7. Elsewhere in *Doggy Bag,* in fact in its title story (subtitled, "A Long Narrative Poem in Prose"), Sukenick parodies the paradigmatic archaeological poem: "What the frag meant: From the feast of their cultures, the fast food of our vultures. Squawk. Yawp. Co co rico. These riffs are sure against their runes. T.S." (52). The story ends in song: "Datta. Yatta. Datta./Yaddadadadada./Shanty, shanty, shanty,/Down in shanty town" (70). Other relevant analogues, apart from *The Waste Land* and *The Tablets,* are Clayton Eshelman's speleological poems inspired by the paleolithic painted caves of the Dordogne, including "Hades in Manganese," "Our Lady of the Three-Proned Devil," "Notes on a Visit to Le Tuc d'Audoubert," and "Visions of the Fathers of Lascaux."

Works Cited

Bakhtin, Mikhail. "Forms of Time and of the Chronotope in the Novel: Notes toward a Historical Poetics." In *The Dialogic Imagination: Four Essays.* Edited and trans. by Michael Holquist and Caryl Emerson. Austin: University of Texas Press, 1981. 84–258.

Banham, Reyner. *Los Angeles: The Architecture of Four Ecologies.* New York: Penguin, 1990.

Belgrad, Daniel. *The Culture of Spontaneity: Improvisation and the Arts in Postwar America.* Chicago: University of Chicago Press, 1998.

Charters, Ann, ed. *The Portable Jack Kerouac.* New York: Penguin, 1995.

———. *Kerouac: A Biography.* San Francisco: Straight Arrow Books, 1973.

Christensen, Paul. *Minding the Underworld: Clayton Eshelman and Late Modernism.* Santa Rose Calif.: Black Sparrow, 1991.

Davidson, Michael. "Palimtexts: George Oppen, Susan Howe, and the Material Text." In *Ghostlier Demarcations: Modern Poetry and the Material Word.* Berkeley: University of California Press, 1997. 64–93.

DeLillo, Don. *Underworld.* New York: Scribner, 1997.

Federman, Raymond. *Double or Nothing.* Boulder, Colo.: Fiction Collective Two, 1992.

———. *Take It or Leave It.* New York: Fiction Collective, 1987.

———. *The Voice In the Closet.* Madison, Wisconsin: Coda Press, 1979.

Mackey, Nathaniel. "That Words Can Be On the Page: The Graphic Aspect of Charles Olson's Poetics." In *Discrepant Engagement: Dissonance, Cross-Culturality, and Experimental Writing.* Cambridge: Cambridge Univeristy Press, 1993. 121–38.

McHale, Brian. "Archaeologies of Knowledge: Hill's Middens, Heaney's Bogs, Schwerner's Tablets," *New Literary History* 30: 1 (Winter 1999): 239–62.

O'Hara, Frank. *Selected Poems.* Ed. Donald Allen. New York: Random House, 1974.

Olson, Charles. "Projective Verse." In *Human Universe.* New York: Grove Press, 1967.

Schwerner, Armand. *The Tablets.* Orono, Me.: National Poetry Foundation, 1999.

Sukenick, Ronald. *Wallace Stevens: Musing the Obscure.* New York: New York University Press, 1967.

———. *The Death of the Novel and Other Stories.* New York: Dial Press, 1969.

———. *Out.* Chicago: Swallow Press, 1973.

———. *98.6.* New York: Fiction Collective, 1975.

———. *In Form: Digressions on the Act of Fiction.* Carbondale: Southern Illinois University Press, 1985.

———. *The Endless Short Story.* New York: Fiction Collective, 1986.

———. *Blown Away.* Los Angeles: Sun & Moon, 1986.

———. *Down and In: Life in the Underground.* New York: William Morrow, 1987.

———. *Doggy Bag: Hyperfictions.* Boulder, Colo.: Fiction Collective Two, 1994.

———. *Mosaic Man.* Normal Ill.: Fiction Collective Two, 1999.

Williams, William Carlos. *Paterson.* New York: New Directions, 1963.

Graphiction: Technological Reality in Ronald Sukenick's *98.6*, *Doggy Bag*, and *Mosaic Man*

Lance Olsen

paper being

"We badly need a new way of thinking about novels that acknowledges their technological reality," Ronald Sukenick advocates in "The New Tradition" (1972), thereby articulating a problematics that will concern him for the rest of his life.

---

blocks

> *We have to learn how to look at fiction as lines of print on a page and we have to ask whether it is always the best arrangement to have a solid block of print from one margin to the other running down the page from top to bottom, except for an occasional paragraph indentation. We have to learn to think about a novel as a concerete structure rather than as an allegory, existing in the realm of experience rather than in the realm of discursive meaning, and available to*

> *multiple interpretation or none, depending on how you feel about it—like the way that girl pressed against you in the subway.* (206)

---

pseudo historicity, graphictional play,
and the reification of the text

Sukenick thus enters into a conversation joined over the course of the last fifteen years or so by such diverse graphictionists as Art Spiegelman in *Maus* (1986, 1992), Derek Pell in *Assassination Rhapsody* (1989), and, perhaps two of the most interesting, Alan Moore and Dave Gibbons in *Watchmen* (1986), whose postmodern equivalent of the illuminated manuscript ludically pastiches drawings together with fake autobiography, a pseudo-history of one of its protagonists, a novel within a novel, notes, police reports, ornithological articles, letters, reviews, interviews, toy brochures, photos, *trompe l'oeil* coffee-cup stains and paper clips, advertisements, and so forth. But Sukenick also enters a conversation already well underway when he published those words in 1972: among, say, Raymond Federman in *Double or Nothing* (1971), concrete poets in general, such surrealist practitioners of the collage-novel as Max Ernst in *La Femme 100 Têtes* (1929), Apollinaire's *calligrammes*, and e. e. cummings's typographical experiments influenced as much by the fragments of ancient texts he studied at Harvard as by the first marketing of the typewriter in 1874 by E. Remington and Sons (famous manufacturers of guns at Ilion, New York, the technological means of creation and decreation abruptly existing at the same locus) exactly twenty years before his birth, and the discovery of Pound's poetry—itself influenced by Chinese ideograms, or at least by Pound's misunderstanding of them.

I don't mean to suggest by way of such a hastily constructed, heterogeneous, and cursory inventory anything resembling an originary site, no matter how tempting it might be to continue tracing a speculative path back to, for instance, the Egyptian hieroglyph or even the pictorial "language" of cave paintings. Nor do I mean to imply some hypothetical causal chain of direct aesthetic impacts throughout history. Rather, I simply mean to give a feel for an admittedly motley constellation of creators with whom Sukenick has consciously or unconsciously entered aesthetic colloquy, who, for the purposes of this essay, I will refer to as **GRAPHICTIONISTS:**

- **i.e., those who attempt to focus our attention on the pageness of the page, and/or (intentionally or unintentionally) work against the conventional structure of Western writing (and hence reading strategies), often by calling attention to writing's mechanical status before us and disrupting it, complicating it—along the way making self-conscious traditional reading assumptions and processes—by means of various graphictional play, a term I employ here in its widest possible sense to include not only the introduction of image into text, but also unexpected typography, layout, spacing, punctuation, collage elements, etc., thereby giving rise to** HETEROMEDIAL INTERTEXTUALITY,

- **i.e., a play and interplay between and among these graphic and verbal elements that allow them to interpenetrate, reminding us of the visual nature of language and the linguistic nature of images, while in a Cubist move that would have delighted Picasso and Gertrude Stein, bringing words and other opticals to the surface of the page, treating them as non-allegorical entities of design, signaling their existence as *objects* and therefore signaling their immediate connection to other tangible items in the extrapaginal world, while at the same time quoting, paraphrasing, and alluding to similiar uses of graphication in synchronic and diachronic texts.**

By doing so, I should like to raise several questions about graphiction in general and Sukenick's version of it in particular, especially by looking at three indicative texts from two different decades in Sukenick's career: *98.6*, one of his earliest novels, published three years after "The New Tradition" appeared, on the one hand, and, on the other, *Doggy Bag*, his 1994 collection, and *Mosaic Man*, his amphibious autobiogranovel from 1999.

What is the advantage of such a graphictional strategy? What does one gain—and what does one lose—by employing it? By learning to think about the novel as a **concrete structure** rather than an **allegory**, do we thus banish the notion of allegory altogether, or simply displace it and reintroduce it at another level of meaning-making? Is it ever really possible to demystify a text without engendering another kind of mystification—here, perhaps, of the technlogical reality of the text itself?

And, finally, what are the implications of graphiction for the act of criticism, or that subversive subset of criticism which elides with innovative narrative tropes to produce a performative **critifiction**?

98.6

Israel is no longer Israel in Sukenick's *98.6*, as Brian McHale points out, but rather "a tissue of deliberate misattributions" where there exist jungles, monorails, barges, and canals; Sukenick's description of the country becomes, as it were, a postmodern parody of an encyclopedia entry that substitutes "for 'encyclopedic' knowledge [its] own *ad hoc*, arbitrary, unsanctioned associations" (48).

In this way, Israel becomes iconic of Sukenick's text as a whole. By means of its graphictional play, *98.6* mimics the aleatoric rhythms of diurnal existence where one sort of event or mode (text or layout) unpredictably metamorphoses into another, the result being a kind of crazy-quilt anecdote to the belief in a single epistemological or ontological cloth. The dystopic, predominantly urban landscape of alienation, cruel will to power, and commodification of desire evident in the first section, "Frankenstein," morphs into the intially pastoral, rural, and imaginative landscape of the second, "Children of Frankenstein," the apparently utopian lives of whose inhabitants slowly unfurl into eerie interchangeability, and then again into the increasingly amped-up linguistic ramble ("Interruption. Discontinuity. Imperfection. It can't be helped." [167]) of the Israel that isn't Israel (except as metaphor for synthesis, invention, and illumination) in the third, "Palestine."

. . . . this novel is based on the Mosaic Law the law of mosaics or how to deal with parts in the absence of wholes. So here I am. (167)

We thus confront the instantiation of Sukenick's Mosaic Law, not soley at the stratum of theme and/or overall internal structural logic, but also at that of the page itself. To journal-like entries that explore and accentuate white space are added scholarly and quasi-scholarly footnotes, the use of unusual punctuation ("Love ÷ power = sadism + mashocism" [7]), the frequent disappearance of standard punctuation such as commas and periods ("No irony no ambiguity No nuances." [30]), a ragged, unjustified righthand margin, the sudden appearance of transcripts of dialogue with directions reminiscent of screenplays, the conflation of adjectives and nouns into miniature concrete poems ("redminiskirt," "seethrublouse" [41]), the utilization of absence as punctuation

the world is flat and getting flatter
no harm no charm come fun come all
Flatima Buck Buck Buck flat as a dollar bill Eve is flattered flatter and flatter by angels by freaks rednecks wetbacks drug zombies
no more Thin King
(162)

the creation of breaks not between punned words but within them ("Bad lang witch. Ize brake you sin tax." [185]), the fusion of many words into a hebephrenic run on

JESSELONGCATFULL
ERJESSEARLYLIFEW
ASSPENTRAMBLING
BETWEENGEORGIA
TEXASANDCALIFOR
NIAWHEREHEEVENT
UALLYSETTLED(187)

and, in perhaps the most unusual graphictional maneuver in the novel, an extended Cubist collage of quotations (45–50) from *The Village Voice*, Tom Wolfe's *The Electric Kool-Aid Acid Test*, and Ed Sander's book on the Manson family, among other documentary sources, all appropriated, repunctuated, and juxtaposed to suggest comparisons among such subjects as Aztec sacrifices, the Tate murders, and state-sanctioned tortures.

a pop person is a vacuum tha
t eats up everything he's mad
e up from what he has seen t
elevision has done it you don
't have to read anymore book
s will be out television will st
ay movies will go out televisi
sion will stay (45)

The consequence of all these visual displays is the development of an intricate piece of textual architecture akin to the assemblage-house called The Monster built at the commune

The Monster looks different from anything he's seen before from anything anyone's seen before he supposes. The reason is first the materials available an odd assortment of weathered wood from the old barn they're building on plus a lot of irregular unfinished redwood planks they got cheap so it's a question of following the suggestions in fact the capabilities of the materials and of course a lot of plywood you can saw into any shape you want.

Plus everybody getting in on the design. . . . And they all agree on a flexibility that disallows fixed interior walls and that allows extension of the basic structure at need or whim. (66)

or (to use another guiding metaphor from the novel) a kind of graphictional Frankensteinian patchwork stitched together in a proto-avant-pop gesture out of the detritus of our culture to mimic a multidimensional polyverse, or what Foucault calls a **HETEROTOPIA,** "the linking together of things that are inappropriate; I mean the disorder in which fragments of a large number of possible orders glitter separately in the dimension, without law or geometry, of the *heteroclite*" (xviii).

In Sukenick's fiction, this is the textual space that endorses the notion, as does the protagonist of *98.6*, that one can overcome the "negative hallucination" of the contemporary by becoming "enchanted" by one's existence, and that one can become "enchanted" by one's existence by "remain[ing] open to the unknown" (11). The carnivalesque impulse evident in the textual thematics of illumination, liberation, and identity fluidity, as well as that evinced by the characters' Borscht-Belt shticks within the narrative ("I used to do an imitation of a guy about to get gassed in a concentration camp it used to crack them up. Too much" [79]), then, are doubled in the carnivalesque impulse in the textual layout itself which inverts, perverts, and defamiliarizes the experience of textuality, slows it down, forces one to read in other ways than from upper left to lower right, reread, rethink, and reexperience the paper being before one.

---

doggy bag

Sukenick impishly instigates graphictional play in the pre-text of his collection *Doggy Bag* by exploring and exploiting keyboard symbols and unusual punctuation in the table of contents (which provides the names of each fiction, but not the page number on which each commences):

> who are these people?}------------------->
>
> name of the dog}=================>
>
> doggy bag}#########::::::::::::::::-------->
>
> a mummy's curse}********++++++==--->
>
> etc.

This motif appears as well between each set of fictions throughout the collection, creating a kind of visual intermission, and forms a complementary bookend on the last page of the volume. Consequently each story title, presented in a manner that recalls concrete poetry, becomes an active part of the reading experience. Moreover, Sukenick often puns visually on the last word or phrase of each fiction, metamorphosing it pictorially into the first word or part of a phrase that opens the next fiction. The effect is to transform language into a tangible entity that can be manipulated the same way that pieces of The Monster in *98.6* can be manipulated, or the recycled scraps in a collage or assemblage.

HETEROTOPIAS are disturbing, probably because they secretly undermine language, because they make it impossible to name this and that, because they destroy "syntax" in advance, and not only the syntax with which we construct sentences but also that less apparent syntax which causes words and things (next to and also opposite to one another) to "hold to-gether."

—Foucault (xviii)

Whatever it is thinks Lance.

—*98.6* (133)

Theory is a sign of ignorance. It becomes important when we are no longer sure what we are doing. We are passing through a time when all the "paradigms" of fiction are called into question and in consequence

"The line starts moving slowly, into the Uffizi," the narrator of "Who Are These People?" begins that story's final paragraph:

> The tourists are wistfully eager to begin their work. They're looking for something, but they don't know what it is.

Then comes the following that segues visually into the first line of the next story, thus:

k n o w w h a t i t i s

h a t i t i s

i t i s

i s

?

t h e

t h e t e x t

t h e t e x t o f l i f e

name of the dog}===========>

> Strange logics dictate the text of life. The first time I travelled to Europe . . . (18)

Sukenick thus creates a literary ecology that suggests visually the larger thematics of the collection: the pirating of past genres (the vampire myth, pornography, cyberpunk SF, etc.) and specific texts (*The Waste Land*, *Naked Lunch*, *The Raven*), and their quotation, transmogrification, and revitalization in a gesture similar to Eliot's in one of the first

we begin to see the development of a poetics of fiction. Preferably the theory should be implicit in the novel, the poetics part of the poem. —Sukenick, "Twelve Digressions" (4)

tell me a story i says lying there in the almost-black and my mama she says **go to bed, girl**, and i says **tell me a story first**

In fact, many modern works are, in a sense, "about themselves—that is, they signify consciousness of themselves as forms in process of being worked out. This is a condition of an art whose paradigms are no longer fixed by a tradition. When consciousness of its own form is incorporated in the dynamic structure of the text—in its composition, as the painters says—theory can once again become part of the story rather than

master cut-ups of Western culture. Unlike Eliot's serious, even nostalgic shoring up of fragments against the ruins, however, Sukenick expresses a devious joy in toying with the cultural shards, often citing them for no other purpose other than to cite them, to riff on them, conflating pop material with that of high art ("As I say, these days high culture sometimes seems to me nothing but a classy conspiracy in the service of an oppressive elite" [72].) to a degree *The Waste Land* finds it impossible to contemplate.

"The soap opera of reality has disintegrated into fragments nobody knows how to deal with" (54), the narrator of the title story writes, once again alluding to Sukenick's Ur-metaphor of the Mosaic Law. Every scrap of leftovers at the textual table can be and is taken home in a figurative doggy bag and eaten, ingested, made into a kind of ludic musical composition because "the intelligence of music. . . . is the only intelligence that is obtuse enough. That moves enough. Because you have to move it move it move it" (70).

In addition to this graphictional ecology, Sukenick underscores the pageness of the page in a number of ways, including placing key nouns in quotation marks for an ironic distancing effect ("My 'companion' strikes up a conversation with a girl from Yale" [10].), generating new systems of punctuation (" 'Then, [?] it is to be dead to be crazy' " [28].), using blank space to indicate the absence of key information ("   she   and he quickly   around her neck.   brought Ram   naked   manacled gagged, to wall   front of bed" [136].), inserting dingbats and a photocopy of a piece of paper into the text, and substituting word-processor keyboard signs for language to demonstrate

about it. One of the tasks of modern ficition, therefore, is to displace, energize, and re-embody its criticism—to literally reunite it with our experience of the text.

—Sukenick, "Twelve Digressions" (5)

tell me a story i says lying there in the almost-black and my mama she says **go to bed, girl,** and i says **tell me a story first mama** and my mama she says **go to bed now, you hear** and i says **just one** and my mama she says **rolling her eyes toward** heaven up in the darkness with that way she has of sucking her cigarette letting its smoke spike out her nose like a cow on a cold autumn morning **just one, girl, just one and then to sleep** and so commences to spin me how "everyone uses language without understanding it" (73).

Each of these unexpected intrusions of the optical into the text serves as an interruption of the conventional reading processs, and as Sukenick affirms through one of his characters:

> You need to understand that understanding is an interruption. Understanding is always an interruption of which you understand in the form of the cryptic. You need to interrupt yourself. (74)

That is the point of always calling attention to the text in my work. It is not a kind of narcissistic phase of consciousness. On the contrary, it is a way of trying to make the reader conscious of his own mind, the functioning of his own imagination as the writer is aware of the functioning of the text. So that the imagination is then activated, ready to go back to reality in some revitalized way. —Sukenick, "Cross Examination"(146–47)

To facilitate understanding means to slow down perception, to jam, snarl, and hence make perpetually self-conscious the processes of understanding themselves.

Fiction, then, becomes a teaching machine, not about the intricacies of the author's mind, about his or her beliefs and perceptions, but about the reader's, and it does so not only through content, by means of thematics, but through the forms it chooses to take, the structures it imposes upon itself—not simply what's through the page in an imagined universe, but what's **on the page itself, how it's constructed, how it presents itself, calls for consideration of itself, announces itself as BEING THERE and as a being, there.**

---

mosaic man

The title of Sukenick's 1999 autobiogranovel returns us to his Ur-metaphor, this time through the appropriated lens of the Old

and so commences to spin me the most beautiful i ever done heard about this kind handsome prince without a

Testament, itself a model of polyphony and rhizomatic nonlinearity.

In a recent interview in *george jr.*, Sukenick accents this view by claiming provocatively that "the whole idea [Western culture has] of narrative is really a mistake." This is the case for two reasons. First, its idea of narrative is rooted in Aristotle's *Poetics*, which foregrounds notions of **mimesis**, rather than his *Rhetoricie*, which foregrounds **argument** (read: **technique**) in the full range of its possibilities. Second, Western culture's idea of narrative derives from a fundamentally **Christian notion of storytelling** evinced in the New Testatment that foregrounds the emblematic mode of the parable rather than from the Old Testament "which is more like a whole panoply of narrative techniques." The Old Testament

> includes something like parable but it also includes argument and catalog and a whole bunch of techniques. Poetry. And narrative sequence that has very little of the imitative in it. If you read Auerbach's *Mimesis* he compares a Greek epic with biblical Old Testament style. He points out that there is very little effort in the biblical style, the Old Testament style, to make you, as Conrad said, see, to create the illusion of reality.

In *Mosaic Man*, Sukenick actuates a corrective anti-mimetic, multivocal paradigm of narrative both by adopting and adapting books from the Old Testatment to his own ends ("Genesis" becomes "Genes," "Exodus" "Ex/Ode," and so on) and by exploit-

name who done got turned into a toad by a evil witch with hairy warts on her face and pink knuckles cuz he did not mind her plus this blindingly pretty princess who only wore white lace and done righted him into what he truly was with a gentle and pure kiss which sent the angels above to weeping and that was it that was all i could not sleep that night no matter what just could not sleep but stayed awake after my mama done finished telling and stayed awake after she done stood and touched my forehead with her rough dry palm thinking i was gone away [**Cloud feels life is a lot like a novel you have to make it up.**] and stayed awake through the carbon hours the opal hours the lilac hours aware-dreaming of that sweetest kiss bar none which brought the world up short and changed everything that god calls human everything that he does not and made the landscape reimagine itself so much the landscape began hurting cuz that is what real love can do it can make you [**That's the**

ing various graphictional gaming that short-circuits a reading experience into whose "illusion of reality" one might be tempted to lose oneself. Doing so, he brackets the question of representation itself, particularly through his conflation of fiction and nonfiction, on the one hand, and, on the other, the thematics of the Golden Calf, idolatry, and his ironic engagement with the story of Moses' reprimand of the Israelites for the need to worship material objects as stand-in signifiers for a transcendental signified, which distantly suggests realism's need to worship mimesis as a stand-in signifier for the diurnal signified of the material world.

Among the graphictional elements exercised in *Mosaic Man* are the use of drawn symbols (chiefly employed in "Ex/Ode" and then as chapter markers); lower-case boldface captions beneath those symbols that recite a personal narrative about discovering the **reel/unreal** nature of narrative itself; untagged and unsituated dialogue mimicking the trasnscripts of tape-recorded interviews and family gatherings; blank spaces as an original form of punctuation and as a way of flagging the absence of key information; the insertion into the text of letters, recipes, road signs, newspaper articles, Raymond Federman's and others' notes on earlier drafts of *Mosaic Man,* and excerpts from a biography of Eisenhower and Chayim Bloch's *The Golem.*

What the reader discovers here, then, as he or she has throughout Sukenick's project, is a replacement of questions concerning epistemology within the textual world with those concerning the onotology of the text itself. Or, closer to the point, the reader discovers an equalization of these two realms by means

point of psychosynthesis in his opinion to pick up the pieces and make something of them.] feel cuz that is what the touch of a princess can do it can make you see how a prince can return from the red undertow called evil so i did not wake up cuz i never went to sleep for happiness but when i heard my mama grinding coffee in the kitchen slamming the fridge feeding our kitties partly cloudy rainy and thunder i slipped out from under my sheets ran down the hall slid into my chair at the table and ate silent like as i hardly knew how no more cuz i was still aware-dreaming [**Psychosynthesis is based on The Mosaic Law. The Mosaic Law is the law of mosaics a way of dealing with parts in the absence of wholes.—*98.6,* 122**] of that perfect state of affairs even as my mama she asks me how i slept cuz i had nothing more to say cuz that was the most beautiful story i suppose i will ever hear in my entire life so when i done concluded i slid off my chair and tugged on my jeans and my sneakers and my pure white t-shirt

of heightening of awareness about the latter: the sensuality of the page, the physicality of the book. One might even go so far as to propose that within Sukenick's project the reader locates one of the earliest realizations of **writing the body** and, quite literally, **writing the body of words.**

---

blocks

> *Opacity implies that we should direct our attention to the surface of a work, and such techniques as graphics and typographical variation, in calling the reader's attention to the technological reality of the book, are useful in keeping his or her mind on that surface instead of undermining it with profundities. The truth of the page is on top of it, not underneath or over at the library. ("The New Tradition" 212)*

---

collages

Although this stress upon the surface of the page is only part of the story (Sukenick's assertion notwithstanding, his texts are not solely about surface; their "profundities," or depth-thematics, involve everything from an examination of the nature of postmodern identity and Jewish history to the politics of commodification), it is a part that most writers simply don't think about—and one that Sukenick probes and extends in highly original ways.

and smack went the trailer door behind me saying **playing** when my mama she done asked after me where i was going to **down by the swamp** as she done told me to mind my feet her voice dropping off behind me like a memory which is where i headed directly with a sky wisteria like the precious stones in the prince's cape and the sun humming like spring bees behind my eyes and the air hot-damp and myriad with fragrances [**this is my fiction, not Ron's**] thinking on elation and lace gowns following the shrimp-pink dirt path behind our trailer into the woods where the earth commences feeling spongy and cicadas fill your brain like the static between radio stations and you leave one way of seeing for another cuz everything there seems so much more real cuz it is all so what is the word **overblowed** which is what you are both thinking and not thinking when you spot the frog on the fallen tree trunk in the shallow avocado-scummed water so you

Perhaps one of the most frequent aesthetic maneuvers by which he does so is the appropriation and juxtaposition of disparate graphictional elements on the same page: in other words, the textual equivalent of collage. Instead of engineering ***trompe l'oeil*** effects that look back to the roots of the form in the work of such nineteenth-century American artists as William Michael Harnett, however, Sukenick engineers **anti-*trompe l'oeil*** effects designed to remind the reader that he or she is reading, and that reading is itself as much an experience in the world as is walking, writing, or making love.

For Sukenick, the structural principle of the collage "is one of the mind's most formidable methods of organizing the disparities of experience" in that it "has the virtue of generating unforeseen connections, and is particularly useful in a time when traditional causes no longer seem adequate to account for observed effects":

> It may produce new systems of order when traditional ones no longer seem persuasive. Since it starts beyond system it is capable of including kinds of experience that given systems might exclude. Or if such a method of organization is considered as a system, then it is an open system. The idea of collage linkage implies discontinuity and the value of the collage fragment in itself, beyond any system. ("Toward a Study of Composition" 14)

In an interview with Patrick Lavallé, Sukenick cites as literary examples of collage Eliot's *The Waste Land*, Pound's *Cantos*, and Joyce's *Ulysses* and *Finnegans Wake*, stressing that the

make a large arc and angle in from behind where the ground is still semi-firm and you crouch you crouch and duck-waddle you crouch and duck-waddle and then sit in absolute stillness for the count of **ten twenty thirty** and then see your hands swooping in from the sides so fast they are not your hands at all anymore but alarmed white swallows and you never thought about setting them in motion but even as that idea flickers up at you the frog is in your cupped palms that were birds and then at your lips which you worry might be too dry cuz of the sunshine but are not you know in your heart cuz it is what is inside that matters that makes the red undertow roll away from the shore of your soul as you kiss quick a brush-kiss like as with the boys brush-kissing on the playground during recess in the great telephone-line of kooties and nothing whatsoever happens but this collage is "a way of pulling in a lot of new material, recombining it in a new form that create[s] something unpremeditated" ("Cross Examination" 130). This emphasis on the aleatoric component in the structuring and reading of collage recalls not only the Cubist work of Braque and Picasso, but also the Surrealist and Dada work of Breton and Duchamp, respectively: interest in the found object, the readymade, the chance encounter.

It also recalls Lévi-Strauss' notion of **bricolage**, as Gregory L. Ulmer points out, foregrounding concepts of already-extant messages, severing, discontinuity, and heterogeneity (84). Ulmer goes on to argue [***ten twenty thirty*** **and then see your hands swooping in from the sides so fast they are not your hands at all anymore but alarmed white swallows**] that collage is a form of citation "carried to an extreme . . . , collage being the 'limit case' of citation" (89), and, as Derrida reminds us in "Signature Event Context," "every sign, linguistic or nonlinguistic . . . can be *cited*, put between quotation marks; in so doing it can break with every given context, engendering an infinity of new contexts in a manner which is absolutely illimitable" (quoted by Ulmer, 89).

Collage, then, through the very process of cutting off opens up. By appropriating and quoting out of context, the form releases new and often unexpected contexts, recontextualizations that can surprise the author as well as the reader. Collage's essential discontinuity thereby generates fresh continuities, its heterogeneity fresh homogeneities. It teaches us how to deal with parts in the absence of conventional wholes by actualizing unconventional innovative ones that offer multiple nonlinear readings, highlight

does not surprise you cuz you know such a minor gesture will never be sufficient for a prince even though mice are running among your organs will not suffice cuz it is not fully felt not felt in the curve behind your knees between your toes in the tail you cannot see but know forms the base of your spine so you bring the frog back to your mouth again and this time you can feel its muscular nervousness in your cupped palms feel the animal's feet scuffling in the cage which is nothing but you and you open your mouth and open a black hole between your thumbs and carefully and lovingly insert your tongue into it and lick what you find there and your breath goes away the bee-sun blossoms behind your eyes the moist granular skin not unlike your mama's hands after vanilla lotion the lungs pulsing like as fly wings [**my fiction, and copyrighted**] the taste honey-salt and green and all the time a kind of frightened agitation within your palms fidgeting back-kicking going nowhere though you go every-

alterity, destabilize "authority" and "origin," and critique representation by continually refocusing the reader's attention on both the act of univocal representation and the act of fractaling univocal representation into resonant polyphony.

---

nonreversible/reversible art

In his essay "The Beginning and the End of Reading—The Beginning and the End of the Novel," Milorad Pavíc distinguishes between two kinds of art: nonreversible and reversible. **Nonreversible art,** such as music and traditional fiction, is unidirectional; instances "look like one-way roads on which everything moves from the beginning to the end, from birth to death." **Reversible art,** on the other hand, such as architecture and sculpture, is prismatic, multi-directional, rhizomatic; instances of these "enable the recipient to approach the work from various sides, or even to go around it and have a good look at it, changing the spot of the perspective, and the direction of the looking at it according to his own preference."

Pavíc predictably endorses the latter variety, affirming that his lifelong goal has been "to make literature, which is a nonreversible art, a reversible one" (143–44)—one that, in a sense, pits itself against the deep-structure propulsion of narrative by rupturing its seemingly unflexible arc from birth to death and celebrating on every page the strength of the human imagination, even in the face of ultimate failure in the final extra-textual assertion of life's linear pith.

Sukenick's project accords well with Pavíc's. Through his use of—among other tech-

where and give it another long gentle lick-kiss which has nothing to do with those that you have till this day delivered upon others nor those that have been delivered upon you and you can sense the red undertow withdrawing can see it feel how right this one sign has been more right than anything you have ever known till that is you retract your tongue and wait and stoop and unfold your palms and wait and set the frog among weeds and watch him watch with his dead gold eyes watching and wait till you realize only gradually you realize only as the afterburn of some thought you had last week that [**people wear trad marks on their narratives**] the world has not changed and the frog is still the frog you are still yourself the sky is still wisteria your heart is still your heart till that is you realize only gradually that you have guessed wrong and at the same time feel the waves commence breaking once more over what up to now you have envisioned as hope though almost immediately understand

niques—graphiction, Sukenick seeks to turn the book into a piece of architecture: a reversible environment that one can enter (never necessarily through the front door), roam around fairly freely in, and always gain new vantage points on, backtracking, digressing, reevaluating, reorienting, reseeing. That is, he seeks to build a space more active, with a greater three-dimensional feel to it, than that found in traditional fiction. Again, we find ourselves recalling the appropriateness of Sukenick's choice of The Monster as guiding metaphor in *98.6*: a lawless architectural amalgam, reminiscent of Frank Gehry's comic composites, in which "everybody [is] getting in on the design" (66):

> What can't be used in any other way they decide to use as building material. Dave makes columns of cans and arches of bottles. Ron makes huge multicolored designs with bottle caps banged into wood. Helen crushes glass and uses the pieces for panels or mosaic. George makes furniture from fruit baskets and Coke crates. Al polishes pieces of rusty metal and welds them into fixtures. Joan fuses colored bottles into windowpanes. Ralph makes a fence of spare parts. Joan and Evelyn lay floors of bricks and tiles and broken dishes and hunks of glass. Paul makes partitions of leftover plastic. The house begins to look like a collage made from the wreckage of a supermarket. (74)

Inside, this acme of the recycled "looks like it's made of eggshells and toothpicks. . . . or maybe more like a crystallized spiderweb or

as the hope of the idea of hope and so you rise into the day into the sunshine the rays your teacher says are all around you and in you and shut your eyes and listen to the bees the cicadas the intermittent chirps scattershot through the branches interlacing above you which puts you in mind of your mama how she sometimes collapses into herself like a collapsing building on the news how sometimes after dinner you discover her alone outside in the lawn chair smoking head tilted back eyes closed as if she can see the twilight through her lids and you ask her what she is doing and she tells you still not opening her eyes **nothing, girl** only that word does not mean what it means it means something so big huge black it can hardly fit into language though she does not say another thing and her lack of saying says more than her saying ever can the sun incrementally turning itself off and the evening coming on and the oversweet summer breeze stirring for maybe fifteen minutes no more without a glass birdnest." In any case, "it looks completely disconnected with his [Ron's] past experiencc which is completely to the good he feels" (66–67).

Just as The Monster separates itself from the careful craft of past architecture by exulting in excess, pastiche, and multiplicity, so too Sukenick's novels separate themselves from the careful craft of past narrative by exulting in, among other things, graphictional play, or what Sukenick calls "the spatialization of form," which he contends can serve "as an alternative to the old novel's sequential organization in plot and narrative": "Through such techniques as juxtaposition [***ten twenty thirty* and then see your hands swooping in from the sides so fast they are not your hands at all anymore but alarmed white swallows**] and manipulation of the print on the space of the page, the novelist can create a structure which communicates by means of pattern rather than sequence in a manner approaching that of the plastic arts" ("The New Tradition" 204).

---

trademark yourself

One intent behind this aesthetic choice is to suggest to readers that they needn't accept habitual narratological conventions any more than they need accept habitual existential or political perceptions. To put it [**and so commences to spin me**] another way, one can and should continually rewrite and reright one's narrative in the same manner that one can and should continually rewrite and reright one's life.

"50,010,008" begins with the question "You know what I hate?" and sets about answering it posthaste:

cooling and you go back into the trailer to watch television trying not to think about all this thinking but after a while you go out again to see and she is still there still sitting in the lawn chair alone precisely as you left her smoking head tilted back eyes closed and so you push on into the woods the thistles skunk cabbage elephant grass where the path forks and reforks like a car with its windshield smashed while the sun goes on getting louder the atmosphere dank tropical like as the inside of a dog's mouth and the you that is me walks singing all the songs i can think of and some that i have to make up till i come upon the pond which is without shore or bank but simply eases into being right under my feet one minute not there and the next there the grass gets wet and wetter and then drops off into hot chocolate swamp liquid as far as the eye can see and so i crab around the side that is not a side quiet as a rattlesnake cuz my mama she says i do not have a daddy and i says that is the silliest thing i

> People who wear trade marks on their clothes. As if to say you are what you buy. But hey, do it yourself. Make up your own mark. Make a statement. Write yourself in the book of life.
>
> It's happening. I see the signs everywhere. They are signs that say, "Hey, I'm me. Pay attention." And the reason is is that nobody is. (*Doggy Bag* 88)

This avant-pop call to empowerment situates itself particularly with respect to the media's technosphere whose reason for existing is to replicate itself by replicating desire for itself. It attains this goal by attempting to script both social and psychological experience in a way that plants within the individual needs the individual doesn't in fact possess. Sukenick advocates retaking that experiential space by turning the technosphere's fetish for speed, design, and hipness back on itself, critiquing and subverting its premises.

As Charlotte Meyer elucidates in her interview with him, Sukenick's "definition of the novel has changed from art-as-illusion to art-as-experience." If art is no longer a mode of mimetic deception, but another mode of experiencing the world, then the artist becomes the embodiment of the Mosaic Man—not only in the sense that the artist continually scripts him or herself, his or her subjectivity, but also in the sense that "the artist becomes the inventor of experience from mere phenomena," the inventor of his or her own being in the world ("Cross Examination" 134).

It follows, then, that we are all artists in the broadest sense—or at least should aspire to

ever done heard everybody got a daddy somewheres and she says **YOU don't, girl** and i says **but everybody got a daddy somewheres** and she says **you just forget about such bullshit right now, you hear** and she even said that word even said it like she was not thinking of saying it nor not saying it and so the you that is me walks sing-crabbing along the side quiet till i spot another frog and get down on my hands and knees and crawl through tall moist limp grass and become a statue and count **ten twenty thirty** and pounce and there it is in my hands the prince and i repeat what i done before only more carefully lovingly yet except this frog is larger than the first and strong and at the last second i decide to put my mouth over the hole between my thumbs and just for a heartbeat just for a single human pulse its amphibious head slips between my lips and everything turns white behind my eyes with the sun the most amazing thing the most perfect thing then it is out again and frozen and nothing

be so. We are responsible for shaping ourselves and hence the world around us, and responsible for struggling against those who would shape ourselves and it for us.

---

blocks

> *We are talking about who controls our imaginations or what controls our imaginations, what has the authority to do so, whether it is proper authority, whether we want it to control our imaginations. Maybe something other than what we want to control our imaginations is controlling them. Then we can really begin to talk about the way our lives go from day to day, whether it is being just, for example, manipulated by politics, the media or the mass market in the United States. There is a slogan that I use for students when I am trying to get them on to the subject, in other words, I am trying to get them into this way of thinking:* ***"If you don't use your own imagination, somebody else is going to use it for you."*** ("Cross Examination" 147)

---

hyperthought

Sukenick decenters the idea of the book as technological object at the moment hypertext and other electronic environments are doing the same, thereby reminding us that the idea of the ~~book~~ (and such related notions as

but a frog and I confess though i do it in tiny augmentations sidling up on the notion that this process will take longer than i suspected but that as my mama says everything you want in life really want does precisely that so i set this frog that is only a frog down and move on till i find another and repeat the process and move on till i find another and repeat the process and move on till i find another and repeat the process before long discovering i can begin to tell the difference between tastes textures smells this frog's back skin or ear plate slightly more marshy than the last or less lumpy or more oily or less substantial or more skitterish and this strikes me with the force of revelation cuz till then every frog has been the same frog every frog only one frog but now i figured each was itself and only itself the light passing above me and this impression made me feel rich in its knowledge and so i moved along the shore that was not a shore and scooped up frogs that were not frogs

~~authorial property~~, ~~originality~~, and even ~~textuality~~) is a transitory, sociohistorically determined one.

Accordingly, his project shares much with those not only of such poststructuralists as Barthes and Derrida, but also of such computer theorists as Vannevar Bush and Theodor Nelson, who, as George P. Landow writes, "begin with the desire to enable us to escape the confinements of print. This common project requires that one first recognize the enormous power of the book, for only after we have made ourselves conscious of the way it has formed and informed our lives can we seek to pry ourselves free from some of its limitations" (46–47). Although Sukenick isn't interested in escaping the confinements of print through the same mechanisms under investigation by hypertext authors, he is engaged in thinking about those confinements and, although still working within the realm of atoms rather than bytes, in putting under erasure traditional post-Gutenberg concepts of textuality and authority.

To this extent, Sukenick's project may be seen as one mathematical point on a long hypothetical line of **antecedents to hypertext** that might include such differing works as Federman's *Double or Nothing*, Cortázar's *Hopscotch*, and Derrida's *Glas*—hardcopy texts that nonetheless evince unpredictable quantum leaps between two or more storylines; typographical/configurative freeplay that ruptures conventional linear reading strategies and foregrounds the reality of the page; an intermixture of prose and poetry, fiction and criticism, novel and drama utilized in order to question traditional genre distinctions; digressive narrative structure where the overarching plotline frequently

and kissed each and every one as if it was the most significant thing i could possibly do except when i picked one the size of my fist up and infolded its head in my mouth and put it down again i thought i saw out the edge of my seeing a rustling in the limp grass and next thing a water rat sliding through the brackishness where the frog had been and i commenced wondering if maybe inside some frogs were neither princes nor frogs but other creatures instead for instance ghosts or fish or dead kitties like partly cloudy rainy and thunder or maybe souls of people who had accidentally fallen into the swamp and drowned cuz they did not mind their feet like their mamas told them or miraculous angels that came down to visit earth but got all mixed up or sinners from before the flood who did not believe in noah nor god or invisible jellyfish from other planets who needed to inhabit other bodies as astronauts need to inhabit spacesuits only ended up inhabiting the wrong bodies cuz they thought frogs were more

turns out to be less important than the individual page before the reader at a given moment; abrupt shifts in point of view; ongoing metafictional contemplation of aesthetic process and product; an appeal to greater readerly freedom and a collaborative model of interpretation; an overall structural feel closer to certain kinds of music than to conventional narrative—one that often creates the impression that a reader can dip into the text at any point for a paginal snippet, because narrative forward force isn't what guides the reading experience any more than it does in lyric poetry or jazz improvisation.

In "The End of Books," a 1992 essay that appeared on the front page of *The New York Times Book Review*, Robert Coover traces the term **hypertext** back nearly twenty-five years to computer-scientist Nelson's coinage "to describe the writing done in the nonlinear or nonsequential space made possible by the computer":

> Unlike print text, hypertext provides multiple paths between text segments, now often called "lexias" in a borrowing from the pre-hypertextual but prescient Roland Barthes. With its webs of linked lexias, its networks of alternate routes (as opposed to print's fixed unidirectional page-turning) hypertext presents a radically divergent technology, interactive and polyvocal, favoring a plurality of discourses over definitive utterance and freeing the reader from domination by the author. Hypertext reader and writer are said to become co-learners and co-writers,

intelligent than people or maybe even my daddy somewheres my daddy out there i remember the sand skin called his beard think i remember cuz he had gotten so sad waiting for me and my mama to return to him waiting for me and my mama to phone him or knock on his screen door wherever his screen door might be that his soul finally just gave up and walked away from his body in profound regret to wander through the countryside alone for all its days in an oyster-gray limbo and that is what i found myself thinking when squatting by the pond that was not a pond i looked up and my heart dropped and i heard the red undertow commence sloshing nearby cuz the daylight above the trees was all of a sudden failing and i had not noticed the hours going by had not listened to my appetite growing inside my tummy had not understood the solemnity of the light bleaching away sky becoming lemon rind becoming the tender flesh beneath your eyes bird chitter all around the long run home and i

> as it were, fellow travelers in the mapping and remapping of textual (and visual, kinetic and aural) components. (23)

The precipitate, Coover argues, possesses "no fixed center, for starters—and no edges either, no ends or boundaries. The traditional narrative time line vanishes into a geographical landscape or exitless maze, with beginnings, middles and ends being no longer part of the immediate display" (23). What develops instead is—to exercise a familiar metaphor among hypertext writers and theorists—a Borgesian **garden of forking paths** without hierarchy. Quoting hypertext authors Carolyn Guyer and Martha Petry, Coover emphasizes that this innovative brand of fiction demands an innovative brand of reading because "the form of the text is rhythmic, looping on itself in patterns and layers that gradually accrete meaning, just as the passage of time and events does in one's lifetime" (23–24).

Sukenick's proto-hypertextual fiction, which in a metafictional passage in *Mosaic Man* he describes as "ongoing, no beginning, no end, just an endless middle of shticks, bits, gags, and routines" (218), strives to approximate what he calls **random consciousenss** ("Art and the Underground" xviii). It is a fiction, then, not of declaration but exploration, not of expectation but of expedition—a method of continual discovery for the reader, of course, but also for the writer, who works

> not from a priori ideas about what will happen and what form it will take, but in and through the text. He does not work from a presiding idea or a preexistent scenario. The next word is always

looked up and my heart dropped and behind the receding bees the overstated real the cicadas filling my brain like [**one kind of allegory replaced with another**] the static between radio stations i could hear the oceanic rise of croaking heavy and clamorous as desire and i came to understand then if only for an instant how many frogs existed in this swamp around me and how many swamps existed in this county around me and how many counties existed in this state around me and how many states existed in this country around me and how many countries existed in this world around me and how many worlds existed in this galaxy around me and how many galaxies existed in this universe around me and [**to capture the kaleidoscopic, multidimensional, random experience**] in that instant i did not turn back toward my mama's trailer but continued my sing-crabbing along the side of the pond that was not a pond [**a mere sublime simulation**] wondering somewhere so far back in my mind that it

> a surprise. The text is generated by the activity of composition in an ongoing interchange between the mind and the page. ("Toward a Study of Composition" 8)

almost seemed like someone else's

"Disengaged from utilitarian ends," he writes, random consciousness "makes contact with the vagrant world . . . and wins insight into the nature of **mind and reality**" ("Art and the Underground" xviii).

Such hyperthought and its graphictional expression distills down to nothing short of a variety **[and so commences to spin me]** of **neo-realism.** It isn't mimetic in what Sukenick would discuss as the illusionism of conventional Aristotlean literature, yet it *is* mimetic—mimetic in the sense that it tries to capture the kaleidoscopic, multidimensional, random experience of the postmodern condition which is in sync with the televisual and digital rhythms of the millennial edge. In this way, it is possible to suggest that it has indeed replaced one kind of allegory (between word and world/consciousness) with another (between structure and world/consciousness). If so, it has simply demystified one sort of text (let us call it **Conventional Fiction**, however we might ultimately define such an elusive beast) by mystifying another sort (let us call it **Graphiction**).

Sukenick's perhaps unintentional discovery, then, has been that **[maybe inside some frogs were neither princes nor frogs but other creatures instead for instance ghosts]** an author is always an author, not of the world, but of a model of the world, an allegory of it, and that writing—all writing, including any performative act of critifictional **[the Baudrillardian outbidding of simulation is the endpoint of the postmodern stylistics of the sublime]** discourse—

is, for better or for worse, the act of textual mystification.

---

death on the supply side

Sometimes they ask me why I write this way when it would be so easy to give the audience a break **[in a sense, the Baudrillardian outbidding of simulation is the endpoint of the postmodern stylistics of the sublime]** *and sell more books by using the kind of plot and character narrative they're used to. I write this way because it's a way of saying* **[and so commences to spin me]** *their whole system is bull. That's why I write this way. To cut the* **[to become the awed witness of the unpresentable]** *bull. (Doggy Bag 149)*

---

the self-implicating limit situation
(Connor 247)

In a sense, the Baudrillardian outbidding of simulation is the end-point of the postmodern stylistics of the sublime, but it is an end-point that demonstrates a potentially dangerous paradox **[wondering somewhere so far back in my mind that it almost seemed like someone else's]***: if the prime responsibility of criticism and theoretical knowledge is not to represent the representable, but to become awed witness of the unpresentable, then what is there to guarantee the subversive effects of that work except in its own inevitably institutionalized forms of self-legitimation? A self-legitimating sublime that denies its positioning by the exigencies of its own material production becomes a mere sublime simulation, a cool professional fiction of subversion which paradoxically brings into being the very effects of simulation, unreality* *and deterrence which its discourse evokes, but in the passive or negative mode of routine and rationalization. . . .*

---

blocks

where does the kissing end?

Works Cited

Connor, Steven. *Postmodernist Culture: An Introduction to Theories of the Contemporary.* Cambridge, Mass.: Blackwell, 1997.

Coover, Robert. "The End of Books." *New York Times Book Review* (June 21, 1992): 1, 23–25.

Foucault, Michel. *The Order of Things: An Archeology of the Human Sciences.* New York: Pantheon, 1970.

Landow, George. *Hypertext 2.0: The Convergence of Contemporary Critical Theory and Technology.* Baltimore, Md.: Johns Hopkins University Press, 1997.

McHale, Brian. *Postmodernist Fiction.* New York: Methuen, 1987.

Sukenick, Ronald. *98.6.* New York: Fiction Collective, 1975.

———. "Art and the Underground." *In Form: Digressions on the Act of Fiction.* Carbondale: Southern Illinois University Press, 1985: xiii–xxii.

———. "Cross Examination." *In Form: Digressions on the Act of Fiction.* Carbondale: Southern Illinois University Press, 1985: 107–55.

———. "The New Tradition." *In Form: Digressions on the Act of Fiction.* Carbondale: Southern Illinois University Press, 1985: 201–13.

———. "Toward a Study of Composition." *In Form: Digressions on the Act of Fiction.* Carbondale: Southern Illinois University Press, 1985: 3–15.

———. *Doggy Bag: Hyperfictions.* Normal, Ill.: Fiction Collective 2/Black Ice, 1994.

———. *Mosaic Man.* Normal, IL: Fiction Collective 2, 1999.

Ulmer, Gregory L. "The Object of Post-Criticism." *The Anti-Aesthetic: Essays on Postmodern Literature.* Ed. Hal Foster. Port Townsend, Wash.: Bay Press, 1983.

Zupp, Adrian. "Skydiving Language: Ronald Sukenick." *george jr.* (June 1997). 25 September 1999. <http://www.georgejr.com/jun97/sukenick.html>.

The Artist is the Medium is the Message: A Ron Sukenick Re-Mix

Mark Amerika

Abstract Expressionism (Part One)

Riffing on Sukenick's dictum that "[g]enre is traditional, medium is technological . . ." and that "[w]e live in a technological culture, not a traditional culture," this experimental essay employs the practice of "surf-sample-manipulate" to create a collage of Sukenick's fiction, theory-digressions, emailings and personal conversations with the author, exploring the programmatological energy that fuels the development of his pseudo-autobiographical narratives and avant-pop rhetoric. The essay/remix also explores how Sukenick's work, along with the work developed by some of his colleagues in the pomo lit scene, anticipates the arrival of more multidisciplinary, networked-narrative environments being created on the World Wide Web. Particular emphasis is placed on the notion of "rhetorical remixing" and "the narrative interface," highlighting Sukenick's conceptual design skills as well as the way he transforms the paginal syntax of conventional novels into "moving visual thinking" that provides not only a learning experience, but a healing experience, enabling readers to purge themselves of bad karma while getting in touch with their *moksha*, or liberatory-potential as interactive Other engaged with the Sukeneitzsche text.

The first thing that happens when readers encounter Sukenick is that they become a medium. They become a medium by surfing the experiential narrative Sukenick rhetorically persuades us to consider while making his case. We then find ourselves "sampling" from Sukenick's own exploratory open-field compositional style, practicing the Sukenick model of composing critifictional digressions, like the ones found in his books *In Form: Digressions on the Act of Fiction, Down and In: Life in the Underground, The Death of the Novel and Other Stories,* and *Narralogues: Truth in Fiction.* Finally, this so-called essay, now story, will attempt to transmit to the reader the "ongoing ungoing" sensibility of the fictional character often referred to as "Ron Sukenick," that is, not the author himself, but the fluid sequence of "de-characterizations" that go by that name in his various writings.

Ron, in Character . . .

He had known from an early age that he was more interested in excitement than stability. If he had been gifted with a talent for sports he probably would have been a whitewater type, surfing the rapids. He liked life in flood, undamned, unruly. He liked experience tuned up to an intensity that was on the edge of control, and over the edge. This carried over into his art—he liked to think of himself as a practitioner of "extreme writing."

Up and at 'em: The Brooklyn Dodger

The jacket copy to Sukenick's first novel, *Up*, says "the story is about the circumstances, ideas, and feelings that hold us in bondage—including our idea of what a novel is supposed to be. Its main character is the writer himself, Sukenick. But there is more than one Sukenick. There is the *adolescent* undergoing both academic and sexual torment in Brooklyn; there is the *young man*, a sometime English teacher who lives on the Lower East Side and tries to write; there is the *witness* who records the lives and conversations of his relatives; and there is the *fantasist* assuming various alter egos (not always friendly to him) that take on the mythic situations of modern life."

"In the matter of style," Sukenick, the young Professor says to his class in *Up*, "the basic virtues, for all ordinary purposes, are clarity, directness, and concision. In realizing these qualities, we must first give our attention to diction, or the choice of words. Diction is a fundamental part of rhetoric."

He proceeds to eyeball the girl who "comes to class dressed like a French whore," as well as the "receptive girl in the front row . . . working her legs up to expose her attentive thighs."

> **She stares at me with big drippy eyes which advertise awe, lust, virginity, and a desire for self-immolation. I would like to keep her, mildly drugged, in my apartment for a week, then quietly sell her into the white slave market.**

But this is fiction, right? The fantasist overtaking the Professor who is, after all, a young man. Or is it pseudo-autobiography, that decidedly narrative application that processes the fundamental parts of a rhetoric willing to take on "the mythic situations of postmodern life?"

These days, the first of the twenty-first century, Sukenick uses the term "Not-fiction" to refer to this streaming pseudo-autobiographical writing style ("loci of consciousness") he's been practicing all of his life. "Not-fiction," he says, is "the most appropriate form to explore and express not-ego," and "its purpose is to gather data in pleasurable complexes, yield information, and argue truths." For Sukenick, "Not-fiction" is the logical outgrowth of postmodernism which, he suggests, leads us to the following grab-bag of possibilities:

postmodern fragmentation will lead to
the jumpy non-sequitur of mosaiced narrative

postmodern pastiche will lead to the predication of truths

postmodern interaction of composition and audience will lead to
decomposition of the virtual artifact and its intervention
in the real world

postmodern illogic and alogic stemming from Duchamp
will resolve into the dialogic

postmodern drift to the language of speech will be mixed and
amplified with the language of writing, graphics, and music

postmodern deconstruction will gravitate toward the
contingencies of rhetorical assertion

postmodern intellectual disintegration will mutate
to a yearning for spiritual reach

postmodern imagination will move toward a hard factuality

postmodern interest in pop genre will result
in a new synthesis of genres

postmodern embrace of the mass market and its values
will turn toward a revival of unmarketed prestige

"Not-fiction," it ends up, will leave postmodernism in the dust, just like e-commerce is poised to leave traditional cash transactions behind. In fact, these changes that Sukenick envisions are rhetorically postulated so that the reader will rethink their position on the value of literary books in our disintermediated, network culture. "What they could add up to," he suggests, "is something that might fit into the category of rhetoric and whose medium could conceivably be the Internet as the only one which could possibly accommodate this kind of variety."

Blurb for the new Alt-X Online Publishing Project composed by the marketing rhetorician whose narrative life is at stake:

The Internet, and digital publishing, present a unique window of opportunity for reaching readers of serious fiction who are not being served by the publishing industry as currently constituted. Our intellectual discourse, including literary publishing, is threatened by a reduction of nonprofit funding on one hand and de facto censorship by the market place on the other. Under the circumstances, the traditional concept of a publisher needs to be reexamined and the very concept of publication needs to be reality-tested and changed to align with new realities. The revolution in new media publishing, bringing with it the ability to produce books profitably for niche, or even micromarkets, promises to bring new life to literary publishing. The problems and excessive costs associated with printing, warehousing, distribution, and book store shelf space will all be swept aside, shifting the focus of publishing back to editorial selection. The Alt-X on-demand book series will thus benefit from the established reputation Alt-X has already achieved for editorial taste. This is due to Alt-X's known ability to reach out and locate (and publish/exhibit) some of the best in the new electronic and Web oriented writing. The driving idea behind this project is to be able to publish books inexpensively for an important tastemaking readership that needs to be served with intelligent literary fiction, and that exists in numbers too small and unprofitable for the mainstream publishing industry.

The Net is where the action is. The excitement of a writing practice unbound from convention.

a woman appears slim dark moving across the terrace with measured stride wearing a loose garment of white linen or miracle fiber black hair falls over her shoulders she smiles balances a vessel in offering to me then sets the drink down on a table I following the mobile arabesques of her obvious unbound body

"Not-fiction," it ends up, is the life-practice people constantly make up, as if they were using their own daily existence as a research and development platform for to reinvent history itself, to MAKE history or make history *Up*, a post-literary history that presents itself in public as an ongoing ungoing digression on the act of fiction (or what was once called fiction but is now not capable of playing that role any longer). "When we talk about 'reality' with regard to fiction, what we're really talking about is the authority to comment plausibly on experience."

But now Sukenick wants to take writing further; he wants it to become an activist, utopian, unbound body of work made of miracle fiber, a practice that will "supplant Surfiction with its tactic of intervening in experience. Where Surfiction was relatively passive and contemplative in its stance toward experience, and in this sense still esthetically oriented, Intervent [short-hand for a more "interventionist not-fiction"] is aggressive, interactive, influencing the course of events, changing attitudes, leading to action, or even itself overflowing into overt gesture, performance, theater, or practical organization, including its own production and distribution—the continuum of effects in Intervent running from meditation to demonstration in all senses of the word."

In other words, an "interventionist not-fiction" writing practice could just as well leave both the book and literary sense and sensibility far behind, leave it to literary history, those days when people read novels because they presupposed a novel gesture on behalf of the author who wrote them, one that could still innovate thoughtful interaction with daily life.

Like all forms of cultural production in twenty-first century daily life, writing too needs upgrading to the latest version. In this case, the latest version would be one you could apply to your web browser, personal digital assistant, mp3 player, or email program, because in this ever-morphing new media environment that writers finds themselves in, what was once a narrative practice in search of an audience of sophisticated readers, has transformed into a networking practice that uses the intuitive (Sukenick might even say "prophetic") role of the writer as a medium, or shamanic filterer. A kind of DJ Deconstructionist or Network Conductor whose disintermediating practice as Cultural Producer leads to a Reconfiguring of the Author into a Virtual Artist.

Our goal should be to "move constantly beyond literature, beyond the definitions of particular linguistic realities, beyond language itself, to change the world we live in."

Bliss Street Utopia Parkway Mount Eden Avenue Olympia Heights

Abstract Expressionism (Part Two)

"When I start writing my first novel, *Up*, a book about the East Side that is a combination of autobiography and invention, I realize that that place and time is one in which we can in fact partly invent our autobiographies, in which life is not something imposed on us but a process in which we are creatively involved."

Sukenick and his colleagues in the lower part of Manhattan are experiencing some pretty heady days back in mid-1960s. Anything can happen, and most of the time, anything does.

"The distinction between art and life in the book is reduced to a quibble of form only partly out of theoretical considerations. It's also a consequence of the kind of life that, after decades of alienation, we are finally positioned to lead."

Of course, alienation is not always a bad thing. In the late 1950s, if you feel like an exile in your own country, you can always just bag it and take off for Europe, write your life-story that "like a cloud, changes as it goes." For Sukenick, the life-story of the author is always already a clean slate, for

The contemporary writer—the writer who is acutely in touch with the life of which he is part—is forced to start from scratch: Reality doesn't exist, time doesn't exist, personality doesn't exist.

Crossing the Atlantic in the late 1950s becomes the perfect opportunity for self-erasure and, consequently, PoMo Nest Building.

"Around the Village, after the myth of collectivism had shattered and the cult of heroic individualism had grown, of necessity, out of the social rejection of the great Black bop jazzmen, the isolation of the early Abstract Expressionists, and disillusion with grand social movements, I sometimes thought of the big pot."

The big pot?

"In an ambience so fragmented that the so-called Abstract Expressionists vehemently rejected any common label and people had a hard time agreeing on common interests, much less the common good, the Spanish Civil War vet's big, communal pot seemed a lot more appetizing than it once had."

Once there, the artist's mind gets thrown into the pot with the rest of the melting brains, and persisting through seasons of euphemistic hell, ideas spring forth—later, in the context of a writing practice:

"Obviously there's no progress in art. Progress toward what? The avant-garde is a convenient propaganda device, but when it wins the war everything is avant-garde, which leaves us just about where we were before. The only thing that's sure is that we move, and as we move we leave things behind—the way we felt yesterday, the way we talked about it. Form is your footprints in the sand when you look back."

What is the post-literary footprint being left in the electro-sand?

you have a peculiar feeling and before you can finish the sentence a throbbing in your back your chest a spasm a blinding pain you hear of those things cutting a steak feeling a girl signing a check stepping off a curb into oblivion you never know helpless nothing to be done all mowed down by death's machine gun

Later, in narralogue, tuning into his extremist writing style while maintaining clarity, directness, and concision, he says: "By rhetoric I mean a kind of ongoing persuasive discourse that, in itself, resembles narrative—agonistic, sophistic, sophisticated, fluid, unpredictable, rhizomatic, affective, inconsistent and even contradictory, improvisational, and provisional in its argument toward contingent resolution that can only be temporary."

He says this, while talking to me in a cafe in Paris, a smoky joint on the Rue de la Roquette that is frequented by writers, artists, and critics. Or at least that is what they think of themselves as. Meanwhile, Sukenick's attention is on the French whore feverishly smoking a cigarette outside the cafe window, a young blond who he has mistaken for an ex-student.

Bohemia is a Country In Europe: Or, The Author Formerly Known as Ronnie, Arrives in Paris to Catch the Virus and Ends Up Feathering His Soon-to-be Pomo Nest

"What are you going to Europe for?"

1958. If you want to see what America is like, go to Paris.

"Paris is like a petri dish for Americans, it isolates the germ and lets it grow. You take a few Americans fresh from the States, drop them into the medium of the dish and wait a few months, sometimes just a few weeks, then examine the resulting growth."

One day while in Paris, Ron gets violently sick in his hotel room. He has no medication, can't afford a doctor, and stops eating. What Ron doesn't realize, because he has no mirror, is not only has he not shaved or gotten out of his clothes for almost a week now, but he's covered with chicken feathers. The whole room is gradually being covered in chicken feathers.

It ends up that the hotel owner's wife chops up chicken feathers to stuff in the pillows and quilts they put in all of the bedrooms. But she doesn't stuff them in sufficiently enough for them to stay there, so they start leaking, and Ron, wearing woolens to keep warm, becomes saturated with feathers all over his body. All over his unshaven face.

Meanwhile, he's reading Celine. It just so happens that the first time he realizes that he's being attacked by an unnamable virus is when he's reading Celine and now, some time later, covered in chicken feathers, he realizes that reading Celine actually immunizes him. Like taking a flu shot to make sure you don't catch the flu. Writing as Pharmakon (very Francaise, when you come to think of it).

But then a voice, another virus, hiding in the closet, asks:

"Immunizes him from what?"

From Obscuring the Muse, is the response.

It's time for Sukenick to start leaving his formal footprints in the papered sands. After experimenting with the poetics of parasitic citation ("it is not the thing described, nor false facsimile"), Sukenick has caught the bug. Transitional Ron, always on the border, a pseudo-autobiographical work in progress, is ready to play Host to his own writerly virus.

In Blanchot's *Thomas The Obscure*, the narrator says: "This head, my head, no longer even sees me, because I am annihilated. For it is I looking at myself and not perceiving myself."

The important thing is to annihilate the important thing.

There are many Americans who come to Paris planning to stay till their money runs out and then when it runs out decide they don't want to go back to the States. Young men and women with no careers, they usually blunder around a few months on a few emergency checks from home, and then they go back anyway. Those who stick with it settle in to a lazy, pleasant, marginal life either admittedly aimless or which they often call something like "painting" or "writing." Now and then it actually is.

Abstract Expressionism (Part Three)

the important thing is a feeling
the important thing is a bug transition
the important thing is a communal pot
the important thing is a mythic situation
the important thing is a hard factuality
the important thing is an unbound body
the important thing is to keep it open
the important thing is to run on sentencing
the important thing is to disembody practice
the important thing is to use experience as base for knowledge
the important thing is to manipulate very similitude
the important thing is to remix net persona
the important thing is to outthink premeditation
the important thing is to decharacterize eros
the important thing is to strip i.d.
the important thing is to ejaculate superego
the important thing is to pla(y)giarize virus
the important thing is to muse continuum
the important thing is to butcher the butcher
the important thing is to see how they run like peegs from a numb see
how they fly
the important thing is to kill our fear of death

Remembering The Sixties: Or, How to Get It Out of Your System

The jacket copy to Sukenick's second novel, *Out*, describes the work as "a novel of immense energy. Sukenick's characters flash into and out of presence; episodes impel themselves so strongly that they are self-obliterating. This is an experiment in narrative and language; at the same time it is an extremely accurate, persistently funny portrayal of the psychic overload we all reached at the end of the Sixties."

We all. Even those of us who weren't there, or if we were, might have been too young to remember.

My heart doesn't remember anything.

Putz. Make it up it's the same thing.

It was a time of idealistic wanderlusting and vulgar distortion. Of eros intensification and hardcore manipulation. Sexual revolution and psychic prostitution. It was difficult to find which way was *Up*:

"Fidelity, jealousy, and exploitation were not problems that were going to be disposed of by ignoring them, though we often did. We quickly learned that it was hard to explore a liberated sexuality without paying a bitter price in terms of humane relations. And I just as quickly decided I would pay the price. There was no way to put the cork back in my bottle, no matter what."

sometimes stays several days seems to be part of his
job. the way they fuck is she never wants it tells him he's
a bore that's all he wants from her he doesn't love her why

doesn't he jerk off with his surfboard he's just a stupid jock
he has no refinement get away from me dammit you're not
getting anything off me no no not again oh shit oh god oh

my god give it to me I love you that's her thing. His thing
is come on cunt cut the crap lie down I'm horny he only
grunts once when he comes he comes like a man driving home a

Both *Up* and *Out* were landmark novels in that they revitalized the rival tradition in literature, an historical brand of storytelling that highlights its deliberate refusal to render itself coherent and accessible while foregrounding a formally (read: politically) conscious narrative strategy reminiscent of Sterne's *Tristram Shandy*. Sukenick's PoMo colleague, Raymond Federman, has called this kind of obliterature "self-reflexive fiction."

Says Federman: "Sukenick's body of fiction exemplifies the way language and narrative structures are exploded in the fiction of the 1970s. He constructs his fiction on the principle of a fundamental and sustained opposition: the construction of a fictional illusion and the laying bare of that illusion. In other words, he creates a fiction and simultaneously makes a statement about the creation of that fiction. The two processes are held together in a formal tension that breaks down the distinction between fact and fiction, between fiction and criticism, between imagination and reflection, and as a result the concepts of creation and interpretation merge into a new type of discourse—a critifictional discourse."

A critifictional discourse not terribly unlike Sukenick's own upgraded version of the narrative-rhetorical blur, "Not-fiction." Sukenick, who has on numerous occasions expressed to me his desire to become his own "second-generation Sukenick," sees the post-pomo writing moment moving beyond the lame inadequacies of a heavily manipulated imagination. Rather, he sees it turning into a synthesis of hybridized genres that produces a "hard factuality." He also claims that this "Not-fiction" writing style will lead to more fluid sexual identities that are so self-reflexive as to strip i.d. (id) from itself, creating a more feminized openendedness. For example, he tells us of a recent conversation he had with a young woman who tells him point blank that "my boyfriend is like a girl with a penis."

This is a trend that's been gaining steam since the 1960s:

"I was just living the kind of erotic life I had always assumed I would lead, but now the world, and not just a special underground milieu, was ready to accommodate me. I found myself making it not only with other subterraneans and assorted art molls, but with Uptown girls and prep school products as well. Oddly, their totally promsicuous behavior began to irritate me from time to time. Their 'liberation' was too facile . . . [a]t times I felt downright exploited. But, what the hell."

What the hell, indeed. The 1960s was a time when heterosexuals were coming out of the closet, willing to experiment with their own radical sexuality even if meant nudging at the edges of their own self-exploitation. Why protect yourself from yourself when you could just as easily go out and turn your writing practice into social practice?

I don't want to remember anything. I want to be numb and ruthless. And beautiful.

98.6: The Novel as Demonst(e)ration (some sampled remixes)

7/14 a birth solidifies in the mist. fog decompresses morning mindset and unglues the letters hanging inside his brain like virtual wallpaper. a message comes in via email: if it moves it's alive, if its stays still it's art. fluid legacy simultaneous multiplicity random interconnection? feed the network. the message is signed RAM. he takes the message and shows it to a friend. explain this, he says. message incomplete says the friend. he turns away from the computer and checks his temp: 98.6. ha, he says, knowing he's all fever. getting away with moider. what to do? he thinks about the difference between earth and air. air is breathing is living is intuiting. earth is gravity is money is being grounded. but there is a counterforce. groovity. where gravity is heavy groovity is light. where gravity is day groovity is night. about midnight. where gravity feeds your stomach groovity feeds your mind. where gravity is power groovity is joy. and like that.

8/22 what is it? myth dream vision joke. prosody of event. conjunction of chance. media landscape with brand name identity. frankenwoof. all bark and no byte. calculated return to the no-load mutual fungus. exploratory routes. abscess of soul. negative hallucination. seeing what's not really there. an albatross telling unicorny jokes to the lock n'est-ce pas monster? a tummler. a psychosynthetic carny controlling the rollercoaster. a transcendentalist suffering from consumption.

5/23 remember he can't remember. remember he can't remember. remember he can't remember. remember he can't remember. remember he can't remember. remember he can't remember. remember he can't remember. remember he can't remember. remember he can't remember. remember he can't remember. remember he can't remember. remember he can't remember. remember he can't remember. remember he can't remember. remember he can't remember. remember he can't remember.

4/13 Lady Drackenstain expectorates a blood clot. covers it with white linen. picks it up and says what does it mean? cheesecloth psychosynthesis. THE REAL ME. a rainmaker in dried-up canyonland. making senses of the menses. think about it. interruption. discontinuity. imperfection. vex'd pig hymn waltz fuck bjorsq. read my lips. part my sea. see what I mean? mean what I say? my pages are red. let my peepholes go. nymphs waltz jig fuck vex rod bq. bisquick and get it over with. hymn waltz fuck sex gip v.d. bjorq. beyond the bjorq and into the.

7/14 he's got virtual sperm. it's not cold hot lukewarm mental. it's HIM. a distributed bodytext impregnating the network. spawning tribes of ingenious wanderlusts camouflaged as Metacommentaries on The Problem. always The Problem.

I've gotta go.
Why.
Cuz the gates are only open so long then it's a nuisance.
You can bypass the gates pass go and collect your tension I mean pension.
Let me think about it.
There's no time.
I don't need time I got all the time I can handle what I need is
What.
What I need is
What.
Let me finish.
Okay. Finish.
What I need is
(the computer says "You've Got Mail")
more.

7/10 autohypnosis. angelic degradations. thrust of want. raw information bodies. dream elixirs. seductive suck-offs. oblivion encounters. maestro of sleep. boneweep.

Interview Digression: An email Q&A

Q
You call your book, *Doggy Bag,* a collection of hyperfictions. What are hyperfictions?

A
Hyperfiction is fiction plus hype. All literary labels are hype. On another level—subhype—hyperfiction is the fixed print equivalent to the computer's hypertext—hyperfiction is interactive and intercuts sources, styles, genres. Hyperfiction is the sequel to surfiction. Hyperfiction is the scraps from the table of the culture feast that you bring home in your avant-pop *Doggy Bag.*

Q
So you're saying that hyperfiction is the sequel to surfiction. When I hear the word surfiction, I think of surrealism and when I hear the word hyperfiction I think of the hyperreal or hyped-up reality. What we're talking about is the interfacing of reality and fiction. But whose reality? And why fiction?

A
The point of hyperfiction is to hype up reality—not to phony it up, but to make it more intense, more inclusive, and more responsive to the needs of the spirit. This is more akin to the function of "art" in a "primitive culture," where it is considered to be instrumental to having an effect on reality (curses, blessings, healings, prophecies) rather than as an end in itself. Euroamerican art is considered to be an end-in-itself, an elitist point of view that results in the imprisonment of art in cultural zoos known as museums and universities.

Q
It sounds as if you're saying writing can be a kind of shamanistic practice. In fact, shamanism as a way of "conducting" one's creative life seems to be at the heart of a number of your characters, not the least of whom would be Ronald Sukenick. Considering that we're now caught

up in the era of multi-national publishing conglomerates, how does a contemporary writer maintain that intense connection with his/her practice so as to feed the needs of the spirit?

A

Do it in the morning, do it at night, do it while you're reading, do it while you write. I.e., keep writing your narrative while doing other things, so as to include them; include the other things in your narrative while you're writing it. I think the answer to this question has something to do with image, or more exactly, lack of one. The international-multiconglomerate culture operates in the currency of images, therefore it becomes important not to have an image. Once you have an image you're caught in the conglomeration web, but if you avoid an image you're still free to glide through the net. Lack of image keeps you mobile. I've noticed that when people meet me they're often surprised because I'm not like their image of me. That's to the good. Not having an image is freedom. Shamans don't have images, they're chameleons. When you don't have an image you can have any image or none. This is the doctrine of anti-imagism.

Q

I've always coiled at the thought of creative writing as an exclusively literary practice. You once said we need to break out of the cage called Literature. What did you mean by that?

A

Literature is a false category. Literature simply doesn't exist. That's all I have to say about it. Literature is a way of saying that a basic human faculty that is supposed to be potent and efficacious isn't. It's just literature. Or you could take it the other way—what you find in a science magazine or nature magazine, the two places where scientific discoveries are published, you could call that literature—if literature exists, that's also literature.

Q

I want to change gears here. Do you think your fiction has been influenced by any of the other arts or, for that matter, television?

A

Fellini films, especially *8 1/2*, were supportive and illuminating at the time. Painting: abstract expressionism in its action painting form. Music: jazz improvisation for sure. Dance: in the revolution of the everyday phase, yes. TV: channel surfing is a biggie. All the arts form an atmosphere which all artists of consequence thrive on breathing.

Q
Which contemporary authors do you feel represent the direction fiction is going in and is likely to continue going in?

A
I can only give a wish list on this and it would include Kafka, Celine, Beckett, Genet, etc.—all pre-postmoderns.

Q
You're one of the few writers I know who is very active in the publishing and nonfiction scene. You publish *American Book Review* and *Black Ice Magazine*, you're a codirector of Fiction Collective Two, your last book (*Down and In*) was a look back at the different undergrounds in New York City over the last fifty years. How do you find time to do it all?

A
You know the old garment industry joke? I lose a dollar on every garment I sell—so how do you make a living?—volume!

Q
How would you describe the kind of interaction you see between what you do as a publisher, a professor, and a nonfiction writer, and what it is you're up to as a fiction writer?

A
Down with phony distinctions. I'm not a novelist and publisher, etc.—I'm an always emerging wordturd—it's all part of the same braunschweiger—chop off a bit to fry up as an essay, another bit to boil as a press release, a hunk slowly roasted as a novel, and, if you keep moving, maybe they won't catch you.

Q
Do the electronic networks and the big push toward electronic publishing interest you?

A
Mais, oui! In fact, here I am doing the trip at this very instant (another chip off the old braunschweiger).

Q
Is your creative process—your writing routine, assuming you have one—the same as it's always been? What is it?

A
I insert a specially designed crank in my left ear and turn, slowly at first, then with increasing vigor, making my tongue dart in and out and my eyeballs roll around in my head like the images in a slot machine till I start ejaculating ink on the page.

Q
Your novel *98.6* is going into its what, fifth printing now, and as I was re-reading it I felt like I was reading about contemporary life. Frankenstein, the mythological landscape where the novel takes place, is America, no doubt, and as I was reading it, I couldn't help but wonder how you view the autobiographical moment in fiction, what some people call pseudo-autobiography. Could you tell me your thoughts on this, on how, say, a novel like *98.6* is or isn't (pseudo)-autobiographical?

A
I use myself as a source of data because I know the data, it's at my disposal. What happens to it when I start writing fiction is another thing.

Q
There's a scene in the endless recycling of scenes in *Blown Away*, where the protagonist goes to a reading—I think it's at UCLA—and gets to shake hands with Henry Miller. Did this actually happen to you?

A
Yes.

Q
I had this strange feeling while reading the book that this was a very important moment for Ccrab? Didn't Anaïs Nin once say you were the next Henry Miller?

A
The new Henry Miller. But she took it back with the publication of *Out* because she felt it was too—vulgar. Sexually coarse. You can see why she was always fighting with Miller, which was why I didn't get to see more of Miller. But it was important for me to at least shake hands,

because Miller was the one who woke me up to the fact that words on the page can be a vital extension of the life of the writer and therefore of the life of the reader, and this was a passing on of the succession, though Miller couldn't have known it, especially since the dead hand of Durrell swept me instantly out of its way.

Q
Can there be a radical edge to language and art nowadays, or are we always already setting ourselves up for immediate consumption/absorption and, as a consequence, neutralization?

A
The radical edge isn't political, or economical, or consumeristical, or selloutical—it's situational. And you have to get yourself into that situation, if you have a taste for it. Some people seem to be there by nature, so maybe you only think you get yourself into it, while you've always been there and simply haven't realized it.

Works Cited

Sukenick, Ronald. *98.6*. Boulder, Colo.: Fiction Collective, 1975.

———. *Doggy Bag: Hyperfictions*. Boulder, Colo.: Fiction Collective, 1994.

———. *Down and In: Life in the Underground*. New York: Macmillan, 1987.

———. *In Form: Digressions on the Act of Fiction*. Carbondale: Southern Illinois University Press, 1985.

———. *Mosaic Man*. Normal, Ill.: Fiction Collective Two, 1999.

———. *Narralogues: Truth in Fiction*. Albany: State University of New York Press, 2000.

———. "Not Fiction." *American Book Review* (November/December 1999), 3.

———. *Out*. Chicago: Swallow Press, 1973.

———. "Turning On." *Alt-X Network* <http://www.altx.com>, 1996.

———. *Up*. New York: Dial Press, 1968.

Unwriting/Rewriting the Master Narratives of "Bankrupt" Modernity: Ronald Sukenick's *Mosaic Man*

Marcel Cornis-Pope

> [Innovative fiction is] an attempt to get at the truth of experience beyond our fossilized formulas of discourse, to get at a new and more inclusive 'reality,' if you will. This is a reality that includes what the conventional novel tends to exclude and that encompasses the vagaries of unofficial experience, the cryptic trivia of the quotidian that help shape our fate, and the tabooed details of life—class, ethnic, sexual—beyond sanctioned descriptions of life.
>
> Ronald Sukenick, "Autogyro" (294)

As Ronald Sukenick made clear in a more recent interview, the type of fiction he has been interested in writing is "interventive" in a double sense: seeking a new narrative contract, a "non-factitious relation" to reality and its readers, while also trying to "intervene in and change reality, experience" ("The Rival Tradition" 4, 6). Representation is reconceived as an "interventive, i. e., aggressive, interactive" performance (4) whose purpose is to immerse fiction in life, reclaiming entire segments of experience obfuscated by conventional narratives. Sukenick's concept of "interventive fiction" challenges the self-reflexive aestheticism of a metafictionist like William Gass, for whom "[f]iction doesn't make a difference" in social reality nor should it try to make one

(*Unspeakable Practices* 253); it also exceeds Robert Coover's notion of an iconoclastic fiction that does not discard traditional narrative forms but rather assaults them from "inside," exploding their ideological strictures in order to "speak the unspeakable" (*Unspeakable Practices* 252, 253–54). Closer to the reformulative projects in postcolonial literature, L=A=N=G=U=A=G=E poetry, or innovative feminist fiction, Sukenick's fiction sets in motion a revisionistic type of "experiential thinking" that seeks to "undercut official versions of reality in favor of our individual sense experience" (*In Form* 67). The novelist's effort begins with an unwriting of "what has been formulated as experience" ("Unwriting" 26), but continues with an imaginative rewriting that allows "a new sense of experience" to evolve. Disarticulation and rearticulation are the complementary sides of this project. As Sukenick puts it, before "we write fact into language again," we need to "unwrite the book of life till the difference between language and the rest of experience is as clear as possible" ("Unwriting" 4).

Sukenick has arrived at this concept of interventive fiction gradually, in an unremitting struggle with narrative conventions and epistemologies. His early fiction—*Up* (1968), *The Death of the Novel and Other Stories* (1969), and *Out* (1973)—is torn between the competing claims of a nonrepresentational style of writing whose "main qualities are abstraction, improvisation and opacity" ("The New Fiction" 1973; rpt. *In Form* 211) and a notion of art as a liberating experiential and cultural medium, "leading to action" ("The Rival Tradition" 4). *98.6* (1975) and *Long Talking Bad Conditions Blues* (1979) continue to shift their modes of narrative articulation (realistic, improvisational, parodic), but they also try to find a provisional balance among them, best illustrated in the technique of "psychosynthesis" (*98.6* 180). Based on "the law of mosaics [which is] a way of dealing with parts in the absence of wholes" (122), the technique of *psychosynthesis* replaces rigid cause-and-effect relationships with moments of "luminous . . . coincidence" between reality and invention, emphasizing: "A way of things happening without happening. A way of dreaming without dreaming. A way of going mad without going mad. We deny nothing. We incorporate the negation in the affirmation" (*98.6* 180). More recent Sukenick narratives (*Blown Away* 1986; *The Endless Short Story* 1986; *Doggy Bag: Hyperfictions* 1994) have enrolled their conflicting compositional modes more clearly in the service of a radically transformative poetics. The very definition of Sukenick's improvisational poetics has been revised: instead of participating in the experiential illusion, improvisation functions as a bridge to the *possible*, articulating the "uncorked stories," the "absent unsung song," releasing us from the "tedium of prefabrication" (*The Endless Short Story* 96).

The general disposition of these narratives is—with a term Sukenick actually dislikes—"experimental," but in the sociocultural, rather than purely formal sense: "Experimental writing is just writing that breaks out of the modes of literature into something resembling the freaky uniqueness of individual experience beyond the usual brainwash of official culture" ("Introduction: The Dirty Secret" 8). At the same time, however, Sukenick's fiction has emphasized with increasing clarity the difficulties encountered by a visionary narrative poetics in an age dominated by cultural reproduction and consumption. Sukenick's books are underwritten by a tension between two approaches to narration, fictional, and cinematic (visual-electronic). As redefined by Sukenick, the fictional approach is improvisational and transgressive, allowing a certain degree of artistic intervention in reality. By contrast, the visual-electronic discourse is reproductive and uncritical, treating everything as a skeletal story. Innovative fiction emphasizes the transformative flow of composition, whereas cinematic discourse exploits fetishistic fragmentation and appearances: "[T]his is a Huge Production. It's big. Very big. It's got everything. . . . You're in it. I'm in it. We're being filmed right now the cameras are rolling all the time we have set them up all over the world what chaos" (*Out* 209). The job of the innovative novelist is to break through the discursive screens of traditional representation to the repressed, authentic data of experience: "Our lives are an appalling slapstick. On the other side of the TV screen real blood flows, I've got to get out of this" (*Out* 115). But he/she also must acknowledge that the two approaches, one reproductive-manipulative, the other re-creative, are facets of the same process of narration; and that innovative fiction, no matter how clever, cannot entirely escape the mastery system of representation.

Sukenick's fiction can thus be read—a fact that has escaped critics until recently—as an unremitting critique of the seductive economy of narration that for Sukenick functions as the chief illusion-building mechanism of modernity. The "story" in *Out* is propelled ahead by moments of escalation/de-escalation: "There's been an escalation of the latest deescalation intensifying protest increasing backlash" (94). These cycles of rising and falling action suggest the charged psychological and political atmosphere of the Vietnam era that provide the background of the novel, but also the libidinal, manipulative economy of narration itself. The usurpation of the real by a seductive fictional economy is also at issue in *Up*. Though the character-author Ronnie is not always aware of his own acts of mystification, he is quick to denounce them in others. When Nancy, the ex-prude turned nude model in *Up*, praises striptease as an epiphanic production that makes her truer self appear in response to the "intensity of the [man's] desire," the narrator counters by calling it a contribution to the institution of "make-believe. The dream trade. . . . It sounds to me like a bad parody of socialism" (187, 254). The Sukenick persona shares with Nancy a somewhat self-indulging desire to "make up [his] own version of everything as [he] goes along" (210), but he has the courage to unlock the uncontrollable potential of his "inventions" (*Out* 2).

In *98.6*, seduction, simulation, and the fantasy of control are intimately connected. *98.6* probes the roots of our postmodern condition, exposing the "grotesqueries . . . of the vast cultural failures of the recent generation" (32): invasive technology, sexual and political violence, cultural simulation. Rape becomes a ubiquitous literal figure in *98.6* that allows a "conscious critical act of reading the violence and sexuality back into texts where it has been deflected, either by the text itself or by the critics: where it has been turned into a metaphor or a symbol or represented rhetorically as titillation, persuasion, ravishment, seduction, or desire . . ." (Higgins and Silver 4). The imagery of rape connects the ritual sacrifices of the Aztec priests and their Spanish usurpers, which submit captive virgins to the deathly rape of "promised gods" (8), to the modern forms of "mind rape nature manipulation exploitation control" (176). The other literal-metaphoric term evoked in *98.6*, "colonization," makes the connection between cultural violence (the bloody conquest of the Aztec Empire) and literal anal rape even clearer.

In *Long Talking Bad Conditions Blues*, the system of male power that makes sexual violence necessary, comes under serious questioning, and so does its matriarchal counterpart. Carl writes a report that disparages maternity, urging women to adopt the "path of power," paternity. Some of the women struggle to develop an alternative to the pervasive system of male rationality, emphasizing analogy over polarity, fluidity over boundaries, and reciprocal responsiveness in place of phallic aggression. But neither approach can save the world of the novel from dispersal into "gaping hole[s]" and "dull null[s]" (58). *Long Talking Bad Conditions Blues* employs the island metaphor to dramatize the deracinated insularity of postmodern culture, but also to suggest an alternative to its "accelerated shatter": a dynamic intermingling of human "units," each capable of self-recreation and of the type of imaginative rewriting that converts the "petty iconography of the quotidian" into a movement of "invention and [even] prophecy" (5). *Blown Away* continues this twofold exploration of contemporary culture, denouncing its ideology of "make-believe" but also reassessing its potential for change. In the "city of [celluloid] dreams," narration plays initially a purely manipulative role. Hollywood is driven by the three "masters of the [fabricated] obvious": Dr. Boris O. Ccrab, "fat, foul-smelling, middle-aged . . . mentist" (28) and subject-finder, Rod Drackenstein, producer-director of hip porn films, and Victor Plotz, the "hack screenwriter" who always wanted to become a novelist but who is content with "moving plots" (144). But *Blown Away* also illustrates the revisionary power of narration, its capacity to move beyond self-imposed limitations. As the characters rewrite their lives, each develops a contradictory, creative side, becoming more human. Dr. Ccrab splits into character "Crab" and narrator "Ccrab," being able to intervene more meaningfully in "the occult crosscurrents of experience" (128). Clover, the porn starlet, enters a phase of self-awareness, disrupting the script of her male handlers with her need to be more than a "fake, a fraud, a cartoon" (142). Drackenstein is also beset by strange dreams, in which he hears his twin brother advocate an art of silent "unwriting" that poses a serious challenge to his own pursuit of cheap visual thrills: "I unwrite the cultural destiny that's been written and over written. I convert the stain of the visible to the pure radiance of the invisible. I repatriate the spirit from the realm of determinism to that of potential" (114).

The struggle to "unwrite" our cultural destiny and "repatriate" the spirit of modernity "from the realm of determinism to that of potential" is also the focus of *Doggy Bag: Hyperfictions* (1994). Sukenick's story-essays engage the competing traditions underlying Western culture ("Egyptian," "Judaic," "Greek-European"), the "postcolonial" position of American culture in relation to European cultures, and of European cultures in relation to U.S. postmodernity, or the entropic processes of a postindustrial culture caught between Western European decadence and American consumerist obsolescence. The cover design—representing a wolf dog holding a green bag with a skull-and-crossbones drawing—provides the key metaphor for the world's "history of voracious looting and scavenging, culture feeding on itself in a progressive comedy of transformation, the spoils of conquest ornamenting the Roman Empire, Roman columns used to build Christian churches, Romanesque frescoes ripped off for baroque buildings, the Pantheon robbed to decorate St. Peter's, antique monuments as marble quarries for newer palazzi" (141). But this process of cannibalization on which modern culture is based can have a more subversive use in the hand of the innovative writer. Against the frozen icons of both traditional and contemporary culture, the authorial alter ego mobilizes a defamiliarizing, "wolfish" tongue that tears apart and rewrites all kinds of narrative traditions, a "cryptic language we don't need to understand until it interrupts, a language that understands us" (77).

Each one of these works deserves, of course, much more than a summarizing paragraph, but what I want to argue here is that they can also be read as rehearsals for Sukenick's most important work to date, *Mosaic Man* (1999), building incrementally his poetics of unwriting/rewriting and comprehensive critique of modernity. *Mosaic Man* reconfigures not only Sukenick's previous work, rewriting episodes and motifs from *Up*, *98.6*, *Blown Away*, and *Doggy Bag*, but also the poetics of post-Holocaust/post-Cold War fiction. In an effort to retrieve repressed experiential potentialities and make "another sense" of reality, *Mosaic Man* engages critically the dominant narratives that have shaped his destiny as a writer: the existential picaresque, the Western quest, the gauche-pornographic novel, the family chronicle, the political thriller, and even the grand narratives of the Hebrew Bible. Unwriting and rewriting function in *Mosaic Man* as strategies of reformulation against a "bankrupt modern" world (188). They submit the author's cultural heritage (European, Jewish, and American) to a thorough reexamination, discarding one-sided definitions in favor of new cross-cultural interactions.

Because, as the authorial narrator states in a section written after the fall of the Berlin Wall, "we're all post humous as Europeans, including the Europeans themselves. Post human" (197), Europe becomes the main focus of Sukenick's critical attention through the early pages of *Mosaic Man*. The book revisits significant sites in Sukenick's European education—Paris in 1958, Venice in the early 1960s, Poland at the time of the Solidarity movement, or Berlin after 1989—mainly to conclude that the "great tradition of Humanism wasn't worth shit in chateau, a fox hole, a death camp, a stately state palace" (197). Ron finds postwar Europe infested with more insidious versions of the "virus" that tore the continent apart during the war, from new-right nationalisms to "anti-semitism without Jews" (76), neofascist attacks on "Blacks, Arabs, and other 'foreigners' " (12), or a more general sense of "dead-ended" history experienced in the "ghost ghettoes" (189) of Poland and Italy. European artistic culture is likewise contaminated, offering the American novice only varieties of decadence: from the "inhuman" fiction of Céline to the sadomasochistic Parisian avant-garde of the late 1950s; and from self-absorbed Lacanian "auto-fiction" (191) to the obsession of the contemporary German intelligentsia with the work of Holocaust survivors (as fellow writer Federman explains to Ron, they are trying to "conduct a sort of autopsy. Now that they've killed off the Jews, they're interested in finding out what Jews were" [187]).

But Europe can still surprise the fictionalized Sukenick persona with a few "luminous coincidences" that reinforce his own iconoclastic art. In Poland, Ron recognizes a "Siamese twin" in Marta, writer, translator, and editor of an underground publication with whom he shares the foolishness of believing in "an impossible promise to meet the impossibility of the situation" (112) and the refusal to "run after . . . golden calves" (114). He is also reconfirmed in his symbolic destiny as a "sukiennik" (114), an imaginative cloth maker whose task it is to cut the "impossible promise . . . out of whole cloth" (113, 114). In Italy, Ron recaptures briefly the brash vision of his own youthful self and is encouraged to continue his pursuit of "an opening to the unworldly in a world that can't honor it" (180). Finally, the post-1989 Berlin inspires a meditation on walls and the danger of ideas frozen in concrete ("All ideas are wrong. Especially the right ones." [189]). The mutilated Berlin Wall suggests to the narrator a collapsed "writing on the wall," its petrified ideological message "all hacked and pocked and pitted," written over with "multicolored multilingual writing . . . epigraphs, pictograms, hieroglyphs, riddles, runes, alphabetic jocularities, plays on words and words playing on themselves" (184). Though this "concrete poetry" cannot do away with the wall's "skeleton of reinforcement rods" (184), its unpredictable hybridity manages to challenge the "bankrupt modern" tradition of the last sixty years of the twentieth century (188).

American culture offers Ron the possibility to stake out a new cultural-aesthetic space beyond the "bankrupt modern." The authorial narrator begins by looking for the defining words/icons of American culture and of the Jewish subnarrative within it, submitting them to a bittersweet reevaluation in the first three sections, "Genes," "Ex/Ode," and "Umbilicus." Echoing William S. Burroughs's metaphor of the virus as "a very small unit of word and image" (*Electronic Revolution* 3), Ron regards traditional words and icons as "viral" (9), disseminating only empty imitations. Against their infectious reproducibility, section 6 of "Numbers" proposes a quixotic concept of (re)generative writing that mixes the Judaic topos of the sacred book of life with Sukenick's iconoclastic emphasis on what "is true beyond illusion" (106) and his postmodern visionarism, "a kind of praying that resembles a kind of wishing that resembles a kind of dreaming" (105). Ron finds models for his projected "Wholly Book" (105) in alternative American culture. Its liminal spaces such as the Colorado frontier absorbs Jews like Ron who have had their "ties cut" but who are willing to "extend [them]selves to re-establish connections as soon as possible" (190). Its "Peasant Crazies," from "Charlie, Groucho, Harpo, Costello, Abbott" (225) to a reinvented Jewish Elvis, teach Ron the art of prophecy in "conundrums, riddles, nonsense, stupidity, slapstick, wordplay, clowning, quips, sometimes in rhymed or alliterative verse" (224). American popular culture also inspires Ron's Captain Midnight expeditions against the neo-fascists of the world and his hilarious avant-pop rewritings ("Great Expectorations" and "Raiders of the Lost Calf") in the second part of the book.

Although postmodern America is more attractive to the innovative writer than "bankrupt modern" Europe, it is by no means impervious to the "virus." According to the author-character Ron, the virus has spread from Europe to America "by air conditioning. . . . He believes it is more than coincidence that the trend to individual air conditioners with their intrinsic environmental selfishness took hold at the same time as the degeneration of political morality during the McCarthy era" (106). Both Ron's Brooklyn boyhood and his struggling days as a young artist in New York are marked by traumatic encounters with prejudice (anti-Semitism, sexism, social discrimination). The "post"-Cold War America of the late 1980s is the choice playfield of the idolatrous, money-driven "Raiders of the Lost Calf" and the instigator of new racial and economic wars (Ron is concerned with the Gulf War and the situation of homeless). But unlike Europe, Ron's America can still hope to be saved one day by the "collective conscious" (105) of its eccentric dreamers.

The utopian-regenerative promise is even stronger in the "Jerusalem" section (118–59) that recreates Sukenick's journey to Israel after his father's death. In this imaginative travelogue, Israel functions (much like in *98.6*) as a metaphor of paradoxical inclusiveness: "Jerusalem, especially, is a place where everything seems to happen at once" (120). Seen from Mount Scopus, the city is an "aggregate repetitively disintegrating into a jumble of pure competing details numinous and hypnotic" (146). The Old City seems "cut off from real time by its wall. Its circular flow outside and inside history at the same time" (129). Likewise, in Israel "everything is happening at the same time . . . because in Israel the past is the present" (136). This historical co-presence gives the country and its religious capital a "hard definition, redefinition, over-definition" (146), but also a sense of self-contradiction. The Holy Land is "full of holes tunneling toward our missing whole" (146) and Jerusalem "is a problem without a solution. Like life" (147). The three major religions resemble the "jewel-like birds that inhabit its parks—bulbul, hopoe, sunbird—each monopolizing the attention in turn with its dazzling, singular and dominating brilliance" (146). The intercultural competition gives the country "a certain state of intensity" (122) that Ron's writer friend Shmulie associates with "the States during Vietnam" (136). This intensity translates into a fratricidal tension both between and within cultures.

Ron gets a taste of the country's "state of intensity" during his trip to the Hezekiah tunnel. Caught in the multilingual throng of people, Ron experiences a claustrophobic sense of the "Babel" of tongues and desires that reduce one another to an indistinguishable "babble" (148). Ron also has a revelation of the infrastructures of his own culture divided between "two tracks, the Mosaic and the Aaronian, . . . the Rabbi and the Mogul" (248). Both tracks become dangerous when absolutized. The "Extreme Rabbi" track leads to new prejudice: "The Israelis are now in the business of telling others they aren't really Jewish, the Orthodox tell it to the Reformed, the Hassidim tell it to the Orthodox, the white Jews tell it to the black Jews" (151–52). The "Mogul track" leads to ruthless competitiveness and mindless consumerism. Deep in the womb of the Hezekiah tunnel, Ron feels threatened by "brutal chtonic powers," "the Minotaur, Zeus as bull, the Golden Calf . . . demanding blood sacrifice" (155). His quest for a spiritual origin is continually detoured by surreptitious messages that send him on a goose chase for the Golden Calf idol. But the Middle East also provides Ron with a fraternity of like-minded writers: Ron's Jewish friend, Shmulie, who wants to write a book about the humanity of the Arabs; an innovative Israeli writer who writes in Ron's familiar self-canceling style, subverting "the virile thrust of his native tongue with a kind of semiotic hysteria" (149); an Arab writer Anton Shammas whose "soft irony" is "more Jewish than the aggressive assertiveness of the Israelis" (149). These writers reconfirm for him the idea that imaginative literature can cross ethnic boundaries, finding an antidote to the European virus of prejudice, the Middle Eastern "multilingual fratricidal Babel" (148), and the "American disease" of no thinking, just buying (151).

In response to all three, Ron chooses the "generative," "algorithmic" word (9), or writing as a "nest of possibilities" (142). The issue of thinking and writing "otherwise" has concerned Sukenick throughout his career. The essays collected in *In Form: Digressions on the Art of Fiction* (1985) and in *Narralogues* (1999), suggest a cumulative, polemical effort to redefine the role of narrative imagination in a post-Holocaust/post-Cold War world. Common to these essays is a concept of "generation" according to which the literary text "is generated by the activity of composition in an ongoing interchange between the mind and the page" (*In Form* 8). First sketched in "The New Tradition" essay (1972), this "generative theory of fiction" allows the novel to define itself in the process of composition, as "a form of invention, a way of bringing into being that which it did not previously exist" (*In Form* 8). Every aspect of the novel participates in a double generative process (textual and existential) that, as Voloshinov/Bakhtin argued several decades earlier, is continually reenergized by its own "living contradiction": "There is nothing in the structure of signification that could be said to transcend the generative process, to be independent of the dialectical expansion of social purview. . . . There is nothing in this that could be said to be absolutely fixed. And this is how it happens that meaning—an abstract, self-identical element—is subsumed under theme and torn apart by the theme's living contradiction so as to return in the shape of a new meaning with a fixity and self-identity only for a while" . . . (106). Although certain of Sukenick's procedures (word and event permutations, thematic montage, divergent endings, intertextual cross-referencing), recall the linguistic and "situational" generators of Raymond Roussel, Georges Perec, and Alain Robbe-Grillet, his generative approach is for all intents and purposes different from the "poetics of formal constraint" (Motte 19) practiced by the French. Sukenick's fiction is concerned with the enabling connection between the compositional and the experiential process, rather than with "constrictive" formal generators. As Sukenick puts it in his latest novel, innovative fiction is the last "holdout against an idolatrous, icon conned, oscar crazed hollywooden world," refusing to participate in the "counterfeit [game], including imagination's sleight-of-mind" (*Mosaic Man* 160). The novelist's struggle is to find the right balance between the "generative" WORD, "[i]conoclastic," "[a]lways beginning," and the analogic language of fiction, "genetic," "chronic," "iconic" (*Mosaic Man* 9). Inevitably the "pictures" generated by the language of fiction become "Multiplied. Viral. Simulacra, i.e. Facsimiles. Androids. Manikins. Gelded. Gilded. Scripted. . . . Story becomes history" (9), so that the novelist needs to seek continually the generative word that can start the process of articulation afresh. This task has an immediate political consequence since, like Federman, Kosinski, Major, or Morrison, Sukenick has used his innovative strategies to disrupt a representational ideology that has often reduced Jews, Blacks, women, or gays to "dummies"/"manikins"/ "androids"/"cyperpods"/ men and women "of parts" (*Mosaic Man* 205).

Revisionist writing turns Ron's search for his Jewish roots into a recreative experience, making a new "bible" out of the "babble" (148) of historical discourses and interests. *Mosaic Man* rewrites the titles of the Books of Moses (Genesis becomes "Genes," Exodus "Ex/Ode," Leviticus "Umbilicus," and Deuteronomy "Autonomy") and some of the plots of the Old and New Testament (the story of Adam and Eve, the motif of the Golden Calf, the last supper) from an iconoclastic perspective that emphasizes the progress from "Testimony," Commandments and "Numbers," to "Writing." In similar ways, the self-indulgent babble of contemporary culture is opened up through rewriting to excluded voices: Holocaust survivors, "unmentionable" Arabs, Mosaic dreamers, homeless Blacks. The narrator feels solidarity with all those "burned in the belly of the whale" (253), adopting the first person plural in the last section of his narrative. Feeling "unhomed" not only in the post human Europe, but also in the fratricidal Middle East and the "Space Bubble" (220) of postmodern America, the authorial narrator makes a home for himself in the "collective conscious" of history's excluded and in the "stupid [b]ut beautiful" (261) art of rewriting that makes the "literally true . . . fundamentally mysterious" (105).

Following a direction outlined in Sukenick's earlier books from *Out* to *Doggy Bag* (1994), *Mosaic Man* attempts a comprehensive recovery of those "leftovers of reality" that "make another kind of sense, a sense that you don't, can't, or don't want to see" (*Doggy Bag* 65, 66). This "other sense" of reality is sought first of all at a personal level: in the story of a post-Holocaust Jewish writer who suffers from "an advanced case of being human, [when] being human may be a terminal disease that's run its course" (16); in the "mosaic text" produced by an innovative, wild-tongued surfictionist punning himself into existence across conflicting identities; in the "cross-fiction" (192) that Sukenick exchanges with his literary friends. The "other-worldly" is sought also at the level of cultural history through an approach that uses improvisation and parody to rewrite the master narratives of the modern world, flushing out the oppressive virus of polarization. Sukenick finds this virus not only in Nazified wartime Europe, but also in McCarthyist and hyper-consumerist America, in the hedonistic machismo of the sixties, in the Cold War geopolitical partitions and their subtle reinvention after the fall of the Berlin War, and even in the "Mosaic" vs. the "Aronian" (Rabbi vs. Mogul) division of his own Jewish heritage (248). Threatened with being "xxxx-ed" by the religious, political, and literary "writing on the wall" (182), the post-Holocaust/post-Cold War writer finds his home not in a particular geocultural location (ancestral Poland, Venice, Paris, Berlin, Jerusalem, Boulder, or New York) but in the re-creative "mosaic" of his fiction that honors the visionary "unworldly" as much as the "worldly-wise" (*Mosaic Man* 180).

From this point of view, *Mosaic Man* participates in an important recent trend of analytic-utopian fiction that challenges our complacency about human history at the end of the second millennium. Against the demobilizing "end-of-history" vision that Francis Fukuyama and others have associated with the end of the Cold War (the 1989 revolutions marked for Fukuyama not only the triumph of Western consumerist capitalism, but also, since this system no longer faced serious competitors, "the end of history" and the "end of man"—*The End of History* xii), recent innovative fiction continues to imagine human strivings that make history "provisional and revisable" (Butler 8). The suggestion in Thomas Pynchon's *Mason & Dixon* (1997), Morrison's *Paradise* (1998), or Ronald Sukenick's *Mosaic Man* (1999), is not that we have exhausted our capacity to think historically, but rather that our historical imaginary is being choked by forces of stagnation, fragmentation, and repolarization—by new myths that "immobilize the world," discouraging "man against inventing himself" (Barthes 142, 155). Against these discouraging odds, these recent books continue to imagine alternative futures and worlds, making clear that contemporary innovative writing has not surrendered its commitment to transformative thinking.

The question that Sukenick's novel asks is how "could one even presume to be a person . . . , or even a human" after being submitted to the "ongoing ego smasher" of twentieth-century history (*Mosaic Man* 181). Confronted with the "progressive ebbing of [his] self," the post-Holocaust/post-Cold War writer resorts to the "metamorphic power of imaginative language" in order to retrieve a "story" (16) from the dissimulations of "history" (25). The story that *Mosaic Man* gradually reconstitutes is that of the innovative (Jewish) writer, threatened by history's repressive "writings on the wall"—from the Nazi ideology that tried to "exx" his identity "off the surface of the planet" (181), through the Cold War hysteria that scapegoated "others," to the incomprehensible post-Cold War "babel of symbols, slogans, signs, messages" (184). Condemned to "progressive invisibility" (182) by official culture, the innovative writer learns to become metamorphic, a "comic, a crazy" (201), a "Mosaic man" (205) punning his "genetic language" against "the Babel of background DNA" (208–09). *Mosaic Man* links the fate of the postwar innovative writer to his capacity to turn history into a story of possibilities, "opening doors" in the dead-ended past (170). Though his final fate in the hands of the "multinational interplanetary conglomerate" (223) remains uncertain, Sukenick's multiplex narrator manages to intrude his subversive "history rap" of "speculative jocularities" and "stochastic extrapolations" (206) in the grand narratives of Western culture. He becomes our rewriter who prods "the tribe to remember itself against the progressive alzheimer's of history. . . .We have met the writer and he is us" (215).

Works Cited

Barthes, Roland. *Mythologies*. Selected and trans. Annette Lavers. New York: Hill and Wang, 1972.

Burroughs, William S. *Electronic Revolution, 1970–1971*. Cambridge, England: Blackmoor Head Press, 1971.

Butler, Judith. "Poststructuralism and Postmarxism." *Diacritics* 23.4 (Winter 1993): 3–11.

Fukuyama, Francis. *The End of History and the Last Man*. New York: Free Press, 1992.

Higgins, Lynn A., and Brenda R. Silver. "Introduction: Rereading Rape." *Rape and Representation*. Ed. Higgins and Silver. New York: Columbia University Press, 1991. 1–11.

Motte, Warren F., Jr. *The Poetics of Experiment: A Study of the Work of Georges Perec*. Lexington, Ky.: French Forum Publishers, 1984.

Pynchon, Thomas. *Mason & Dixon*. New York: Henry Holt, 1997.

Sukenick, Ronald. "Autogyro: My Life in Fiction." *Contemporary Authors Autobiography Series*. Vol. 8. Ed. Mark Zadrezny. Detroit, Mich.: Gale Research. 283–95.

———. *Blown Away*. Los Angeles: Sun & Moon Press, 1986.

———. *The Death of the Novel and Other Stories*. New York: Dial Press, 1969.

———. *Doggy Bag: Hyperfictions*. Boulder, Colo.: Black Ice Books, 1994.

———. *The Endless Short Story*. New York: Fiction Collective, 1986.

———. *In Form: Digressions on the Act of Fiction*. Carbondale: Southern Illinois University Press. 1985.

———. "Introduction: The Dirty Secret." *Experimental Fiction*. Special issue of *Witness* 3.2/3 (Summer–Fall 1989): 7–9.

———. *Long Talking Bad Conditions Blues*. New York: Fiction Collective, 1979.

———. *Mosaic Man*. Normal, Ill.: Fiction Collective Two, 1999.

———. *Narralogues: Truth in Fictions*. Albany: State Univeristy of New York Press, 1999.

———. "The New Tradition." *Partisan Review* 39 (1972): 580–88. Rpt. in *In Form* 202–13.

———. *98.6*. New York: Fiction Collective, 1975.

———. *Out*. 1973.

———. "The Rival Tradition." Interview with Jack Foley. *FlashPoint* (Summer 1996): 1–12.

———. "Unwriting: Talmudic Fiction." *American Book Review* (December 1991–January 1992): 4, 26– 27.

———. *Up*. New York: Dial Press, 1968.

Unspeakable Practices: A Celebration of Iconoclastic American Fiction. Symposium held at Brown University, April 1988. *Critique: Studies in Contemporary Fiction*. 21.4 (Summer 1990): 233–75.

Voloshinov, V. N. *Marxism and the Philosophy of Language*. Trans. L. Matejka and I. R. Titunik. Cambridge, Mass.: Harvard University Press, 1986.

Down as Up, Out as In: Memoir as Manifesto

JR Foley

Down and In: Life in the Underground descends into a paradisal hell of sex, art, and money: plenty of the first two, none of the third—or . . . golden pots of it, if the media decide you make good copy, and the markets find you marketable.

Money is what you get for Selling Out. To Sell Out is to be a shmuck, "[a]n idolater of Things, a consumer at the feet of the Golden Calf" (12). So Not Selling Out was a big concern among anti-shmucks at Midwood High (Brooklyn, New York) in the late '40s. Newly arrived on middle-class Ocean Parkway from tough working-class Gravesend Avenue, young Ronny Sukenick had no particular politics beyond a raging annoyance with folk-singing, folk-dancing, and leftish-talking upwardly mobile doctors- and lawyers-to-be. "Every bright kid in Midwood in the middle of middle-class Brooklyn is campaigning his ass off for Henry Wallace" (13). But try debating in favor of socialized medicine! "You'd think I'd got up there and told them—ultimate insult—that they were 'bujwah.' " The hail of sarcasm and scorn drives the arriviste more than off-stage. In Brooklyn there might not have been much of an alternative to the "caution, conformity, and mercenary values" (12) of "those who assumed the moral superiority of leftish views while maintaining shmuck-materialist values about money, success, and sexuality" (17). But any "moderately well-informed kid around 1950" (12) knew that just across the Manhattan Bridge lay a Village where money was not important—and just as important, sex was not "a commodity you traded for marriage" (13). ("The value of art," says

Sukenick, "is taken for granted" (17).) So Ronny would light out for the Territory of MacDougal and Bleecker Streets—and with his ex-Yale Art School fellow anti-shmuck sister Gloria at the San Remo—drop down and into the underground.

But *Life in the Underground* as *Down and In* recounts it yields precious few biographical facts about Ronald Sukenick himself. He gives us enough to locate him at any particular time, and certainly makes us intimate with his attitude. Like Dos Passos in *USA*, however, he's essentially a Camera Eye—or, better, a voiceover listening to the answers of fellow subterraneans he focuses the Eye upon. ("I always seem to assume the position of an outsider looking in, even when looking in at outsiders" [14].) The book is actually a collective memoir, or "collective autobiographical experience . . . an experiential history out of which an art-literary movement came," and the point of the account is to "justify [that experience] as a legitimate creative sphere" (275).

It's a wonderful, enthralling read that succeeds in placing *l'hypocrite lecteur* vicariously at a crowded table in every dark teeming bar in 1940s–1960s Greenwich Village, eavesdropping on everyone, famous, brilliant, and otherwise.

The individual memoirists include the well-known: Allen Ginsberg, Gregory Corso, Judith Malina, Robert Creeley, Ted Joans, once-upon-a-time-Fugs Ed Sanders and Tuli Kupferberg, Diane Wakoski, Jackson MacLow. Like most underground denizens, though, more of the memoirists range from the less well-known (*Village Voice* writers Howard Smith, John Wilcock, and Ross Wetzsteon, performance artist Carolee Schneeman, poet-novelist-editor Carol Berge) to the obscure. (Supplementing live voices are anecdotes from the writings of Amiri Baraka, Diane Di Prima, Yuri Kapralov, Bill Amidon, and others.) Gloria Sukenick helps her brother remember the lower-than-obscure, all-but-forgotten—suicides most of them—whose self-obliteration shows both the rebellious risks and sometimes unforgiving consequences of rejecting the great world of the Golden Calf for the purity of marginalized resistance.

Although successful artists like Jackson Pollock can destroy themselves, too, the "myth of Bohemia," notes Sukenick, paraphrasing its 19th century chronicler, Henri Murger, "can be devastating for hangers-on who have no strong artistic vocation providing a purpose for that kind of life." Of one such suicide, Marilyn Duport, he writes that her problem: ". . . was that she needed not only to seek [her freedom] but to define it as well, requiring an open and experimental attitude toward experience as demanding as that which an artist, working at the cutting edge, must maintain toward his or her art" (63).

Defining freedom is, in part, what the collective voices of the underground here recorded are always doing. Sukenick orchestrates them for his own purposes; but noting the many failures of definition, he reflects: "When I discover the underground, I see it solely as an enclave providing the chance for a principled resistance to an unacceptable status quo. It will take some years for me to desentimentalize the underground, differentiate the interesting from the merely seedy, and begin to acknowledge its darker, unredeemed, infernal aspects. It might be argued that tapping the infernal is necessary to release the darker powers of consciousness that energize art, but not everyone is an artist and not everyone can handle it" (65).

Tapping the infernal without merely going to seed is a task Sukenick did not set himself in the early years; but defining freedom was very much a task, especially beyond the Village as he went off to Cornell and later Brandeis. Defining freedom is also inventing or reinventing identity, an ordeal for which the stakes only kept increasing for Sukenick on the one kind of campus, as well as for fellow subterraneans and artists on the other.

Guided by Gloria and others, the young Sukenick had observed how older habitues of the underground like Maxwell Bodenheim and Joe Gould coped with various challenges to identity. Living legends of the old *entre deux guerres* Bohemia, Bodenheim recited his poems for drinks, Gould flapped his arms and made sea gull cries . . . for drinks. What strikes Sukenick is the way these "bitter clowns" (in Seymour Krim's phrase) "throw themselves on the mercy of others, their willed destruction of pride, self-respect, and even ego itself. If you are seeking distinctions from the aggressive egoism of the 1950's success cult, Gould and Bodenheim are especially instructive examples."

But they represent only one end of the underground. At the opposite end, just five blocks to the east and north, stood the Cedar Tavern, nearly lightless retreat of the abstract expressionists on the verge of international fame, relaxing after a hard day at the studio, talking shop over beers. Jackson Pollock, Franz Kline, Hans Hofmann, Willem De Kooning, Joan Mitchell, many others. For the young Sukenick going to the Cedar for a beer "has . . . the power of a ritual that puts me in communion with the gods. I stand and watch the blur of activity, people talk to me casually, and though I have no idea who they are, I'm aware that, as in the Homeric epics, any disreputable-looking half-drunk bullshit artist might turn out to be an Abstract Expressionist Apollo, Dionysus, or even, hopefully, Aphrodite. You have the feeling that everything has become an open question that everybody is trying to answer at once from the bar up front to the wooden booths in back" (53).

The blur of people will soon not only catch the attention of *TIME-LIFE-LUCE*, and so the rest of American society—they will become to the world of art what America, since winning World War II, has become to the entire world. And not long after, commercial artists like James Rosenquist, Andy Warhol, and Jasper Johns will leave advertising behind, "moving successfully into serious painting, a development that helped fuzz the distinction between the art underground and the commercial mainstream" (55). And also pressed the underground toward a crisis of identity beyond the hopes or despair of the old bitter clowns.

At Cornell and especially Brandeis Sukenick faced a similar crisis. He assumed that "you had to live underground—lie, present a facade, never say what you really thought . . . *Nothing seemed possible.* We were scared and threatened and defiant" (77). He entered Brandeis ostensibly to earn a doctorate—actually, to continue his draft deferment—but also to sit at the feet of "precisely . . . the intellectuals I assumed were the vanguard of the underground, and whom I took to be in tune with my real self" (96).

Many of these vanguard intellectuals were refugees from the Nazis, like Herbert Marcuse and Abraham Maslow. But Sukenick was stunned to hear his teachers—Irving Howe and poet J. V. Cunningham in particular—try to persuade him to "choose security," because a writer's life was "precarious," and become "a good academic" (97) who writes on the side. It is best to quote Sukenick at length, as this is the core issue of the whole book.

> At stake here was that vague humunculus I chose to call my real self, independent of middle-class definitions of success and failure. This was the phenomenon vulgarized at the time as "identity crisis," but it was a real issue and it will remain a real issue. Is the American personality simply the sum of success-driven responses to the network of cultural pressures? Or is it the stubborn assertion of a virtuous independence, however unexamined? Horatio Alger or the Lone Ranger? Is there such a thing as a real self, and if there isn't, what makes life worth living? Consumption of products? Liberty and justice for clones? Social welfare for pods? . . . (97)
>
> . . . In the schizoid dialogue of the American psyche, the real self is Emersonian, passive, innocent, and spontaneous, while the public self needs to be aggressive, power oriented, and politic. . . . [T]he idea that it's sometimes better to be nega-

> tively capable than positively impotent was still news unless you happened to be a certain kind of artist. . . . (98)
>
> . . . I did not know yet that in America artists and intellectuals are necessarily different sorts of critters, committed to the schizy split that pits the real self against the public self, even when the two selves are part of the same psyche. A public self, insofar as it is divorced from the emotional life, which it puts to one side in the interests of calculation, policy, and power, can register feeling of any kind only in a limited way. In such a situation, the creative arts will always have a potentially subversive force, the more so the more they are innovative and unassimilated at the public level. The effect of such art can be disruptive and without regard to received ideas of what is right and good, as conservative critics and authoritarian regimes are well aware. American intellectuals have tended to be sociopolitical in orientation, and do their best to redirect the erotic force of art toward their concerns with good and bad, right and wrong. . . . (99)

The sudden media attention received by the abstract expressionists of the Cedar Tavern forced "real selves" to face the dilemma of "public selves" or at least public images thrust upon them by well-heeled nonartists who not only found them good copy but could smell the money in their paint. They were good copy in part because their work was already big money in the arts market and soaring fast. How the painters dealt with their own several identity crises is beyond the scope of this essay (or indeed of *Down and In*); and although Sukenick gives a good deal of reflection to how individuals in the next group of subterraneans, the Beats, dealt with their several shocks of fame, I pass over that, too. But one big difference between the abstract expressionists and the Beats is that the former were (passively) discovered, but the latter were actively self-promoted, certainly by Allen Ginsberg, himself a drop-out from an ad agency.

On the old question of selling out Ginsberg's attitude was quite fresh: "Selling out is one of those cornball ideas that people who didn't have anything to do got hung up on. I wouldn't have minded doing it if I could find what to sell out to. Geniuses don't sell out, in the sense that genius bursts the bounds of either selling out or not selling out" (122). His own advice, to Jack Kerouac in point of fact, was that "the less selfish course is to risk corruption by the world, sell out, and 'turn shit to gold' " (82).

Sukenick notes that, yes, there is "a difference between selling and selling out. . . . Why shouldn't everybody have the chance of buying into a good thing once it's discovered?" (39). Selling one's wares—paintings, poetry chapbooks, novels, songs—does not necessarily involve divorcing one's real self from a false but more marketable public self, or at least disguising one's real self in order to make the sale. Ginsberg is a fine illustration of real self *made* into public self—and that success certainly shattered the apparent market demand of the conformist 1950s to keep the underground self invisible. But that very success carries a new risk to the artist. If selling out is, in Steve Katz's definition, "doing something for someone else, rather than for yourself or your own vision" (239)—and Ginsberg certainly sang his own vision, not some sponsor's—the *succès de scandale* of flaunting a forbidden life-style may paradoxically betray the art anyway. ". . . [W]hen you start selling yourself, you may stop selling your art and wind up selling your life style" (39). (One can argue that Ginsberg managed to do both, but his own later self-assessment is severe: "I had my chance, and lost it. . . . Allen Ginsberg warns you: Don't follow my path to extinction!" ("After Lalon").)

Unlike the abstract expressionists who, despite their public success, avoided celebrity, Ginsberg sought it out, albeit on his own terms, and this for Sukenick represented a turning point in the development of the artistic underground in America. Eighty years earlier, in 1870s Paris, "a handful of clever entrepreneurs started a series of Bohemian cabarets whose function was basically to vend Bohemia to the middle class" (119). As Ginsberg and friends drew new media interest to Greenwich Village, tourists, merchandisers, and real estate speculators began pouring money into Bleecker Street, and raised rents as well as allergy to middle class values drove artists and writers, Sukenick among them, to the Lower East Side.

By this time Sukenick had made the choice confronting him at Brandeis. Although he continued to teach college from time to time, and dutifully completed his Ph.D. dissertation on Wallace Stevens (later published as *Wallace Stevens: Musing the Obscure*), he opted for the "precarious," dropped out of academic life, took a flat at East 12th Street and Avenue B, and resumed writing fiction.

> I . . . remember a sense of community during those days on the East Side. . . . The neighborhood was for a while the model of the American melting pot, polyglot with Poles, Jews, Ukrainians, Blacks, White Russians, Puerto Ricans, Italians, and us [writers, painters, underground film makers, perfor-

> mance artists, musicians], all willing to live and let live with, even, a certain amount of neighborliness. . . .
>
> When I start writing my first novel, *Up*, a book about the East Side that is a combination of autobiography and invention, I realize that that place and time is one in which we can in fact partly invent our autobiographies, in which life is not something imposed on us but a process in which we are creatively involved. The distinction between art and life in the book is reduced to a quibble of form only partly out of theoretical considerations. It's also a consequence of the kind of life that, after decades of alienation, we are finally positioned to lead. What critics don't realize when they foam, or even effervesce, about "Postmodernism" in fiction is that it did not come out of arbitrary literary considerations but out of a kind of life. It is a way of living in which you participate in a communal imagination, rather than having to struggle continuously with an intrusive public vision imposed by the mass market. "Use your imagination," I tell my students these days, "or someone else is going to use it for you." (149)

The smaller community of artists and writers found new places to meet (the Tenth Street Coffee House, Les Deux Megots, Stanley's) and perform (Café Le Metro, St. Mark's Church). They also found a common enterprise in "[d]issolving the boundaries between art and life": ". . . the breakdown of conventional limits for the imagination places art in the service of the actual, to the enrichment of both. In the hands of a skilled social critic an analysis of the part imagination plays in what we call reality helps demystify our experience. In the hands of an untutored teen-ager zonked on acid, or a monomaniac theoretician trapped by an idea, the results will be predictably vulgar" (149–50).

The general "push of the creative community [in the Lower East Side] to democratize high culture" also ran the risk of promoting vulgarization, with commercialism either close behind or leading the charge. This happened in several ways. The advent of the Hippies in the mid-1960s resulted directly from, and further stimulated, the mass media image of Village Bohemia:

> It's an exaggeration, but one that has truth, to say that the Hippies who were then beginning to drift into the East Village were picking up on the hedonistic side of the artist's life, elaborating on Beat culture, without themselves having the intense drive for accomplishment characteristic of the Beats

> or of any serious artist. These people were not interested in the artist's life—they were living as if art were life, given over to pleasure and excitement without practical consequences. This may have been partly the result of a too-literal take on the problematic relation between performer and audience, between art and life itself, that was one of the innovations to come out of the art of the sixties. In a nontraditional country like America, where art has constantly to justify itself, if art is too closely identified with life, one of the inevitable reactions you're going to get is "All right, if art is life, who needs art?" . . . (170)

One result of the advent of the Hippies was their increasing desperation to pay for drugs, and even bread, which led to the selling of whatever could be sold, ultimately their own bodies in prostitution. Although this was nothing new in the underground, never before had it happened on such a scale. Certainly the influx of Hippies upset the delicate symbiosis (or truce) of artists and locals on the Lower East Side; and to an extent Sukenick is clearly saying, "There went the neighborhood!" His attitude is not so simple, though, partly because he witnessed daily the human cost to the Hippies themselves, who in many ways relived what earlier immigrants to the neighborhood had suffered. Still, selling oneself remained the Ur-meaning of selling out; and in the larger picture Hippies represented a massive invasion of the margins by the mass market. But Sukenick sees the Hippies as more symptom than cause. What troubles him much more is what writers in particular had been doing for some time to undermine their own underground.

As early as 1957, if we use the publication of Kerouac's *On the Road* as a marker, the subterranean-as-hustler began emerging from the underground into the klieg lights of the marketplace. The type of this hustler for Sukenick is not Kerouac or even Ginsberg, but Norman Mailer—himself assuredly *not* a subterranean, but very much an apologist for the "white negro" hipster, as he saw him. Mailer materializes in *Down and In* whenever Sukenick speaks of the devil of playing to the market. What he objects to is the crafting and projecting of a public self, always keeping a weather eye on the marketplace. But he sees Mailer, too, as merely symptomatic. He quotes Seymour Krim's famous essay, "Making It!" (circa 1959–60), that "[m]iddle-class ideals of success once curled the lip of the intellectual; today he grins not, neither does he snide . . . The only enemy today is failure, failure, failure, and the only true friend is—success!" (112) (also in *What's* This *Cat's Story?: The Best of Seymour Krim*).

Emerging access to the bestseller list constituted one temptation to estrangement from the underground-as-refuge-from-the-middle-class. More subtle temptations also emerged. On the Lower East Side (already adopting a new Hippie name, the East Village), the cafe community of poets regrouped at St. Mark's Church as a stage and audience. "Poets became more like performers, even entertainers, rather than artists engaged in dialogue with other artists" (154). Show biz could not be far behind.

But when show biz arrived, it came not as anyone expected. It came, with startling twists, as Andy Warhol. ". . . Warhol's serial photo silk screens of Marilyn Monroe are about as sentimental as Fords coming off an assembly line, each one a different color but each one the same as every other. . . . Carolee Schneemann refers to his . . . vampiristic invention of art as commodity that was absolutely correct for the cultural moment, an art that was superficially available but that lacked the sacred quality of art that satisfies underlying human needs" (221–22).

Moreover:

> Warhol deflated the mystifications connected with high culture, but at the same time he devastated the adversary position of avant-garde art in relation to the middle class, the position that in America had generated the avant-garde's vitality, if not its reason for being. As [Peter] Schjeldahl says, "he was the prophet of the embrace, of the integration of the avant-garde and the middle class." There's also the point of view that, as a young artist who was part of his entourage says, "everyone took Andy seriously as an artist because he sold," a remark in itself indicative of the new criterion he promoted. (222)

Warhol did not promote in a vacuum; he thrived in a particular, hospitable setting which was all of hip New York City in a single bar/cafe called Max's Kansas City—known to intimates as The Store. It was a Store in every way—and although it was a place where the artists and writers of the underground sold themselves to reps and agents of the mainstream, the mainstream could never love it. But Sukenick did. "Part of the Max's scene was a quality Studio 54 would later pick up on that was alien to an artists' bar, so in a way what you liked about it was what you didn't like about it. *I must be doing something wrong*" (206). The whole narrative of *Down and In* leads us to The Store.

Lovingly but unsentimentally Sukenick evokes The Store from morning to night to very wee hours of next morning. His roving camera eye takes it all in. But it takes in a much larger picture, too.

> What was important for people . . . was image. For previous subterraneans, image was incidental to a vision of change in society and the self, while for these newer movements image was an end in itself. Insofar as the inner life was concerned, it was important only in order to exorcise it through a kind of ritualized psychodrama, whether in slam dancing or performance art. Image is safe because it's disembodied—you get around better as an image than you can as a self. It allows you flexibility and ironic distance, and it allows you to reject an idea without taking its alternative seriously either. . . . (270)

For Sukenick, the reduction of self to image is precisely what he's been fighting against since Cornell, if not since Midwood High; and in the marvelous circus of contradictions that is The Store he faces afresh the old underground crisis of identity. For he too, with the publication to rave reviews of his first novel, *Up*, has been propelled into imagehood as well, and he enjoys and plays with it even as he fears: "*I must be doing something wrong*" (198). If the example of Norman Mailer is the Bad Angel, there are also Good Angels like the Diggers, who (in the words of Peter Coyote) "did everything for free. We fed people for free, we got the crash pads and the medical clinics for free." As a result they became "free in a deeper sense" which could be harrowing: it "also meant no identity. The Diggers were always anonymous. . . ." (187)

Sukenick reflects that, "In a country such as ours, with a tenuous attachment to tradition, it is possible that concepts like 'free identity,' and 'twenty-four hour improvisational spontaneous self-creation,' are more than symptoms of a brief period of the underground, but stand against a culture in which the reality of self is constantly defined and redefined, and finally called into question, by the complex of exterior circumstance, by 'reality' " (198).

The implied challenge for Sukenick was to avoid selling out self like a Warhol "Superstar" on the one hand; avoid reducing self to a "bitter clown" like Maxwell Bodenheim and Joe Gould on the other; enjoy personal liberation (especially sexual), dealing honestly with all the consequences of that, pleasant and otherwise; and still, as a determined artist, complete important, innovative work . . . that won't make money.

Down and In is never mere nostalgia trip; it does not look backward only. In his extended reflection over the final chapters on The Store, Sukenick raises memoir to something very close to manifesto; indeed retro-charges everything that's gone before with the question of the underground as adversary culture. Defining what the underground was and how "adversary artists" must redefine or re-realize it in changing circumstances is what Sukenick has been orchestrating his subterranean voices to address.

Sukenick makes three large points: (1) the underground is independent, not alienated from mainstream culture; (2) it is inside, not outside, society; and (3) it's a stance, not a place.

> A cultural underground sustains the distinction between artistic achievement and worldly success. . . . The underground audience of peers and hip critics may not be disinterested, but it probably provides the most authentic consensus today for artistic success as such in a culture increasingly dominated by commercial factors. This is in part because an underground calls status quo values into question rather than reinforcing them, thus asserting an independence of judgment. An underground is neither necessarily a physical place nor a particular life style, but precisely this mutinous attitude. It is an attitude conspired in by dissidents inside the establishment and those at its fringes, without participating in the dependent duet with the middle class called alienation. . . . It is from this vantage point of difference, rather than alienation, that an underground serves as part of the conscience of a culture, and a culture may be measured by the degree to which it can accommodate such a critical force. . . . When an underground loses that kind of independence [and adversarial freedom] it is no longer an underground. (240)

Sukenick declares that "we can no longer pretend that the underground is positioned outside society. We now have to realize that no one is outside society. Even the most marginal minorities are conditioned by the social discourse, dropping out of which is not an option. You cannot drop out of that discourse, you can only change it. . . . There can be no simple opposition to culture, no transcendent perspective or language, no secure singular self-definition, for all find their meaning only within a social framework" (264–65).

Where, then, can you find the underground, post-Warhol?

> The drop-out must now be replaced by the hold-out, working stubbornly in the wasteland of the mass market, ruthless in his effort to define and dominate his appropriate territory.

> He (or she) is not on the make. Money is insufficient reward and celebrity is an insult. He may be a loner or not. The hold-out may prowl with a pack on the impoverished margins of the culture or he may emerge from within the heart of the establishment. . . . He may find refuge in the tenements of the city or the underground of the psyche. He uses whatever he can use, cultural guerilla tactics or lobbying and applied grantsmanship, to call into question the values of the status quo. An adversary culture must now acknowledge a more complex situation than it has faced heretofore, requiring more sophistication and less indulgence in image and flashy gestures of style. No more Lone Ranger, silver bullets, or white horses. The hold-out looks just like you, and could be you. (265–66)

Lest this sound like wishful thinking, Sukenick gets down to practicalities, albeit difficult ones. The first is: *organize.*

> . . . At the start of the seventies the squeeze was on . . . to neutralize creative life. From secret government suppression, as of the underground presses, to exclusion or co-optation, as of the literary arts, the situation left few options between surrender and organization. And, since the opportunity to organize was at hand, if you didn't do it, you knew somebody else would, maybe even some ghoul who actually enjoyed doing it, someone with culture commisar potential, or culture czar, as the case may be. In a country of organizations, it's hard to avoid them if you want to exert any amount of economic or political control over your creative life, rather than leaving it to people who have no idea about—or perhaps contempt for—what you're doing. And maybe the most important payoff of the effort of organization is the network of associations it produces, with its consequent broadening of cultural vision. (258)

There's an element of seizing the means of production in this. "Considering the process of production part of the reality of any work of art immediately resolves the schizoid conflict between purity of art and the experience out of which it comes" (274).

What Sukenick himself has done is help found the writer-controlled small press, Fiction Collective (now FC2), establish the *American Book Review* covering innovative fiction and poetry mainstream reviews ignore, participate on the Coordinating Council of Literary Magazines, teach, and do anything he can, not to raid the mass market, but rather "cultivate your own market" (269). "A creative community with its own criteria in resistance to the business establishment is essential to any kind of alternative culture. This quality is the minimal requirement for a culture underground" (273).

(In the 1980s, when he wrote *Down and In,* Sukenick did not consider the possibilities of the Internet for extending the "creative community" and cultivating "your own market" worldwide. But when those possibilities exploded in the 1990s, he was quick to take advantage. His observations as well as new work (and some old, like his second novel, *Out*) can be found at such websites as *Alt-X* (http://www.altx.com) and *FlashPøint* (http://www.flashpointmag.com).)

Ultimately *Down and In* is about going down and into "unconsciousness" (which Andrei Codrescu tells Sukenick is *the* "enemy") and wrestling it up to consciousness—wrestling the real self free of socially imposed, but unself-conscious, images of self. To the extent that *Down and In* is an Odyssean descent into the underworld of the underground of the 1940s, 1950s, and 1960s, the whole purpose is to seek directions for the present and the future of an adversary culture—not just for the "real selves" of Sukenick and friends but for "you," Hold-out Reader. So Sukenick takes readers down and in with him to seek directions together. Unlike the proclamations of the Futurists and other avant-garde art movements, this is manifesto by process. And the process is necessarily open-ended, the directions not definitive but suggestive, provocative. It is then for us, readers who would be artists, on our own to make our way . . . Up and Out.

Works Cited

Ginsberg, Allen. *Holy Soul Jelly Roll: Poems and Songs 1949–1993*. Los Angeles: Rhino Records, 1994

Krim, Seymour. *What's* This *Cat's Story?: The Best of Seymour Krim*. Ed. Peggy Brooks. New York: Paragon House, 1991.

Sukenick, Ronald. *Down and In: Life in the Underground*. New York: Macmillan, 1987.

———. *Up*. New York: Dial Press, 1968.

———. *Wallace Stevens: Musing the Obscure*. New York: New York University Press, 1967.

Exploring the Question of Values: An Interview with Ronald Sukenick

Larry McCaffery

Boulder, Colorado
September 30, 1999

Larry McCaffery: Your most recent book is entitled *Narralogues*. Could you talk a bit about the origins and meaning of this notion of "narralogues"?

Ronald Sukenick: Basically I wanted to write a book about the nature of "truth in fiction" (that's the book's subtitle) in a style combining narrative and dialogue. Its premise is that the more fruitful and useful way to look at narrative is as a kind of rhetoric. Rhetoric as a formal practice and conception is an entity that began to lose prestige during the nineteenth century because it got so overblown. For centuries before that, rhetoric was the main core of education and intellectual activity in the humanities, as well as being the main source of narrative until the novel and its concept of imitation took over. Actually, throughout the rise of the novel, you can see a basic conflict at work between the role of rhetoric and imitation. Several important early novels show this conflict very clearly: *Don Quixote*, for example, is clearly based on such a clash of rhetoric and mimesis, and in *Tristram Shandy* Laurence Sterne was working out of the rhetorical tradition he was grounded in as a preacher by exposing the pretenses and pretensions of the whole notion of representation. But gradually realism as a consumer artifact took over. The end result is that with postmodernism the usefulness of imitation as the basis for fiction has now collapsed. This being the case, it's now better to look at the rhetorical basis of fiction once again.

LM: What sorts of advantages does looking at narrative like this have?

RS: Rhetoric is argument and therefore once you accept that the novel is rhetorically based, then you're able to reestablish fiction as an intellectual activity.

LM:—As opposed to a static representation?

RS:—Or a dynamic representation, for that matter. My point isn't that representation isn't involved in the novel—it is—but that representation can't be the basic rubric of fiction. It's just another element like scope or plot.

LM: *Narralogues* includes sections written in different styles, though they all employ dialogue.

RS: Yeah—hence the name: narralogue. My intention all along was to integrate dialogue with other narrative modes. The first essay is a kind of joke—a deconstructing of deconstruction—but it begins in pure essay form. The next piece is pure Platonic dialogue but it's also specifically a *Jewish* Platonic dialogue that argues that the Platonic dialogue isn't appropriate for Jews. Then the next one is a combination of story and dialogue, and so on.

LM: Isn't basing a fictive aesthetic on argument taking the risk that readers are going to be turned off by didacticism?

RS: *Everything* is didactic. Faulkner and Hemingway are didactic. Detective stories are certainly didactic because they teach you that the world is a certain kind of place available to rational analysis and to a solution. Even the most formulaic, pot-boileresque romance novel imaginable has a message, usually just some lesson about how people should be acculturated, that's repeated endlessly because its been ingrained in the writers and the audience. That makes it really a form of mind-control, a closed loop that actively inhibits readers from thinking about any other option. So it's didactic. It's not a matter of eliminating didacticism, it's just that didactic qualities have been forgotten. It's like a vestigial part of literature: gone but still there. My point is, why not bring out that didactic level into an arena where authors and readers can argue and think about it?

LM: Did you conceive of these pieces with a specific sequence in mind—so that there would be some kind of "progression" to your overall argument? Or does the chapter order here mainly follow the order that you wrote them?

RS: They appear in a logical order, but the progression is based on formal principles rather than on developing an argument *per se*—that is, it's based on a movement from a reliance on traditional essay forms to pure fiction, with gradations between, so as you move through the book, you are advancing more and more out of essay into fiction.

LM: Why not present your ideas in a more traditional format?

RS: Because imitation has become corrupted by being taken over by the entertainment industry and the electronic media. We don't trust images anymore—at least I don't. Anybody who trusts images today is just a sucker. To take an extreme example, think about how untrustworthy the images were which people were shown throughout the managed reportage of the Iraq War. We heard that Saddam Hussein had released oil into the Persian Gulf that was killing all the seabirds, and we were shown pictures of seabirds gunked up with oil. Those images were certainly going to attract the attention of the ecologically concerned mind-set among us, but it was only later that we discovered that the televised pictures of the seabirds were just stock footage and not taken in the Persian Gulf at all. In other words, the images are, at best, phony, even for telling the truth, and at worst highly misleading and deceptive.

LM: Given the important role that images have always played in fiction, this corruption of images by the media, together with the resulting distrust people feel about them, would seem to have important consequences for fiction.

RS: Sure. And if images are now totally to be distrusted, then people are going to have to *think* about things rather than passively accepting whatever images the local media or CNN choose to broadcast. The notion of using rhetoric as the main basis of fiction seems especially important today because rhetoric is an *active* process (it grows out of speech making) rather than a process of passive acceptance. You can't write a book with a rhetorical basis on automatic pilot, you have to think—and the audience reading this kind of book also has to think instead of sitting back and being image-receptors. Another factor is that I've grown to think that the rhetoric underlying traditional notions of commentary is specifically Jewish as opposed to the Christian idea of imitation—the imitation of Christ as a model, for example. In fact, the idea of imitation is very important in Christian tradition generally. I'm not sure how to put this without being offensive, but this tradition is not as intellectually active as the process of Talmudic commentary. So I see what I'm doing as basically reclaiming my tradition. It's no accident there was such a high number of Jewish literary innovators who changed American fiction in the 1960s and 70s. Their work probably reflected a semiconscious or unconscious reversion to Jewish traditions, in which the graven image is forbidden and we instead have commentary.

LM: One of the key concepts you explore in *Narralogues* is Emerson's "transparent eyeball." Isn't there a contradiction between your attraction to this notion of a "transparent eyeball"—something providing human consciousness with a direct link (or perception) of the process it's seeing—and your pessimistic assessment that people have lost their trust in visual images?

RS: Emerson's transparent eyeball posits a direct link between consciousness and the real world, but it's a spiritual link rather than visual. Emerson was talking about the *visionary*, not about the visual—about how human consciousness relates to the phenomena of the real world, a part of the real world being in some sense spiritual. So there's no contradiction.

LM: Most writers today compose their works on a word processor. This shift away from the typewriter strikes me as being enormously important (it's certainly changed my own perception of what I'm doing when I'm writing). Word processors encourage writers to think of what they're doing as, well, *processing* or "assembling" words or texts. What's your own take on this topic? Do you agree that the process of writing on the computer screen is different from, say, the act of simply writing on a typewriter?

RS: Sure it is. Being able to move the words on the computer screen makes writing a very plastic activity analogous to the plasticity the visual arts have always been involved with. When you're writing on a computer screen, you can literally see how writing emerges from drawing as a graphic art. That's a very liberating feeling. I don't feel as if I'm struggling against the grain of the medium, the way I always used to with the typewriter. That struggle is now anachronistic. How can you "struggle" to do something that any word processor can take care of in a few seconds? It makes it easy to work with a new conception of the space of the page. Plus there is the sense that composition is temporally a collage process rather than a serial process.

LM: This exploration of the possibilities of using the page as a space that can be used for creating designs and other typographical experiments—and of generally taking advantage of the book's physical characteristics (what Butor referred to as "the book as object")—was one of the commonalties your early work shared with that of Federman, Katz, Gass, Barthelme, Michel Butor, LeClezio, and many others associated with postmodernism.

RS: My experiments with typography were mainly an outgrowth of reexamining representation generally. Especially early in my career, I was trying to work against the rigid formats imposed on most fiction in those days by trying to come up with new ideas for ways to use the space of the book and the page. And there's no question that word processors have made a huge difference in this regard. Just think of the tremendous amount of labor and ingenuity Ray Federman had to invest to create on his typewriter (and an old manual one at that!) all those elaborate patterns in those early books like *Double or Nothing* and *Take It or Leave It*. It took Ray several years just to type those goddam pages! But as complicated and fabulous as they are, those kinds of designs would be a cinch to do today on a computer, which really lends itself to that sort of thing, whereas the typewriter still basically demands people to think of writing as a left-right, top-to-the-bottom-of-the page process. My response to those arbitrary constraints has pretty much always been to work against these demands, so that you can see how writing has more capabilities as a graphics medium. The word processor just makes this a lot easier. The computer screen is a writing tablet on which I can do any number of things: I can hand write on the screen, I can draw pictures, insert photographs, or do all of these in combination with print. Maurice Roche, the French novelist who died a year or two ago, used to write books that relied not just on words, or even typographical designs, but on actual images to a certain extent. Rather than introducing his own images into his books, he tended to use typographical symbols in a limited way—drawings of skulls and things like that; and since he was a musician, he would also occasionally include musical scores in his line. If you were musically inclined you could whistle or hum part of his sentences. I don't know if that's an effective way of writing fiction, but it brings out the other side of writing—that is, when writing comes from drawing, it disappears again into music if you're using it poetically. The main thing about a computer is that its vast capacities for manipulating language and sounds make it perfectly self-evident that writing is, on the one hand, a kind of drawing and on the other, a kind of sound that you can make music out of. I've always considered myself as a novelist who uses language poetically; and in fact, I don't like the distinction between "poetic" and ordinary prose.

LM: As early as "The Death of the Novel," you had a character announce that the enormous upheavals we've undergone—not just in reality itself but also in the way we conceive of the world scientifically and philosophically—had already made the realistic-novel obsolete, unrealistic. And of course, these upheavals have only accelerated since then. As a writer seeking to present some truths about our contemporary world, what have been the most significant changes in the world or in the world of art and literature, since you began your career? Have these changes altered your task as a fiction writer?

RS: In terms of literature, art, and culture, the biggest and most positive side of what's happened since the War has been the shift away from art as an elite practice for an elite audience to art as a progressively more democratic, popular phenomenon. That change has unquestionably been very good for just about everybody involved. On the whole, however, the agents of that change didn't understand what they were dealing with—and they corrupted it. Andy Warhol destroyed a lot of crap that was coming out of the gallery scene, especially the mystique of the artist as macho and addict and all that shit, but he also shamelessly exploited his situation and turned it into pure commercialism; by the 1960s, his enormous popularity, financial success, and influence, not to mention his celebrityhood, had convinced a lot of artists that, for better or worse, they all now shared the same common horizon with Warhol—mass culture—and ultimately the same goal: to make money and court celebrity. In that sense, Warhol almost single handedly devastated the adversarial position of the avant-garde art in relation to the middle class, which had up until then had accepted the mythology of the avant-garde and consequently saw it as the ultimate source of artistic vitality and longevity. Warhol is only the most visible example of what happened to many other artists from that period. You can see the same commercialization of the avant-garde impulses just about everywhere—Norman Mailer's *Advertisements for Myself* is another famous example (the title pretty much says it all). There was a move away from the idea of high art to a democratization but at the loss of the integrity of art. Art got completely confused with the entertainment industry, which meant that it totally lost its adversarial position.

LM: One of the notions we shared when we started up the Black Ice Books series and began promoting the notion of avant-pop was to encourage writers to reanimate this adversarial position. But is it really possible for contemporary authors to enter into the belly of the pop-cultural beast without getting swallowed up by it?

RS: One approach, not mine, is to simply embrace it and forget about being oppositional. This expansion of the media since the 1950s hasn't been all bad—it's expanded people's concept of reality enormously and this seems like a good thing. It's been a liberating process that at best exposes or opens up more possibilities for life, for living, for interacting with other people, and provides other new options as well. But all this talk about the expansion of reality has to be balanced with the recognition that the *primary reality* for all humans still resides in the body—and that the body suffers and eventually dies. That's not an image or a media construct. It's a simple statement of fact.

I think that you and I are split on this issue. That was my complaint about your attachment to avant-pop as opposed to my attachment to avant-pop. I mean, I *like it* that Jello Biafra didn't know how to play any instruments when he started the Dead Kennedys—for the kind of music he wanted to create, he didn't need to. But on the other hand I wouldn't confuse Bruce Springsteen with Bach either.

LM: Actually, I'd say a more relevant comparison would be with Brahms. And I think you're entirely wrong to bring up the example of Springsteen as proof that I'm confusing entertainment and serious art—sure, Bruce is mighty entertaining, but he's also a serious artist (probably a more relevant comparison would be with Steinbeck). I'd argue that Springsteen may well be the *most* significant American artist of any kind during the past quarter century in terms of his contributions to rock music as an art form, the quality of his songs and albums, and his impact on audiences. But I suspect your opinion that my appreciation for Springsteen indicates a confusion between high and low culture isn't nearly as informed as it would be if I were obsessed with, say, Charlie Parker.

RS: That may be true—and I have to say that as long as Bach is the criteria, Charlie Parker has his moments. But leaving aside your situation, I'm disturbed to see that for the most part this sort of criteria—in fact just about *any* sense of criteria—has been eroded, even lost completely. There's no authority in the art world today (and when I say the "art world," I mean all the arts, literature included) and there's a total lack of conscience and morality; it's become a scene without credibility and without culture. I know that there are efforts to recuperate that situation, especially in the graphic arts and through the women's movement, through conceptual art and through phenomena like the Gorilla Girls. I like their impulse but I don't like that kind of solution because it reduces art to propaganda.

LM: Even the term "propaganda" implies a diminished capacity to function as serious art. And certainly you can't judge a work's greatness on the basis of "content," no matter how admirable or disgusting that content is.

RS: That's why an artist like Celine, who's a son of a bitch and whose message is morally and politically disgusting, can still be called a great artist. The morality of art functions at a different level from the obvious message level. Celine's genius partly has to do with the way his work wound up changing the very grammar of the French language. Or take the case of painting: it's a medium concerned with how we see, so you could conceivably have a great painter who produces admiring works about the Nazis—a situation not at all unlike Celine's.

LM: Leni Riefenstahl would be an analogous example.

RS: Yeah, Leni Riefenstahl is a perfect example: the obvious Nazi message in her films is not what ultimately counts, although it's also important to remember that her content *does* count. Like you just said: content is always a factor in any work of art—it's just not the *basic factor* in judging a work's greatness. Of course, to one degree or other, there are going to be times when immediate social pressures dictate your responses to art. I'm sure I would have boycotted Celine during World War II while the death camps were operating and he was being such a dedicated Nazi. I'm just bringing up Celine as an extreme example to show that the criteria for art, even among the most well intentioned artists (and there are precious few of those anyway), are other than the obvious "content" of their work. All of this is complicated by the fact that in a broader view an art work is of course all content, and that ultimately style/form is just a way of discovering new content. Right now we seem to be in a disastrous transition period from restrictive or elitist criteria to no criteria at all. As a result, what we badly need these days is a reevaluation of values.

LM: What sort of values do you have in mind—moral, social, aesthetic?

RS: To the extent that art opens up new experiences for its audience, it's valuable. But even more important is the ability of art to offer audiences new ways of thinking about things and expressing those thoughts.

LM: The democratization of art and culture seems related to the attack on the canon that's been occurring within the academy recently. It often also reveals a widespread absence in universities today of any means of judging artistic value other than via political, gender, or racial correctness.

RS: I agree that most people in universities have no way to judge anything other than on commercial or political criteria. I'm constantly shocked by the vulgarity of the judgments made by my non-specialist colleagues whenever they have to confront so-called postmodernist fiction or whatever you want to call "edge-work" of our era. More often than not, their discussion winds up talking about current best-sellers. That wouldn't have happened in the sixties, perhaps for the wrong reasons. There's a kind of snobbism about liking Joyce and Beckett, and it's true that Joyce and Beckett aren't available to the common reader—which is why universities should be making more of an effort to get their students to read them.

I'd like us to talk about that article you wrote for *American Book Review*[1] where you basically said your idea of solving the problem of where postmodernism has taken us is by returning to modernism. I can understand how you got to that position, but I think your idea is definitely the wrong track.

LM: That *American Book Review* article grew out of my growing disillusionment, disgust even, with the way the P-word has evolved over the years. This recent brand of "postmodernism" has very little to do with the kinds of serious, formally daring works I had been using the P-phrase to describe back in the mid-1970s; back then I associated "postmodernism" with a general reaction against the traditions and aesthetic assumptions associated with High Modernism—whose innovations had themselves begun to feel oppressive to artists by the 1960s. But by the late 1980s, pomo had been hijacked by semioticians and critical theorists like Lyotard and Baudrillard and by Marxists like Fredric Jameson, who began using the term to describe a much broader shift in post-World War II Western culture that included everything from the loss of "grand narratives," Baudrillard's "Precession of Simulacra," and (the most influential of all), Jameson's "cultural logic of late capitalism." These guys all seemed to share the view that the rise of the media culture, along with the impact of hyperconsumerism, had essentially resulted in a culture of bewildering profusion, excess, confusion, and an aesthetic based on the random interplay of images and texts (often ones cannibalized from other contexts) that were highly stimulating (though, as Burroughs pointed out back in the 1950s, they were also highly addictive). Once deconstruction seemed to demonstrate that all values and explanations are culturally based, you've got a lot of artists and tenure track professors deciding to ride this wave of relativism to fame, fortune, or promotion. For instance, right now you've got a lot of literary and cultural critics arguing that the quintessential contemporary example of postmodernist art is advertising—all the jagged cuts and pastiching of prior forms, all the fancy technical stuff visually allow ads to seduce people with fifteen or twenty seconds of vivid but ultimately meaningless sensory input whose only function is to grab our attention momentarily to sell us something. Well, okay, fine, maybe this *is* the way to define pomo aesthetic practices—but ultimately this brand of pomo has no coherency, no morality, no real aesthetic purpose beyond that of grabbing people's attention.

There was also a set of deeply pessimistic sub-themes to most of these theorists—an emphasis on philosophical skepticism, indeterminacy, a loss of confidence in any system of belief, Jameson's insistence that we now live in a world where people literally have no egos, where schizophrenia is the norm due to the "breakdown of the signifier chain," and where the recent rise of the culture industry has succeeded in infiltrating even people's imaginations and unconscious. Not to mention, of course, an almost gleeful joy in the whole process of "deconstructing" any system of thought they could get their hands on. Now some of this deconstructive impulse had some relevance to the earlier postmodernist attack on the status quo, on dogmas of all kinds, including not only politics and social issues, but literary dogmas like "realism." But there's a crucial difference—there was something grandly ambitious and optimistic about that first wave of postmodernist experimentation, and despite all of its emphasis on dismantling the assumptions of the Modernists, there was also a "reconstructive" impulse that was just as crucial, some recognition that new values, new set of aesthetic assumptions would have to be erected after everything had been torn down. So while there were plenty of satire, anger, and outrage at the insanity, brutality, and banality we had inflicted on ourselves, there was also an exhilarating sense in that these dogmas could be replaced by more flexible systems, that new literary models were being invented to replace outmoded ones.

But today's version of postmodernism is mainly associated with a kind of radical relativism and trendy nihilism—a pluralism so thoroughgoing that it's capable of embracing any cultural product but incapable of making any judgments about its moral or aesthetic values. If anything, postmodernism today seems basically a synonym for decadence, or a rationalization for not having values, for refusing to make judgments, for abandoning any set of criteria and instead just joyfully accepting the free play of signifiers. Now there's a niche for artists who employ randomness and chaos as formal methods (Cage, Burroughs, dada, etc.), but pomo artists often seem to employ these strategies because they don't want to bother going through the process of drawing conclusions or arranging the elements of their works into coherent patterns.

RS: I agree with most of what you said there, but how is a return to modernism going to solve anything? There's no going back to the culture that modernism came out of. And the avant-garde is also completely dead at this point—or if not dead, then it's become just another product, another commodity.

LM: My call wasn't for a return to modernist culture but to its basic assumption that it was still possible, even necessary, for artists to create new models and lingoes and formal methods, capable of representing and making sense of this new world we're living in—this despite all the massive changes in peoples lives and understanding, and despite the personal and cultural confusions these changes have wrought. Otherwise you wind up with the despairing attitude the P-word is associated with today—trendy nihilism and radical relativism.

RS: A slightly different take on why we need to dispense with the notion of postmodernism is because it's been commodified. Look at what happened with the recent *Norton Anthology of Postmodernism*—the editors took the term to be the mark of a generation rather than the mark of an idea and so consequently, I'm left out of it, Federman is left out of it, Katz is left out of it, and a lot of other people don't show up. Yet another example of how the whole notion of postmodernism has been totally corrupted. At any rate, most writers I know today seem completely demoralized by having to write in a literary scene of know-nothing workshoppery and of crass, conglomerate-owned commercial publishers who no longer have any interest in serious fiction. To make things worse, the productive literary community of writers and critics who created postmodernism in this country has splintered into factions. I've been shocked recently by the alarming amount of name-calling, in-fighting and thinly disguised personal attacks (including several aimed directly at me) that we've seen lately by people who were once part of the community of writers and critics who helped launch postmodernism. I guess we've all been guilty at some point of negative gestures, but there's no excuse for the sort of mean-spirited, deliberately vindictive attacks I've experienced in just the past few months from people I once felt a connection with. I'm referring, for example, to Jerry Klinkowitz attacking the Fiction Collective (and me personally) in his review of the new FC2 *Into the Slipstream* anthology, and John O'Brien attacking Klinkowitz in *Review of Contemporary Fiction* and then getting back at me for defending Klinkowitz by killing a favorable review of *Mosaic Man*—I mean, how petty can you get? Finally there was Kostelanetz's ad hominum attack on Charles Bernstein in a recent *American Book Review*. These things aren't particularly earth-shattering, but the fact that they all originated from people I once felt some kinship with has hit me pretty hard.

LM: What's responsible for this breakdown of the literary community?

RS: It's traceable to this lack of core values we've been discussing. When those disappear, people lose a sense of connections with other people. Back when postmodernism was just emerging, a lot of us felt we were part of real change that was taking place in literature; it wasn't so much a matter of being "influenced" by each other, or even sharing specific innovative practices, as sharing a sense that we were all contributing our part to produce this change. Today that sense of shared goals, a sense of direction has changed. Nobody knows which direction to move in anymore, and so most people move in the most convenient direction by knee-jerk reactions. Therefore the most important thing for writers to do right now is to go off on a hunt for what is in fact valuable, something that can legitimately hold us together. In the years that are left to me, I see my main job as exploring the question of values, where they come from, how they're created, and how we can get in touch with them again. That was one of the underlying impulses behind *Narralogues*.

LM: Pomo's connection with the ascendancy of theory and cultural studies has unfortunately seemed to marginalize the actual reading and study of literature. It's as if everyone has been so busy promoting and analyzing the interlocking aspects of theory needed to sustain their version of the term that they don't have the time anymore to read and write about postmodern literature. It's revealing that probably the most influential critic of postmodernism—Fredric Jameson—is primarily nonliterary based.

RS: Jameson is very smart and a good writer about some aspects of contemporary culture—but I'd argue that he's basically proposing a version of postmodernism that he can dislike. And when it comes to fiction, I don't think he knows what he's talking about; in fact, his preferred form is fairly conventional, realistic fiction. But his idea of the political unconscious is a very useful concept that has played a part in helping us understand what's been involved in the commodification of postmodernism. A good example of this involves the one negative review *Mosaic Man* received (and it was viciously negative) which appeared in *Publishers Weekly*; when I saw it, it was transparent what was going on: the review had obviously been written by a neocon who was highly irritated and irritable about just about everything in the book. Finally at the end the reviewer remarked something about Sukenick and "his left wing ideas"—meaning that there's a political component to postmodernism that is very close to the surface. It's taken for granted by the right that postmodernism is associated with the left but meanwhile the left has washed its hands of anything avant-garde in any contemporary sense. The end result is that postmodernism winds up being caught between the two opposing political forces, between the left and the right, and has thus been politically castrated.

LM: Your work has always struck me as being *extremely* political . . .

RS: It's deeply political but a lot of critics don't pick up on this because it's not the sort of politics reducible to dogma or simple left-wing/right-wing oppositions. It's what I call "no-wing." Anybody who takes the point of view of *The Nation* for gospel is a sucker to begin with. Now I read *The Nation* regularly, and I'm grateful for its reportage; it's an indispensable publication. But after awhile you begin to see that you can write an issue of *The Nation* yourself—it's that formulaic. It's as much a part of the New York establishment as the neocon publications are. It's all coming out of the same ideological matrix, and the people writing for them get infuriated if you're "no-wing." So I can't win—my work winds up getting attacked from the left and from the right.

LM: Irrespective of its obvious political "content," the formal processes that your writing has been embedded in—and the different kinds of liberations implied by these methods—seem *deeply* political. I'm thinking, for instance, of your emphasis on process, improvisation, a willingness to explore the self and its relationship to the world, not in terms of some kind of pre-determined narrative structure but in the process of the free-play of the imagination. Those all suggest a model of thinking that encourages people to approach life more creatively, to move outside the usual sources of control and exercise their own imaginations.

RS: It's no coincidence that the first thing that's controlled in a blatantly oppressive totalitarian regime is thought—or that the beginning of this process always involves censorship of the arts. Just to illustrate on a practical level what's going on in this country, a Fiction Collective author was told by a high-up official in the National Endowment for the Arts not to bother applying for N.E.A. grants again because the FC2 was never going to get another one. That's due to that Congressional flap over alleged N.E.A. funding for my book, *Doggy Bag*, Doug Rice's *Blood of Mugwump* book, Jeffery Deshell's *S&M*, and Rob Hardin's *Distorture*.

LM: I suppose we should be thankful they didn't notice we had published Samuel Delany's *Hogg*. That would have *really* sent Jesse Helms into a tizzy.

RS: No doubt—even though *Hogg*, which is much more shocking and transgressive than the Black Ice Books the Congressmen attacked, is much more sensitive too. But it's probably no accident that *Hogg* didn't get attacked. Delaney is black and he's gay, and the people in Washington know that those two big pressure groups will fight back. Meanwhile, us poor white males are left sort of defenseless! I'm just joking but there's not a concentrated lobbying group behind us that can get riled up. But these N.E.A.'s threats amount to what is defacto censorship. You can't run a publishing company without money, and you can't run a non-profit organization without somebody giving you money, which is what the N.E.A. is presumably in business to do. A current dispute in New York illustrates the way the left and the right are both being nullified. There's a British exhibition which opened at the Brooklyn Museum last week which is very shocking. It contains things like pigs sawed in half and preserved in formaldehyde, slightly rotting sharks, and other grisly, gruesome stuff whose message seems to be that "art is shock." This exhibition had already created a big scandal in England, but the show went on, as they say, and got a lot of note. When Giuliani got wind that the exhibition included one guy's works featuring the Virgin Mary smeared with elephant dung, he immediately threatened to withdraw all funding from the Brooklyn Museum (which I think gets a third of its funding from the city); furthermore he said he'd withdraw its museum license so the show could not go on. Giuliani has been extremely stupid about this, to the point where the *New York Times* wrote an editorial saying that a cultivated city like New York is being made a fool of by his vulgarity. On the other hand, this is not a show I would go to see.

LM: You don't feel that shock is a legitimate artistic value in and of itself?

RS: I don't like to be shocked to no purpose. I haven't seen this exhibit so I can't really say for sure, but there are some things you can make prior judgments about. I feel that art should include among its tools the ability to shock when shock is legitimately appropriate for an artwork. I certainly use shock this way msyelf. But I don't like *gratuitous* shock—which is what I gather this Brooklyn show is about. I also note that the show comes from the collection of one of the Saatchi brothers who is among the biggest advertising moguls in the world; he has the power to create artistic commodities more than perhaps any other person in the world except maybe the head of the Modern Museum. I'm exaggerating, but my point is that this isn't a left-right dispute; you don't choose sides because both sides stink. I can no more endorse Giuliani's attitude than I can endorse what this "avant-garde" exhibition has come to via its commodification by one of the biggest, if not *the* biggest, advertising firms in the world. What it's come to is literally art as advertising.

LM: I suspect a lot of readers are going to be shocked by the chapter in *Narralogues* that begins something like, "I think it's a good idea for professors to sleep with their students."

RS: I was deliberately making fun of the whole p.c. mind-set there, but I also wanted to make the serious point that sometimes affairs between professors and students work out just fine. I used to know a guy (I won't mention who or where) who was chair of an English department who said that he'd fire anybody if he ever got any hint he was going out with a student. But this department chair himself had married one of his students, so what the fuck was he talking about? These affairs can wind up being as fruitful as any other kind, and in fact a lot of teachers marry their students. That's not to say there aren't unfortunate incidents or that you shouldn't have strict guidelines so that students understand their rights and know what to do if one of their teachers starts harassing them. There are cads around who take advantage of their situation but, hey, you can't prevent cads from being around. That's just part of life. I know of cases where professors proposed sleeping with students for grades, but I also know of cases where students proposed sleeping with professors for grades. So the exploitation sometimes is mutual, or it can go either way. But there's also instances where it's not exploitation at all. Sexual harassment educational meetings have been held here at the Boulder campus that everybody is supposed to attend or risk getting a bad letter in your file. I didn't know whether to be flattered or insulted about being required to do this, but I haven't gone because I figure that at age 67 my harassment days are over.

LM: Another point to be made here is something you've referred to frequently in your books—that knowledge and wisdom aren't just a function of the mind but are connected to the sexual too.

RS: Yes, of course. Having sex is one of the best ways to learn.

LM: There seems to have been an "extremity progression" occurring in most of the "edgy" art forms (rock, horror films, pornography, and so on) ever since the 1960s. Somebody comes along who manages to shock people by pushing the envelope in terms of sexual explicitness or violence, and then it's just a matter of waiting around until the next guy figures out how to up the ante. I mean, Elvis shocked the hell out of people back in the mid-1950s, but during the 1960s it took the Stones and then the Doors, Jimmy Hendrix, and the Velvet Underground to produce an equivalent effect on that generation; by the early 1970s, you've got the Stooges and David Bowie laying the groundwork for punk and rap, which upped the ante even more. That direction seems to be a dead-end for rock (though I'll admit that I was genuinely shocked in the early 1990s when I went to a club and saw G. G. Allen take a shit on stage—but Allen was less into the aesthetic of extremity than he was suicidal).

RS: Let me fill in a little. I'd say that this progression actually began happening back in the 1950s after the rise of the abstract expressionists and their eventual commodification. That removal of criteria you found with the abstract expressionists pretty much set the whole scene, even though a lot of people today associate this lack of criteria with the conceptual artists, the pop artists and everybody starting with Warhol and that art dealer, Leo Castelli, who made the pop art movement. Once the art world accepted the idea that they no longer needed criteria—even *bad* criteria—as a basis for judging a work's worth, then the stage is set for the avant-garde's descent during the 1960s into a kind of personality cult and sheer egomania. At that point, the art hustle became more a matter of celebrity than of art. You can see this in the career of Basquiat, who toward the end of his life wound up (not by accident) becoming associated with Warhol; at the height of his career, Basquiat was complaining that his agent or gallery was grabbing his canvases before he finished them. Basquiat was a spectacular figure and a genius at personal publicity, but you could already see the art world moving in that direction back in the early 1950s, when the abstract expressionists became such successes after they were cultified.

LM: Wasn't the avant-garde already being appropriated and cultified back during the early days of Modernism just as surely it was during the 1950s and 1960s? French razor blade companies were already using cubist imagery in their ads within less than a year or so after Picasso and Braque began to make names for themselves.

RS: That's quite true. I personally think Picasso's genius is overrated and his work often terribly repetitive, but there's no denying he was also a publicity genius. So were the Dadaists and surrealists, but nobody was of Picasso's caliber. But that was a different situation because there you had artists who were not kowtowing to the culture nor being used by the culture. You had artists aggressively staking out ideological and artistic positions and functioning as public intellectuals within a strong intellectual tradition that was far more powerful than the bourgeois establishment in the long run. We don't have that in the States. Over here, art is not taken seriously, and to that extent, artists and intellectuals here are at odds with each other. Our intellectuals, especially left-wing intellectuals, just make things worse because, while they pay lip service to art, they really hate or despise it because they think it's not about important political issues.

LM: Doesn't the ever-accelerating ability of The System to instantaneously appropriate even the most radical artistic gestures and then download it into the soundtrack for the next Nike ad make it increasingly difficult for artists to establish any sort of oppositional status vis a vis the establishment? Or is that even relevant to you at this point?

RS: Well, if I haven't been co-opted by now I don't think I'll ever be. But there are still certain things that the commercial culture can't digest and rejects because they can't fit it in. It's very hard for the system to fit the thoughtful, the meditative, the sensitive, and (if I may use this word) the spiritual into the system of commodification because these qualities are basically unreifiable—"anti-commodities," you might say. One of the good impulses in the installation and conceptual art movements is that they're searching for things that can't be co-opted. Conceptual art actually began as a revolt against the gallery system's whole "what-are-we going-to-show, there's-nothing-to-show" attitude, which reduced art to something like a Hollywood treatment—you know: give it to me in one sentence and *that's* what it's about—so in the end, it was easy to co-opt.

LM: You've been spending part of each year in France recently, and I'm wondering if you've sensed that the global rise of mass media hasn't begun to erode the sort of intellectual tradition and appreciation for what the avant-garde does that one associates with France and Europe generally.

RS: There is still a strong tradition of making you think in European art that doesn't exist in the States, which is something we need to capture and learn how to use. Americans tend to see artists (if we recognize them at all) as celebrities to be gossiped about, but basically artists are simply marginalized as public figures who might have something important to say. That's a shame. Artists-as-intellectuals have more arrows in their quiver than intellectuals per se because they have more than rational intelligence available to pursue their ends. The best example I can think of as the artist-as-intellectual-and-social critic was Joseph Beuys, who did it with interactive works with art-as-message but not necessarily through propaganda. As I've said, art-as-propaganda simply doesn't interest me. I like Lucy Lippard's work and her impulses, but I'm also turned off by her didacticism. Right now I'm reading a book by a woman named Deborah Haynes, which is largely about religion and art and is trying to reactivate the concept of the spiritual and art. I see eye to eye with her about that, but I don't like her examples because she's of that generation that deals in installations, earth art, and other things related to that, such as conceptual art. Her notion of the political influence of art also verges on being crude in that it verges too close to propaganda.

LM: How does this criticism you're leveling at the artist-as-cult (or celebrity) phenomenon relate to the admiration you've expressed to me several times for someone like Allen Ginsberg, who was also very successful as a self-promoter.

RS: Ginsberg is one of the pivotal figures in the American scene for all kinds of reasons. He once told me that he never wanted to be an outsider; in fact he had always really wanted to be an insider—it was just that the inside wouldn't let him in. That's disputable (it certainly seems a distortion of his own history), but, in any case, he was clearly ambitious from the word go and he was an object of great suspicion in the New York poetry scene for that.

LM: In *Down and In* you wrote about that period during the 1930s and 1940s when the notion of the artist living totally outside the mainstream, disdaining its attention, and so forth, was part of the whole mythology about the truly dedicated artist.

RS: Yeah, exactly. Then Ginsberg and Warhol and Mailer came along and split open that whole mythology. But even though Ginsberg helped create the new myth of the artist as celebrity, what saved Allen personally was his generosity. He was always willing to pull everybody he liked and admired along. Because he was a great networker himself and incredibly organized, he always seemed to be able to put you in touch with the right people at the right time anywhere in the world. He had prodigious files, and if he heard you were going to Czechoslovakia, he'd say, "You want to meet someone in Czechoslovakia? Go see *this* guy—he translates Burroughs! You want to see somebody in Moscow? Here's an address." He had it all at his fingertips. He spent some time in advertising, too, as Warhol did (in fact, Warhol had a whole successful career in advertising before he made it big with the Pop Art scene). But Allen wasn't *just* a self-promoter and networker, he also had ideals he really believed in and wanted to live up to. For example, he went to a lot of trouble to research the CIA's involvement in the drug trade and produced a book by the New York P.E.N. Club about how the alternative newspapers were being smashed by a combination of establishment police units, the FBI, local police, red squads, and so on. It's a classic book, heavily documented, and utterly convincing. And let's not forget that Allen came out of a very Jewish, left-wing, communist family background and that he remained true to that old-style counter-establishment mentality his whole life. There's a huge and telling difference between Ginsberg and some guy coming out of today's postmodern scene who doesn't really have any ideal other than wanting to be a big success. Now this postmodern guy may have Ginsberg's drive for celebrityhood, but he hasn't got the idealism and generosity of spirit Allen had to balance off his thirst for celebrity.

LM: One lesson you taught me early on is that there's nothing wrong with an artist or even a critic doing self-promotion.

RS: Yes, although this depends on how the self promotion is being done and its basis. I've been doing a lot of it lately myself to help get people interested in *Mosaic Man* and *Narralogues*. Most writers have to do some of this because the publishing industry doesn't do it for you anymore; that's true even with the big houses, of which there are now a grand total of six left if you're counting conglomerates in New York. The publishers save their resources for the blockbusters, while all the rest of us have to either get the word out ourselves or risk having the book never being heard of again. What's involved is really not so much a question of "self-promotion," which has a nasty ring to it, like you're trying to hype something that isn't worth a shit, but simply of getting your books to the right audience. Before an author is in a position to do that, he's got a lot of layers of resistance to get through commercially, starting with being able to identify your audience. By the way, I've discovered that the Internet is a great tool to do just that. You can reach so-called niche audiences at low cost—basically the cost of the labor. But as much as this promotion business is necessary for individual artists, it's also only a secondary consideration. What we really need more of right now is less self-promotion and more people who are actually *thinking* about what they're doing. Because people who supposedly want to be serious artists today have totally lost track of what they're supposed to be doing. They go directly from idea to promotion and skip all the intermediate steps—like the actual creation of serious art in the first place. To their mind, the whole process is very simple: first comes the idea, then how you package it, then how you sell it. That's all there is to it—certainly a lot easier than having to ponder any considerations as to the morality, the spirituality, the quality of the work, etc., etc. That's what I have against conceptual art, by the way: it's not worked through; it's just an idea that functions on the same level of promotion, except that it's counter-promotion. That's a good way to put it: conceptual art is counter-promotion. A slogan I thought up at lunch that is apropos here goes like this: "If it doesn't make you think, it's entertainment."

LM: Your work was often said to be "un-" or "anti-realistic" when it began appearing back in the 1960s. And yet your books have always seened in tune with emerging paradigms about reality as a dynamic process rather than as something made of discrete elements than can be represented via the usual notions of imitation, linearity, causality, etc. Maybe that makes your work more "realistic" than so-called realistic fiction.

RS: I like to think so. In terms of my understanding of scientific paradigms, I've picked up some ideas in various places, but I can't claim to understand a lot of the concepts or know if they're really in line with the actual models proposed by the physical sciences. My work has never grown out of any deep understanding of science or philosophy, or even psychology or the social sciences; the key for me has always been to write strictly at the level of language, sentence by sentence, since that's the way I perceive. I'd also argue that what we've been calling "postmodern" is really what we might call "pre-rhetorical." We could look at the whole movement of contemporary French criticism as constituting a rediscovery of rhetoric without the Frenchies knowing what they were discovering. But at least in France, there's been an emphasis on the way language is used that intersects with a level of social utility. Baudrillard, for example, recognizes the way language is used as a power ploy in class warfare and in social organization. That attempt to correct this sort of manipulation grew out of the deconstruction movement, despite its excesses and mystifying language. So French deconstruction provides a key tool for repairing the social mechanism via language; language is not the *only* tool—and certainly in France things have usually happened by revolution rather than rhetorical persuasion—but it's an important one.

LM: One specific way your books operate at this level of language is your use of puns to generate "movement" from one moment (or sentence) to the next.

RS: The way I approach language to crack it open to reveal what's there. Puns are just one of the most obvious ways of cracking language open. I believe along with some strands of the deconstruction movement that we're spoken by language rather than language speaking us. It's the language that contains all of the information, all of the collective wisdom of human experience, so if you open it up, you discover things that you didn't know were there before.

LM: Your use of puns seems related to the distinction you make in *Narralogues* between play (which is open-ended, chaotic) and games (which have rules and specific ends). Punning seems to be a perfect example of play because it's such an unpredictable process—you don't know where one word is going to take you.

RS: Right. That difference between play and game is an important distinction. Game is like a ritual acting out a fear of death. When you play a game, somebody always wins and somebody loses, so it's like dying. Play is a more creative activity that has no end point; it exists purely on a level of fun and even celebration. Play is literally endless: you can play forever.

LM: There's an analogy, too, between your use of puns and the way you employ pop-cultural icons almost as open-ended signifiers that act as springboards for your imagination. So in *Mosaic Man*, you use a figure like Elvis not as a static icon but as an image containing all sorts of other associations that need to be let out, released.

RS: Any artist who takes pop images at face value is utterly lost. That's part of why my work has always been based on rhetorical play. Even *Up* comes pretty heavily out of Joyce and various other modernists, but it also comes out of Sterne and Henry Miller, whose books were grounded within the rhetorical tradition—in fact, Henry Miller would be one of my prime examples of a modern rhetorician. Mark Twain would be another example. Come to think of it, perhaps this is the difference between what some people call the romance as opposed to the novel. Melville and Twain are highly rhetorical writers (what book is more rhetorical than *Moby Dick*?). And Twain took great care and pride in examining the language of different kinds of rhetoric in the United States and cataloging them; in fact, there's a beginning note to *Huckleberry Finn* where he indicates this. Hawthorne not so much, although he was maybe the tamest of those three from a formal standpoint. Poe also functions on a level of high rhetoric and Faulkner as well. My theory for why Faulkner is such a rhetorical writer is that the tradition of rhetoric was preserved in the South because the South was outside industrial culture for a long time and had close relations to Europe, especially France. Even into my youth, in politics there was the paradigm of the Southern Senator who gave endless Fourth of July speeches in exalted rhetoric. This seemed to be specifically a Southern rhetorical tradition that Faulkner picked up on, and in my opinion, it accounts for his best work.

While I'm thinking of it, I noticed that *Up* was the only one of my books you included in your *American Book Review* list of this century's top hundred novels.[2] It just occurred to me that maybe the reason you still like *Up* best of all my books is that its sensibility is still about half modernist, while the other half was into something new.

LM: I included *Up* there mainly because it had such a big impact on me and my thinking about metafiction back in the 1970s. The reason my favorite book of yours—*Mosaic Man*—didn't make the list was that I had only read the early drafts you showed me when I was making up the list.

RS: You saw it in the very early stages, and it's very different now. A lot of editing went into *Mosaic Man*. I got a lot of good advice on it, including your input. A lot of people say that *Up* had a big impact on them because of the time it came out and the way it shattered a lot of things that were very shatterable at that point. Because of the kinds of feedback I'm getting from people about *Mosaic Man*, I think that it's going to be the other book of mine that's going to have that kind of impact. *Mosaic Man* seems to appeal to two groups—my young, hip audience and, surprisingly, the Jewish audience.

LM: So Jewish readers seem to understand what you're doing?

RS: It's been a mixed reaction. The day before yesterday I was at a Jewish reading group that used *Mosaic Man* as its book of the month. They were people who were my age (that is to say, old coots), but even though most of their tastes seemed stuck back in the fifties, some of them really loved the book. A few were highly disturbed about some of the content and asked questions about certain specific incidents; for instance, they wanted to know whether or not the brutal Paris incidents really happened. They were ready to pounce on me, but when I gave them the rationale for including such shocking material, I de-fanged them, so at least some of them are win over-able, partly because they can see where I'm coming from in *Mosaic Man*, if not necessarily where I ended up. That intensely old style Jewish content in the beginning is one of the keys to the book because that's the environment and mind-set I'm getting out of. They don't understand where I came out *to* exactly, but they understand the early stuff about the boyhood in Brooklyn, and if they can get hooked on that, then some will read it all the way through. Who knows? It might be a revelation to them because it's a new take on that kind of life.

LM: Was one of the original impulses behind writing *Mosaic Man* a sense that you'd never specifically explored the Jewish aspect of your life very deeply?

RS: A lot of things came together for me with *Mosaic Man*. There was the intellectual tradition via rhetoric and commentary that more and more began to fascinate me. Then there's the third commandment's prohibition against creating graven images. Another factor was that I got started on that book while I was in Paris at about the time Le Pen phenomenon and other revisionist movements seemed to be taking hold in France and Europe in general. Seeing supposedly enlightened, regular line politicians suddenly falling in line behind Le Pen was really very scary—it was like the Holocaust had never happened.

LM: Has your approach to the process of writing changed in any significant ways from when you started out as a writer?

RS: I'm mostly picking up different strands of what I've invented before and elaborating on them. It's like strands of spaghetti: you shlerp up one and you shlerp up another.

Notes

1. See Larry McCaffery, "Bringing Up Baby: The Avant Pop Controversy," *American Book Review* 19.3 (March–April 1998): 3.

2. See Larry McCaffery, "The 20th Century's Greatest Hits: The 100 Greatest English Language Books of the 20th Century," *American Book Review* 20.6 (Winter 2000): 3, 16.

$8\frac{1}{2}$ Ronnies

Jerome Klinkowitz

Ronald Sukenick began his writing career from a minimum of two perspectives, those of a critic and of a novelist. But from this very start, there were more than two Ronnies involved. His critical study, *Wallace Stevens: Musing the Obscure*, had much of the fictive about it, dedicated as it is to a subject larger than Stevens's mere craft—exploring "less an ideological question" than "one of stance or posture: with what tenable attitude may one confront the difficult circumstances of contemporary American secular life and avail oneself of the good in it? How, in short, does one get along?" (1). Likewise, *Up*, with the heft, range, and substance of a doctoral dissertation, used the novel's format to explore the various ways of writing a novel and question the nature of fiction itself. Hence two Ronnies become four. And then a fifth, as through their author's biographical notes each book recommended the other. And so right at the start there were five Ronnies: critic, novelist, fictively inclined scholar, scholastically inclined fictionist, and the publicized image of a fifth figure who does all these things and more.

This combination was, of course, a 1960s phenomenon. The evolving counter-culture had broken down previously defining limits of self-expression. Just as importantly, such multidimensionality as Sukenick pursued was made economically feasible by an eight-year economic boom that underwrote a decade of expansion in academics and experiment in commercial publishing. The Stevens book was a doctoral dissertation from the days when postgraduate programs flourished well beyond any thought of eventual accountability or even practicality; for the time being, enrollments were growing at all levels and colleges were hiring new faculty in droves. Mentored at Brandeis by J. V. Cunningham and Irving Howe, Sukenick had what seemed to be an assured entry into this academic boom, with early promotion guaranteed by a prestigious university press publication. As for fiction, that market was growing as well. Publishers' stocks soared, rewarding investors with split after split. A free range for acquisition drew the best literary minds to editing: Sukenick's editor at Dial Press was E. L. Doctorow, and *Up* was poised to join the heady world already populated by Pynchon's *V*, Barth's *Giles Goat-Boy*, Barthelme's *Snow White*, and a host of other convention-breaking novels that gleefully disrupted the traditions of oldtime fiction. The world of 1967–1968 could accommodate any number of Ronnies with ease.

Then, in December 1968, the supporting economic structure of that world fell apart. Unpaid bills for a Vietnam War that had grown too expensive ended the stock market's bullish surge; overvalued stocks fell, with those of publishers among the worst; freewheeling editors were reeled in, while the smaller and formerly most adventuresome houses were either engulfed and devoured by larger firms or left to die unattended. As badly as this month opened on Wall Street, the scene on American graduate campuses was worse, for job-hunting doctoral candidates returned from the year-ending Modern Language Association convention in Denver with few or no prospects of employment—all positions had been filled, and the academic boom was over. What had been somewhat playfully called "the death of the novel" a decade earlier was now a grim fact, as both likely publishers for such books and the professorial prospects for the authors who would write them had just gone belly-up.

Tough enough for a conventional novelist or academic hack, but imagine the curtain falling on the bright young star of *Wallace Stevens: Musing the Obscure* and *Up*. One more book would have time to appear, a collection titled *The Death of the Novel and Other Stories*, but after this the going would be rough. Who could now pay the bills for the multidimensioned Ronnie pictured in the quartet of Warhol-like silkscreen mug shots gracing the paperback cover of *Up*, his one and only mass market publication? There he was, four of him in the same pose but differentiated by color and pointillistic dots, its composite giving readers a fifth Ronnie that by all accounts the culture could no longer sustain. Yet like a Fellini self-portrait Sukenick survived, projecting at least three and a half more identities until by the century's end his magic number was attained. It is within this development that Sukenick's work is most profitably read.

❖ ❖ ❖

Like "The Two Ronnies" of (unexported) British television fame, whose complementary styles of comedy summed up an era's entertainment, the Ronald Sukenick who signed his name to these first two books epitomized critical and fictive trends that were coming to fruition as this decade ended. Indeed, newer trends, of which this author would not be a part, were just beginning. *Wallace Stevens: Musing the Obscure* is the last major example in serious literary criticism of sustained textual explication. Deconstruction had already made its first visit from France, and up the road at Yale critics a generation younger than Cunningham and Howe were adapting its methods to the American scene. Sukenick's decision was a radical one, as Stevens's poetry had always been read with an eye to its inherent theory; but lining up the poems for explication, in the New Critical manner so useful for other writers these past three decades, was a method that soon fell into disuse. As for the metafictive and self-reflexive properties of *Up*, they were familiar enough from experiments by Donald Barthelme, Robert Coover, and many others; within a few years Gilbert Sorrentino would rather viciously exhaust the technique in *Mulligan Stew*, leaving things clear for his own stylistic self-absorption and a new era's minimal realism.

Yet it is not as an explicator or metafictionist that either of the first two Ronnies claims his fame, although in each case he was clarifying how these respective techniques were being taken as far as they could go. Explicate a theorist, metafictionalize not just the product but the actual process of art—here are the endgames our two Ronnies play in the publishing season of 1967–1968.

For a novelist who'd forever challenge the assumptions of mimesis, the novice critic setting out to explicate Wallace Stevens pays great attention to the poet's wrestlings with the real. Although Sukenick has argued against attempts to read his doctoral dissertation as any sort of plan for his subsequent fiction, his fascination with the problematic forces of reality is more than coincidental. Against those who would study Stevens only for his theory, Sukenick reminds readers that the poet was less concerned with discoveries of The Good than with discovering "good things" (1); such discoveries are happy when the poet maintains serenity in the face of "the pressure of reality" (2). Thus myth, a common refuge from such pressures, is a falsification—the first sign that in Ronald Sukenick's aesthetic the problem is not reality itself but what some people do with it, how they adjust. Do their postures stiffen or remain flexible? "Adequate adjustment to the present can only be achieved through ever fresh perception of it," he writes, anticipating the roles of his protagonists from *Up* to *Mosaic Man*. "A fiction is not an ideological formulation of belief but a statement of favorable rapport with reality sufficiently convincing that disbelief may be suspended" (3), a reminder that to be effective such suspension must be willing and never automatic.

"In Stevens's conception, history is a process in which no idea of reality is final, poetry is a progressive metamorphosis of reality, and reality itself is an entity whose chief characteristic is flux" (5)—this formulation could serve as an epigraph to Sukenick's second novel, *Out*, whose protagonist is said to change like a cloud as he goes. "In a world whose fundamental condition is change," we read in the Stevens book, "the only tenable kind of belief must involve an affirmation of change" (6). Above all, reality is not an idealistic projection, an understanding that would have spared any number of critics from mistaking the author of *Up* and *Out* as a Cartesian (and hence dismissable as a valid novelist who should otherwise be grappling with the world and offering accounts of its news). Instead, "The mind orders reality not by imposing ideas on it but by discovering significant relations within it, as the artist abstracts and composes the elements of reality in significant integrations that are works of art," (12) an excellent appraisal of what happens in *Up* and many of the stories in *The Death of the Novel.* True, Sukenick's fiction privileges the imagination; that's why he's loath to suspend his disbelief without a careful act of the will, always heedful of letting someone else do his imagining for him (as cultural manipulators are always trying to do). But look at the fair play he gives to each side in the act of perception. "When, through the imagination the ego manages to reconcile reality with its own needs, the formerly insipid landscape is infused with the ego's emotion," he appreciates, grateful that "reality, since it now seems intensely relevant to the ego, suddenly seems more real" (14–15).

"The imagination for Stevens is not a way of creating, but of knowing," as his poetic truth is not something idealistically absolute but rather a statement that "says something about reality we can believe" (16)—here's another term, *credibility*, that early critics (or even most critics today) would be better off discerning in *Up* rather than assuming its author had no desire for it whatsoever. At basis, metafiction restores the ultimate credibility by unmasking the act of composition; but the protagonist of *Up* has a lot more going for him than that, and again the rubrics Sukenick discerned in Stevens's poetry help us understand the novelist' s goal. "Though we exist in reality we are bound by the mind," the young critic writes, "and thus it is not the nature of reality that matters so much as our sense of it, the sense that the imagination gives us" (28). Hence the need for balance, for "an agreement with reality" (30) rather than a transcription of it, to which *Up* aspires.

Wallace Stevens: Musing the Obscure is not a backward-looking dissertation to be filed away with other remnants of its author's doctoral studies. Instead, it presents, in an effectively dramatic way, the specific nature of this young man's beliefs in what literature can do and how it does it. Thanks to its paperback reprint in the NYU Press Gotham Library series (where it accompanied Jonathan Baumbach's *The Landscape of Nightmare: Studies in the Contemporary Novel*, another dissertation from a budding innovative fictionist) the Stevens book became influential not just among scholars of modern poetry but for the new generation of academics, presently buying such affordable volumes to enhance their graduate studies, who recognized Sukenick's name from the splashy, university-directed publicity for *Up* in its own Delta edition. And although Sukenick would discourage attempts to read it as an explication for his own fiction, he did make its first section (including the initial thirty-six pages of material cited here) part of his canon by including it among the essays collected as *In Form: Digressions on the Act of Fiction*. Note the distinction: not "art of fiction," but "act." In the first Ronnie's doctoral dissertation, then, we see not just explications of the art of poetry but something more fundamentally related to the fictive act he'd be undertaking less than a year later with the publication of *Up*.

In fact, the two books were written simultaneously as the real-life Ronald Sukenick lived in his slum apartment (in the yet-to-be-hippified East Village) and commuted to an insipidly dead-end job as a part-timer at Hofstra University on Long Island. This residency is recalled in a third volume, *Down and In: Life In the Underground*, and its cultural context is itself ripe with suggestions for the inspirational sources of both books. But the author of this later work is still another Ronnie, a successor to the authors of not just the Stevens book and *Up* but of another two decades of fiction and criticism that had struggled against a new aesthetic conservativism that seemed set against all of Sukenick's beliefs. As it happens, the creator of *Up* is sufficiently embattled within its pages, struggling to make the same connections to reality that Wallace Stevens strove for in his poems.

The most important thing to note about this first novel is that its author is not simply metafictionalizing to the tune of examining a narrative as it is being composed, or even anti-illusionistically regarding himself in the process of his work, but that a story is being told of identifiable characters trying first of all to live a happily successful life. Only because he happens to be a novelist by trade do the practices of fiction become an issue; because he is one, the narrator-protagonist draws on everything he knows about the art to see if it will be useful in making sense of his existence. (A more recent example of this same strategy is stand-up comedian Jerry Seinfeld's situation of portraying the life of a stand-up comedian named Jerry, whose attempts at facing quotidian challenges necessarily involve his comic work.) The Ron Sukenick who occupies the pages of *Up* is a fictionist, just as the Wallace Stevens who generated all those poems another Ron Sukenick studied was a poet; that alone does not make either of their works "meta-," whether metafictive or metapoetic. Instead, both the fiction and the poetry can be appreciated for what they are in themselves: attempts that by the imagination's reconciliation of reality with its own needs infuse the landscape with the ego's presence and make this suddenly more relevant reality seem, quite naturally, more real.

The big mistake in how hostile critics read *Up* was their ignorance of how a palpably human presence inhabits its center and determines every narrative act. Unlike most metafiction, which is cerebral or programmatically angry, *Up* is a very funny book—funny because readers can identify with the protagonist's problems, even funnier because his methods recall the strategies of countless novels they've already read, but which here don't seem to take themselves so damned seriously. When characters in the story berate the author, their acts are a comic deflation the reader can accept with sympathy. When Ronnie's sexual fantasy finally lets him have some action but then asks if at least *he* enjoyed it and then another character near the end thumbs the manuscript and asks if he really thinks it's finished, we take the author's side—so different from the reader-response to Flann O'Brien's *At Swim-Two-Birds* and Gilbert Sorrentino's *Mulligan Stew*, where the provocation is toward nastiness. But look at the difference: in these latter works the self-reflexive character is neither O'Brien nor Sorrentino, but rather an outright asshole each author wishes (with readerly concurrence) to punish. In *Up*, the creator is Sukenick himself, who with the hands-in-pockets pose of a hopelessly loveable schlemiel is only trying to do in his own life what the eminently WASPish poet Wallace Stevens did in his: create a fiction that makes life a meaningful if not totally manageable affair.

Think of the world our first five Ronnies might have inherited. A presidential candidate named Eugene McCarthy would have kept otherwise disaffected voters in the ranks and defeated Richard Nixon; the Vietnam War would have ended just before its costs broke the economy; the worst cultural divisions would not have had time to happen, and any resultant cultural conservativism would never have been organized. Publishers would have remained rich and independent, editors free and inspired, authors encouraged to push beyond their first reflexive experiments into a genuinely new way of writing. Continuing to boom themselves, universities would have hired a fresh crop of new faculty not in the least fearful or defensive, but rather dedicated to a renaissance instead of a reaction. But now all of these hopes dissolved into a literal nightmare, and an author like Sukenick had to settle into the prospect of a career in opposition.

Our sixth Ronnie is the combative (if not embattled) figure of the 1970s, writing three novels which are defiantly countercultural. Although there was yet to be an equal to the Stevens book, critical and theoretical essays appeared in great number. The most important of these would be collected as *In Form*, but their alliance with the novels must not be discounted. What appears in the latter volume as "Innovative Fiction / Innovative Criteria" (241–43), itself reprinted from *fiction international*, is in fact Sukenick's somewhat defensive argument that accompanied the Swallow Press publicity materials for his new novel, *Out*. As he presents himself to potential critics, the author launches his program of discounting "innovation" as a proper label for his fiction. By definition, all novels should be innovative. But overly conventional ones no longer are, having become frozen into "literary" postures and therefore falling short of the Stevens measure that lets people believe in art because it "gets at the truth of their lives" (*In Form* 241). Feeling, energy, excitement—these are the factors of relevance that let fiction convey not just the news but our response to it. And as the 1970s were getting underway, the news was not very good at all.

In his thirty years of constructing a thirteen-book canon, Sukenick displays no greater developmental contrast in his work than between *Up* and *Out*. Each volume challenges convention and tradition, right down to typology on the page. But whereas *Up* looks backward for its effect, spoofing and pastiching (if not outrightly exhausting) customary approaches to narrative, *Out* invents an entirely new one. To *Up's* collages, marginalia, and generally spatial form of organization (as protagonist Ronald Sukenick explores all avenues of escape from the stasis he he fears might become his life), *Out* offers the contrast of unlimited, accelerating, forward movement. Its chapters are numbered backwards, like the countdown for a rocket launch, and are arranged in block paragraphs with one less line of print (and one more line of print) for each; as Sukenick liked to say, the book moves faster and faster, with readers flipping. pages at increasing speed until they are shot out the end of it like a cannon ball (in *8½* fashion, the last chapter is blank). Sentences themselves run on, tumbling forward into both visual and linguistic nothingness—not nihilistically, but as the perfection to which this deconstructive grammar accedes. The plot cooperates with this design, moving from the clutter and hassle of New York City to the openness of the Great Plains until its narrative runs off the edge of California's coast into a purity of nothingness. Though the effects are dazzling as narrative display, there's also a theme being served, transmitting the feeling, energy, and excitement of such daily life. In *Up*, the fact of that life could be crushing. Here in his first 1970s novel the author breaks out, liberating himself from spatial constraints even the unfettered Sixties had kept in place.

The California emptiness toward which *Out* directs itself is only superficially a destination. More important than product (which is, after all, a blankness) is process, and that process involves the protagonist's continual sense of reinvention. The "Ronald Sukenick" of *Up* becomes any number of Ronnies in *Out*, until in the next novel he is able to change himself into the person named Cloud whose identity changes as he goes, just like a cloud swept along in the air. Yet neither is the coastal commune of *98.6* a destination. Instead, the novel's structure places it as a stage halfway between the nightmare of "Frankenstein" (part one) and the dream of "Palestine" (part three) that is most properly described as "The Children of Frankenstein" (the title for part two). All three are stages of energy: uncontrolled in savagery of primitive ritual, trying to be creatively channeled in a counterculture's revolt against the corporate ritualism of tradition, and finally liberated for pure enjoyment in a psychological condition known as the state of Israel. Here Mosaic Law helps the narrator understand mosaics, learning "how to deal with parts in the absence of wholes" (167). When the parts fit together magically, he achieves the desired state.

Although this new novel went out to reviewers without any professed theory to support it, the period surrounding its publication is distinguished as Sukenick's most active as a commentator. It was now that seven of his "Digressions" pieces, later to become the heart of *In Form*, would appear in *Partisan Review, New Literary History, SubStance,* and *Studies in American Fiction*—a broad range of academic journals that in sum would catch the bulk of this novel's readership. The task these essays had to support was a major one. The Stevens/*Up* connection had been easy. For *Out*, more explicit connections needed to be forged—not just the publicity essay, but a piece on Carlos Castaneda for *The Village Voice* (collected in *In Form* as "Castaneda, Upward and Juanward") that drew parallels between the fictionist's artful description and the sorcerer's persuasive account. Unquestioned descriptions are the ones that culture pounds into us from birth; alternate descriptions, ones that disrupt the normal flow of interpretation, are what Sukenick and Don Juan provide. Given that all reality is merely a description, the question is how persuasive any one description is. As Sukenick would remind his critical readers, fiction itself is not about experience but is, instead, more experience—in *98.6*, a matter of levels of experience. Which one is normal, corresponding to the ideal body temperature of the novel's title? None of them, as witnessed by the cruel falsity of such measure when applied to the miscarriage a character suffers: through all her affliction, the thermometer reads "normal," giving an account that is anything but persuasively real.

Having read the "Digressions" essays, a reader of *98.6* is likely to say that the thermometer is too distantly abstracted from experience to be of much use. Like a deadly conventional novel, it is more *about* experience than it is *of* that experience. Consider how the author, in his first "Digression," discounts that cornerstone of traditional fiction, verisimilitude, as conveying the idea "that it can represent our control over reality," a "voodoo . . . that helps account for its tenacity" (4). The truth is just the opposite, because the more we make statements about reality, "the less we participate in it; the less we are engaged by the experience of it" (5). Subject matter is important, but only as one part; more central is how "narrative would be the movement of the mind as it organizes the open field of the text," an act that both for writer and reader results in "a new experience" (13). If fiction is not about experience but consists of more experience, then its heart is "An essentialized narrative" that "embodies the progression of mind as it confronts and affects experience" (14). Or, more simply, "Art is not imitation; it is example" (25).

In these "Digressions" essays Sukenick cites plenty of positive examples, from the spontaneous bop prosody of the Beats and the more postmodernist I-do-this/I-do-that continuity of Frank O'Hara's poems to the example of Henry Miller, who was able to "reconnect our art with our experience" (26). Thinking back to Wallace Stevens, Sukenick recalls the joy of rhetoric that connects readers to the world, rather than separating them from it: "Art delivers us from abstraction and solipsism with a newly vitalized (lively) sense of experience. It does not cage us in the crystal perfection of art" (39). As far as the levels of experience in *98.6*, Sukenick's approach to fiction is especially helpful. For him, the novel is "an instrument that undercuts official versions of reality in favor of our individual sense of experience, now constantly threatened by the brainwash of politics and the mass market" (67). The narrator of *98.6*'s first section suffers just such brainwashing, and pressures of mass market culture are forever impinging on the impossibly utopian world of section two. These young people are not at all liberated from their fears but remain children of the Frankenstein so terrifying in section one, where official versions of reality were the only ones available. Back there, people suffered from "negative hallucinations" of culture, a factor of not seeing something that's really there (11). The children of Frankenstein create a new life, but it too is a monster, something created to do something *for* them but which winds up doing something *to* them—another consequence of abstraction from experience. Hence the preferability of section three, "Palestine," where reality is perceived as a rhythn in synch with one's breath and heart beat, and experience can be enjoyed in the pleasure of its flow. This approach is presented fictively, of course, as the nightmare-dreamer of "Frankenstein" and the communard of "The Children of Frankenstein" heeds the narratives of Yitzak Fawsi (a philosopher who acts more like a storyteller) and Tanta Goldie (ostensibly the former Israel Prime Minister, Golda Meier, but having the effects of an aunt's scoldings and coaxings from Ron's Brooklyn childhood). Yet what Fawzi and Goldie say can be taken from any of the Digressions essays, as both novel and commentary are driven by the same aesthetic: "Only experience can restore that lost synthesis which analysis has forced us to shatter. Experience alone can decide on truth." One of the "Digressions"? No, page 186 of *98.6*, where Tanta Goldie quotes her old friend, Albert Einstein.

Sukenick's third novel of the 1970s, *Long Talking Bad Conditions Blues*, picks up where *98.6* left off—quite literally so in its resynthesis of the present with childhood memories in the manner of Jesse Lone Cat Fuller's long talking blues that gives *98.6* a format for conclusion. There, amidst repetitions of the phrase "AT THE SAME TIME" (187–88), the author did a rap by making a wrap of the otherwise disparate parts of his existence, all of them pulled together by the fact of his coincidental experience of them. *Long Talking Bad Conditions Blues* accepts this hard-won condition as its given, weaving Sukenick's apparently separate lives into a seamlessly whole cloth of energized narrative. Isn't it odd that a distinguished professor of English conducts so many of his professional duties with his mind running rampant through the sites of his childhood in Brooklyn? And even odder that this American professor lives so much of the year in Paris, where he'd Fulbrighted as a student but now escapes the hassles of academic life? Are these the diverse experiences of a single person? And who on earth is he? The culture in this novel is itself experiencing something called "shatter," in which there are no longer any reliable structures for existence. All that remains is one's experience; people have to make of it what they can, with some doing well while others do poorly. Doing well involves catching on to the rhythms, taking what in *98.6* was natural to the state of Israel and universalizing it by means of a music available to anyone: the blues, America's one original contribution to global culture that translates almost anywhere.

Long Talking Bad Conditions Blues fulfills the aesthetic ideals of our sixth Ronnie. Its forward-leaning, run-on sentences employ the narrative method of *Out*, while its synthesis of various periods and levels of experience embraces the philosophy of *98.6*. There is even a winsomely unthreatening sense of magic to its seamlessness, as each *quai* and *place* of its Paris setting is named not for a famous general or classic literary figure but for reverently remembered players from the late 1940s Brooklyn Dodgers. It completes the vision Sukenick has proposed. But only as that of the sixth Ronnie. At least two and one-half more of him await succeeding decades, the social, cultural, political, and economic changes of which demand still newer fictive strategies. If the twentieth century had encompassed more change than the two previous millenia all put together, then the last third of this century accelerated the pace even more. This change would incorporate not just Sukenick's style of fiction, but his manner of presenting it to the critics and to the public as well.

As the end of the 1960s had seen the support structure for innovative fiction collapse and the 1970s had witnessed the bad conditions that resulted because of it, the next decade came to distinguish itself for its remakings. The 1980s became the time in which multiculturalism reconstructed the academic literary canon, even as critical deconstruction forced a radical reconfiguration of how previously accepted texts were understood. By now Sukenick himself was a senior academic, well established at the University of Colorado, and from this base he undertook several projects that can only be described as a realignment of power. Beyond escaping the confines of a restricting cultural definition, as he'd aimed to do in the Seventies, the 1980s found Sukenick redefining such terms. Starting at the most immediately practical levels, he used his senior position to recruit new colleagues at Colorado, including two of the most important innovative fictionists around, Clarence Major and Steve Katz. To make sure literature like his and theirs could be published, he took over the Fiction Collective, relocating it from New York to Boulder. To insure that such work got reviewed, he did the same with the *American Book Review*. To his work with the Coordinating Council of Literary Magazines, which distributed funds from the National Endowment for the Arts, he added service on the Executive Council of the Modern Language Association. And from campus to campus, he read his fiction and took part in critical symposia everywhere; fifty pages of *In Form*, subtitled "Cross Examination," provide a sampling of this activity that kept the new seventh Ronnie at the center of literary debates in an era when John Gardner's *On Moral Fiction* and Gerald *Graff's Literature Against Itself* had innovators with their backs against the wall. Personally, Ron's long talking blues had done its job in making him comfortable with a simultaneity of residences and identities. With well-established homes in Boulder (near the Continental Divide), Paris (just west of the redeveloped Beaubourg), and New York (in a new high-rise on the Battery), he could function as an academic, as an intellectual, and as an expatriate novelist all at once. These were, to be sure, important aspects of his existence, even if at present they defined just another stage of development.

Between 1985 and 1987 this seventh Ronnie published four books. *In Form* began the string, helping relaunch the Crosscurrents series with the Southern Illinois University Press. *Blown Away* was an emphatically Eighties novel, whereas *The Endless Short Story* integrated shorter fictive pieces done since *The Death of the Novel.* The most significant of Sukenick's texts in the 1980s, emblematic of how he was presenting his new literary personality, was *Down and In: Life in the Underground*, published in 1987 with some fanfare by William Morrow in New York.

Down and In identifies the new Ron Sukenick as a writer interested not just in the imaginative self and not just in the self's experience but as a figure concerned with cultural power—concerned to the extent of being willing to broker it. Not that such aspirations are in any sense meglomanic. Having admitted that government, news media, advertising agencies, the publishing establishment, and the university-based academy deal in the manipulations of such power, it only seems reasonable to organize and fight back. From the historical vantage point of a generation later, that is just what the underground culture of Greenwich Village accomplished: first undermining the dominant culture, then subverting it, and finally emerging as a powerful cultural stream in itself. Obviously the seventh Ronnie would like to do this himself. But the question is whether it is too late. Told in narrative format, *Down and In* depicts not just the era and its creative artists but a bright young kid from Brooklyn who crosses the East River on weekend evenings to visit the place where all this new stuff is happening. He's not alone; his sister Gloria has dropped out of art school at Yale "To become a belle of Bleecker Street" (19). Will he make the move himself? Or will his good grades, middle class background, and Ivy League prospects hold him back in Brooklyn 'til it's time for Cornell? In fact, he didn't make the move until the late 1960s, when as a resident of the East Village he'd embarked on his writer's career:

> When I start writing my first novel, *Up*, a book about the East Side that is a combination of autobiography and inven-

> tion, I realize that that place and time is one in which we can in fact partly invent our autobiographies, in which life is not something imposed on us but a process in which we are creatively involved. The distinction between art and life in the book is reduced to a quibble of form only partly out of theoretical considerations. It's also a consequence of the kind of life that, after decades of alienation, we are finally positioned to lead. What critics don't realize when they foam, or even effervesce, about "Postmodernism" in fiction is that it did not come out of arbitrary literary considerations but out of a kind of life. It is a way of living in which you participate in a communal imagination, rather than having to struggle continuously with an intrusive public vision imposed by the mass market. "Use your imagination," I like to tell my students these days, "or someone else is going to use it for you." (149)

Note the juxtaposition of postures, all of which now relate to power. Postmodernism emerges not from literature but from life, specifically as a way of tracking the imagination's remaking of life. Personal control fights back against the mass market. By writing *Up* in the East Village, its author learns a lesson; and now twenty years later he's equipped as a distinguished full professor ("tenured" is even specified in his back-jacket biographical note to *The Endless Short Story*) to teach it to his students in Colorado. That Wallace Stevens did the same thing in more literary terms is deemphasized, but it cannot be forgotten, no more than *Down and In* can forget that 1960s Village counterculture is rooted in the Beat culture that preceded it. Hence a new configuration of the self and society obtains "that epiphany of self-recognition that is a discovery of a real self beyond the claims of official existence," the ticket to "participation as a singular individual in a shared public life that subverts the claims of our homogenized mass-market culture" (251). What was once preciously modern, a bit alien and very much obscure, becomes broadly democratic; Wallace Stevens becomes Allen Ginsberg. And then comes Carlos Castaneda, whose exercise of the imagination on experience "implies, among other faculties, the power of feeling to the world" (254).

Sukenick's linking of the Don Juan books of his 1970s counterculture with his own 1980s power culture is instructive. Looking both ways, it explains the vibrancy of the Beat movement, suggests a reason for the cultural cohensiveness in present Village life, and anticipates how what is initially an underground can establish a functional level of its own. What fascinates the seventh Ronnie (as opposed to the sixth, who admired Castaneda's fictive persuasiveness) is that this writer "is exercising his spell directly on the world rather than through an intermediate fable," interrupting the flow of normal interpretation so that the world becomes not a given but "a nest of possibilities." And why is this view "so popular with a waning counterculture"? Because it suggests that "an adversarial vision can function in the mass market and probably always has" (255).

Hence Sukenick's hopes for a better future, one in which "instead of its romance with the outsider and the subversive, the underground is strong enough to make a stand for its point of view within the mainstream of the culture," moving "from mere resistance to outright attack" (264). Is this very likely? Well, with Solidarity's writers it happened in Poland, one of them telling Ron why she and her colleagues did not hide behind pseudonyms: "We are not subversives. This is our country" (279). *Blown Away* and *The Endless Short Story* are similarly direct confrontations with power and how it operates, with no need for fiction to adopt even a critically digressive *nom de guerre*. The latter collection was conceived as something Sukenick could compose without "limits but readily cut off and sell by the yard," while the novel sets in action in the world where the creative imagination most successfully commodifies itself: the film industry of Hollywood. *Blown Away* stands well beyond the musings of both *98.6* and the "Digressions" essays—just listen to what its protagonist, director Boris Ccrab, has to say about Sukenick's favorite subject: "Maybe experience is a number done on nothing by infinity" (19). As far as working with this more radical formulation, "The big idea is not to drown in your experience" (21). As always, the author can call on Castaneda, Henry Miller, and Anaïs Nin, but those who work for Ccrab, such as the starlet Clover Bottom, have nothing more than the texture a more postmodern figure, Roland Barthes, had for meaning, as Clover herself complains: "Onions every time I peel a layer inside me there's another layer it won't stop till there's nothing left" (94). For her, experience is being peeled away and sold by the yard—by someone else. Only by doing as Charlie Chaplin did, forming United Artists so that film actors and actresses can "control their own professional lives" (99), may Clover's experiences be something more than celluloid fantasties by and for others.

A more hopeful image for artistic control of one's own experience is the act that initiates *The Endless Short Story*: the making of the Watts Towers. Made from detritus as something for the people, it survives as a donation to common experience, helping viewers create meanings for themselves as they need them. Created by a working class laborer for the poor who remained in this decaying neighborhood, the Towers fill a lack, as producer Rod Drackenstein (Boris Ccrab's nemesis) explains: "For the middle class life is unreal, for the poor it's too real, that's all it amounts to. The poor and the rich are in touch with the powers that shape their lives, but the middle class lives in a manipulated revery. I should know, I'm one of the manipulators" (127).

Blown Away ends not with a successful film but with Henry Miller's assurance that ongoing experience is still the best tonic, subject only to one's ability to taste it. *The Endless Short Story* sustains that tonic, moving beyond the need for any one piece of intelligence to explain another. Beyond the moviemakers' narrative in *Blown Away,* one that got short-circuited into a metafictive display of the production process itself, Sukenick's newly discontinuous narratives dismiss the need for continuity at all. For what is the ultimate end of such narrative progression? "If someone could explain death nobody would need to explain everything else" (126), so why bother?

The Endless Short Story anticipates Sukenick's latest work, but also looks back to the most experientially flowing parts of *The Death of the Novel and Other Stories,* the collection with which Ronald Sukenick exited the 1960s before it had the chance to collapse around him. The postmodern condition itself was examined in the title piece, a fitting coda to both *Up* and the Stevens book. "The Birds" anticipates the countercultural Ronnie of *Out* and *98.6*, while "Momentum" defines the essence of his style: an ongoing rush that eclipses limits of grammar and syntax, with reflection reserved for brief comments in a parallel column. This would be the manner of Sukenick's three decades to follow, an attempt not so much explain experience as understand it—an Emersonian distinction the author was proud to advertise.

The eighth Ronnie is a transitional figure who writes just one book, *Doggy Bag*, that examines all he has made of himself before moving on to more work by a Ronnie still in progress, the eighth and one-half. Much of *Doggy Bag* is set in contemporary Europe, a somewhat transformed world thanks to the European Union—but also changed by a generation of visits from Americans, starting with Sukenick's own Fulbright year so long ago and now grown to a flood of tourists. Are they seeking what he sought as a young man? If so, does this speak well or ill of his past motives? Thinking that "Europe was the solution" (23) is the connection, a typically American miscalculation (dating back to Henry James and Gertrude Stein) that Europe is history, and that if history doesn't work right, just fix it, as James imagined Europe could fix his vision of Hawthorne. But by missing the fact that all new frontiers are within, such Americans suffer a "denial of introspection" and become "Zombies" (39). The same eighth Ronnie who writes this work contributes a preface to the second edition of *98.6,* "Love Conks Us All." Here he relates Hawthorne's utopianism at Brook Farm with his own 1960s idealism, a dream that fizzled out for lack of "mediating institutions" (ii). Why go to Palestine? Because the state of Israel was nowhere Sukenick had really visited, but rather was a mental state that let his book "resolve itself in the imagination" (iii) and hence avoid both official and literary versions of reality. Introducing "sustained mental and emotional disequilibrium" (v) is, we must remember, a talent in the sixth Ronnie only perceived by the eighth.

In the meantime, the Ronnie in between had both visited the real Israel and reestablished close contact with his Jewish-American childhood in Brooklyn. The former experience allowed him to study firsthand an actual utopia in progress, much as Hawthorne had visited the Brook Farm of Transcendentalist days. The latter put Sukenick in touch with experiences of half a century before, something his parents' lives had buffered. As the parents declined, he found himself back in New York more often to aid them and deal with their affairs, to the point of establishing a third residence to complement his home in Boulder and apartment in Paris. Yet deepest was the emotional experience. Between one's old ways of childhood and the present fact of living (often elsewhere) as an adult stand one's parents. The old neighborhood, the old customs, the old values are theirs; even memories of being a kid are tied to their proprietorship. When the mother and father die, that buffer is removed, the last barrier to one's own mortality falling away. As for past and future, you yourself are now it, just as after half a lifetime of entertaining the idea of Israel is, by virtue of an actual visit, transformed into an experience of the place itself.

Mosaic Man is, as its title implies, Ronald Sukenick's most complete work, a mosaic of all the themes and styles that distinguish the canon compiled by no less than eight Ronnies before him. Its strategy is to assemble these parts (each of which retains its integrity) into a new composition organized by the author's appreciation of his Jewish-American culture and the long traditions (both Jewish and American) surrounding it. The starting point is "Genes," a genesis of words for experiences that exceed customary articulation (the Holocaust being one of them, but not the only example by far). "What's the story?" the narrator asks. "Am I a Jew?" The question is not parochial, because a civilization that makes no sense by one set of rules might be better perceived by others. "How many of you have had the feeling that you're from another world, not this one?" (151).

New rules for composition are in order, most principally the rule for mosaics. Here parts must retain evidence of their source while contributing to a larger picture. "What's your story?" can be asked of any of them, and—more importantly—answered with confidence and credibility. Family oral histories (including gaps and breaks) have their place; so do bad-news phone calls coming at five in the morning. What are the best dying words? "Now I see the story" (38) , the sentiment that sums up *Mosaic Man*'s second section, "Ex/Ode." Thus empowered, the narrative can proceed with "Umbilicus," a long series of childhood memories that combine the Brooklyn Ron was always expected to write about realistically (never forget he is an almost exact contemporary of Philip Roth) with elaborate yet compelling fantasies about carrying his childish inventions out into the real world. Here comic books and history books, cartoons and newsreels intertwine, a combination of hilarity and nightmare that captures one part of the mosaic: how a ten-year-old might face a looming reality that includes Hitler, Mussolini, and the camps.

Section four, "Numbers," matures the picture, matching the author's sense of intellectualization with his experience of Europe. Here are the characters from his young manhood who would organize existence: Wallace Stevens and, from *Up*, Strop Banally. To do the same, these first and second Ronnies would become a novelist—but not a conventional novelist. "The idea of making things up" is boring, a children's game, mere Hollywood. But from a distance, viewing the mosaic of all eight Ronnies, he can see that "his dislike for making things up is deeply connected with Jewish rules," the struggle against imitation that warns against graven images, the "false liberty" of Art that yields just a Golden Calf: "Once you start making things up you start indulging yourself. You erect idols that are wish fantasies. But idols are always cheap imitations of treacherous gods. This is what Art has come to in our tradition" (96).

Out and the first two sections of *98.6* convey this understanding, but to the "Palestine" of *98.6* this new *Mosaic Man* counterposes "Autonomy," four subsectioned visits to specifically Jewish sites in Poland, Israel, Italy, and Germany. Here are the large doses of history that balance the earlier novel's Palestine as the ideal of an ideal. But this history is not anyone's story, rather something found in the Shrine of the Book, where once more Jewish rules make the author's case that "The Book is not about anything it engenders everything, joins everything with the Word" (145). In the Jewish cemetery of Berlin the author feels at peace, laying to rest feelings that have been disorganized since the death of his father, just as in Italy his vision of himself as a young man is shocked into realization (a Hawthornesque device, pure innovative fiction) by the young man's complementary vision of himself forty years hence. By the end of "Autonomy," the mosaic man is whole.

Taken together, these constitute the novel's first grouping, "Testimony." Having given it, the mosaic man can then commence the second, "Writing." Here are "Profits," a retelling of the golem legend, and "Hand Writing on the Wall," where a conflux of myths well beyond the constraints of history conspire to tell his story. Men of clay, calves of gold—the Golem of Prague, Jesus Christ, and Elvis Presley seem remarkably the same in terms of effect. The "Hand Writing" narrative moves beyond such simulacra to embrace experience itself, the mosaic man's most personal in terms of components, including two decisions regarding his aging, ailing parents that strike to the heart of his own identity. Each is a test. Each is passed, with neither case demanding any graven images, just the thing in itself that the mosaic man writes.

The eighth and a half Ronnie, nearly complete but not yet finished, writes a second book. *Narralogues: Truth in Fiction* finds the dynamic of narratives (such as *Mosaic Man*) in their rhetoric, an argument not represented by a subject but undertaken in its author's act.

> Thinking in the moment of composition calls up faculties distinct from those that dominate more logical thought. Less linear, more embedded in the situational flow, more open to the wisdom of the feelings and emotions, more dependent on the power of example; more open to preconceptual information registered by the senses, more responsive to the moment and what is said to be a form of very short term memory that defines the purview of the present, more governed by quick reflex and instinct, these faculties add up to the word intuition or maybe, imagination, and constitute a powerful alternative to abstract thought. It's not much of a stretch to see that they also form a base for narrative thinking. (82)

Thus criticism yields to commentary, and commentary to story, the last as "one story" that "leads to another in an ongoing narrative" (89), assembled as a mosaic that depicts nothing else so much as the central intelligence that makes it—not the disparate parts of modernist collage, but the postmodern mosaic that takes those disparate parts and "turns them into new wholes. It's the beginning of something else" (91). This new whole, the beginning of something new, was first suggested by the two Ronnies who wrote *Wallace Stevens: Musing the Obscure* and

Up, and even more so by the several Ronnies called into being by the mutual presences of these books. Yet here were just the beginnings of a writer who would take thirty years to construct evolving identities sufficiently rich in imaginatively considered experience to be presented as a true mosaic man. One self, but known in a multitide of ways, with each act of knowing constituting its own story—this is the infinity of being that the truly fictive writer commands in his fiction of truth.

Works Cited

Sukenick, Ronald. *98.6*. New York: Fiction Collective, 1975.

———. *98.6*. Boulder, Colo.: Fiction Collective Two, 1994.

———. *Blown Away*. Los Angeles: Sun & Moon Press, 1986.

———. *The Death of the Novel and Other Stories*. New York: Dial Press, 1969.

———. *Doggy Bag: Hyperfictions*. Boulder, Colo.: Black Ice Books, 1994.

———. *Down and In: Life in the Underground*. New York: Morrow, 1987.

———. *The Endless Short Story*. New York: Fiction Collective, 1987.

———. *In Form: Digressions on the Act of Fiction*. Carbondale: Southern Illinois University Press, 1985.

———. *Long Talking Bad Conditions Blues*. New York: Fiction Collective, 1979.

———. *Mosaic Man*. Normal, Ill.: Fiction Collective Two, 1999.

———. *Narralogues: Truth in Fiction*. Albany: State University of New York Press, 2000.

———. *Out*. Chicago: Swallow Press, 1973.

———. *Up*. New York: Dial Press, 1968.

———. *Up*. New York: Delta Books/Dell, 1970.

———. *Wallace Stevens: Musing the Obscure*. New York: New York University Press, 1967.

Selected Bibliography

A full Sukenick bibliography is available at http://www.mosaicman.com.

Books

98.6. New York: Fiction Collective, 1975.

Blown Away. Los Angeles: Sun & Moon Press, 1986.

Cows. AltX Press ebooks. <http://www.altx.com/ebooks/> 2002.

The Death of the Novel and Other Stories. New York: Dial Press, 1969.

Degenerative Prose, ed., with Mark Amerika. Normal, Ill.: Fiction Collective Two/Black Ice Books, 1995.

Doggy Bag. Normal, Ill.: Fiction Collective Two/Black Ice Books, 1994.

Down and In: Life in the Underground. New York: Beech Tree Books, 1987.

The Endless Short Story. New York: Fiction Collective, 1986.

In Form: Digressions on the Act of Fiction. Carbondale: Southern Illinois University Press, 1985.

In The Slipstream: An FC2 Reader, ed., with Curtis White. Normal, Ill.: Fiction Collective Two/Black Ice Books, 1999.

Long Talking Bad Conditions Blues. New York: Fiction Collective, 1979.

Mosaic Man. Normal, Ill.: Fiction Collective Two, 1999.

Narralogues: Truth in Fiction. Albany: State University of New York Press, 2000.

Out. Chicago: Swallow Press, 1973.

Up. New York: Dial Press, 1968.

"A Wallace Stevens Handbook: A Reading of His Major Poems and an Exposition of His Theory and Practice." Ph.D. diss. Brandeis University, 1962.

Wallace Stevens: Musing the Obscure. New York: New York University Press, 1967.

Films

"The Great Peace Scare." Screenplay written for Roger Corman.

OUT. Dir. Eli Hollander. Perf. Peter Coyote, Danny Glover. Edde Entertainment, 1994.

Fiction in Periodicals

"50,010,008." *IO* (1993) 77–86.

"A Long Way from Nowhere." *Epoch* 14 (1964): 69–77.

"An Attack." *South Atlantic Quarterly* 93.2 (1994): 462–68.

"At This Very Instant." *Fiction International* 15.1 (1984): 92–96. Rpt. in *American Made*. Ed. Mark Leyner et al. Boulder, Colo.: Fiction Collective, 1986. 189–96.

"The Doctor." *Caprice* (1994): 5.

"Ecco." *Boulevard* 12/13 (1990): 71–89. Rpt. in *O. Henry Prize Stories*. Ed. William Abrahams. New York: Doubleday, 1991. 301–22.

"Extract from The Fortune Teller." *Trema* 2 (1977): 143–46.

"Fin de Siecle." *Sensitive Skin* 2 (1994): 8–9, 35.

"Flakes: A Serial." *Black Ice Online*. Changing of the Garde Issue. <www.altx.com/profiles/archives/index.html>.

"The Flood." *Fiction International* 22 (1992): 327–334.

"How to Screw a Coot." *Nerve Magazine*. (1997). <www.nervemag.com/Sukenick/Coot/1997>.

"The Key." *Fiction*, 1:3 (1972): 2–3.

"Life/Art: Static Story for Small Screen." *FlashPoint* 1:1 (1996): 13–17.

"Lit Comix." *Exquisite Corpse* (1983).

"Momentum." *Innovative Fiction*. Eds. Jerome Klinkowitz and John Somer. New York: Dell-Laurel, 1972. 177–214.

"The Monster." *Iowa Review* 6 (1975) 33–46. Rpt. in *Pushcart Prize, I: Best of the Small Presses*. Ed. Bill Henderson. New York: Pushcart/Avon, 1976.

"On the Wing." *North American Review* 258 (1973): 29–48.

"One Every Minute." *Carolina Quarterly* 13 (1961): 57–64.

"The Permanent Crisis." *Epoch* 10 (1960): 211–17.

"Sublet." *Chelsea 64* (1998): 148.

"Tiger." *Denver Quarterly* 24:3 (1990): 46–47.

"What's Your Story." *Paris Review* 11:44 (1968): 33–51.

"Who Are These People?" *Fiction International* (1990): 45–50.

"The Wondering Jew and the Black Widow Murders, or the Return of the Planet of the Apes." *Southern Plains Review* (1993): 25–34.

Articles

"Art and the Underground." *American Book Review* (January–February 1984): 2–3.

"Author as Editor and Publisher." *New York Times Book Review* 15 September 1974: 55.

"Autogyro: My Life In Fiction." *Contemporary Authors Autobiography Series*. Vol. 8. Ed. Mark Zadrozny. Detroit, Mich.: Gale Research, 1989. 283–96.

"Changing of the Garde." *Black Ice* 9 (1992): v, vi.

"The Ecology of Literature." *Village Voice* 18 (April 5, 1973): 26–28.

"Eight Digressions on the Politics of Language." *New Literary History* 10 (1979): 467–77.

"The Fiction Collective." *New York Times Book Review* 22 December 1974: 16.

"Fiction in the Seventies: Ten Digressions on Ten Digressions." *Studies in American Fiction* 5 (1977): 99–108. Rpt. in *American Fiction*. Ed. James Nagel. Boston: Northeastern University Press, 1977. 99–108.

"Get Thee a Grant: Why Writers Must Play Politics." *Nation* 3 October 1981: 199–302.

"How To Be Jewish." *Autobiographie & Avant-Garde*. Eds. Alfred Hornung and Ernstpeter Ruhe. Tubingen, Germany: Gunter Narr Verlag, 1992. 387–400.

"Literature at the End of the Century." *Literary Review* (1990): 1983–84.

"My Life in Fiction." *Konoch* 1:1 (1990): 24–27.

"Movie Digression." *Writing in a Film Age*. Ed. Keith Cohen. Boulder: University Press of Colorado, 1991. 155–66.

"Narrative Thinking vs. Conglomerate Culture." *Critical Quarterly* 27:4 (1995): 27–33.

"The NEA: Art and Money." *American Book Review* (March–April, 1990): 3.

"The N.E.A. & the Avant-Garde." *Nation* 11 October 1993: 400–01.

"The New Innovative Fiction" (with Raymond Federman). *Antaeus* 20 (1976): 138–49.

"The New Tradition." *Partisan Review* 39 (1972): 580–88. Rpt. as "The New Tradition in Fiction." *Surfiction*. Ed. Raymond Federman. Chicago: Swallow Press, 1975. 35–45.

"News from Utopia." *Harper's Bookletter* 2 (August 18, 1975): 1.

"Not-Fiction." *American Book Review* 21:1 (1999): 3.

"Novel as Novel." *American Notes and Queries* 5:4 (1992): 244–46.

"On Reinventing the Novel." *Fiction International* 2:3 (1974).

"On the New Cultural Conservativism." *Partisan Review*: 39 (1972): 448–51. Rpt. *in New York Times Week in Review* 20 August 1972.

"Publishing, 2001." *American Book Review* 16:4 (1994): 3, 6, 7.

"Ronald Sukenick." *The Literary Review* (1990): 183–84.

"The Situation of American Writing 1999." *American Literary History* 2:2 (1999): 324–31.

"Statement." *Fiction International* 22 (1992): 48–51.

"Statement." *Statements: New Fiction from the Fiction Collective*. Ed. Jonathan Baumbach. New York: Braziller, 1975. 7–8.

"On Steve Katz, Raymond Federman, Tom Glynn, George Chambers, Douglas Woolf, Peter Speilberg, Frank Waters." *Writers Choice*. Ed. Bill Katz and Linda Sternberg Katz. Reston/Prentice Hall, 1983.

"Taboo or Not Taboo." *Village Voice* 19 (January 3, 1974): 4.

"The Underground." *American Book Review* 16:1 (1994): 31.

"The Underground Exposed." *Cups* 72 (1996): 12–16.

"Unwriting." *American Book Review* 13:5 (1992): 4, 26–27. Rpt. in *The Novel of the Americas*. Ed. Raymond Leslie Williams. Boulder: University Press of Colorado, 1992. 48–51.

"Upward & Juanward: The Possible Dream." *Village Voice* 18 (January 25, 1973): 27–28, 30–31. Rpt. in *Seeing Castaneda*. Ed. Daniel Noel. New York: Putnam's, 1976. 110–20.

"Writers for Carter." *Partisan Review* 44 (1977): 108–09.

"A Writers Forum on Moral Fiction." *Fiction International* 12 (1980): 21.

"Writer's Roundtable." *South Atlantic Quarterly* 93:2 (1994): 461–62.

Interviews

Sukenick, Ronald. "The Sarah Lawrence Orgies of 1968: An Interview with Ronald Sukenick." By Christian Ettinger and Alexander Lawrence. <www.altx.com>.

———. "Sukenick's *Mosaic Man* is his novel—and his life." By Kathryn Bernheimer. *Intermountain Jewish News* (October 8, 1999): 16.

———. "Ron Sukenick: The Rival Tradition." JR Foley. *FlashPoint*" 1 (Summer 1996): 1–12.

———. "The Fiction of Fiction: An Interview with Ronald Sukenick." By Ted Rooney. *Poetry Flash* (May/June 1995): 1, 4–11.

———. "Interview with Ronald Sukenick." By Alexander Lawrence. *Cups* 3 (1995): 12–13.

———. "Turning On: An Electronic Interview with Ronald Sukenick." By Mark Amerika. *Interzone* <www.altx.com>.

———. "An Interview with Ronald Sukenick." By David Seed. *Over Here* (Summer 1990): 1–7.

———. "A Talk With Ronald Sukenick." By Zolton Abady-Nagy. *Hungarian Studies in English* XVI (1983): 5–22.

———. Interview. By Tom LeClair and Larry McCaffery. *Anything Can Happen*. Urbana: University of Illinois Press, 1983. 279–97.

———. Interview. By Charlotte M. Meyer. *Contemporary Literature* 23:2 (1982): 129–44.

———. Interview. By Janos Szeky. *Elet es Irodalom* (December 3, 1982): 7.

———. Interview. By Bruce Kawin. *Arts at Santa Cruz* 1:1 (1981).

———. "A Conversation in Boston." By James Nagel. *American Fiction*. Boston: Northeastern University Press, 1977. 175–202.

———. "Imagination as Perception." By Joe David Bellamy. *Chicago Review* 23 (Winter, 1972): 59–72. Rpt. in *The New Fiction: Interviews with Innovative American Writers*. Urbana: University of Illinois Press, 1974. 55–74.

———. Interview. Videotape. Center for Twentieth Century Studies, University of Wisconsin, Milwaukee, 1972.

———. "The Tape Recorder Records." By Joe David Bellamy. *Falcon* 2–3 (April 1971): 5–25.

Criticism on Ronald Sukenick (Excluding Reviews)

Adams, Timothy Dow. "Obscuring the Muse: The Mock-Autobiographies of Ronald Sukenick." *Critique* 20:1 (1978): 27–39.

Aldridge, John W. *The American Novel and the Way We Live Now*. New York: Oxford University Press, 1982.

Barth, John. "The State of the Art." *WQ* (Spring 1996): 36–45.

Beebe, Maurice. "Reflective and Reflexive Trends in Modern Fiction." *Bucknell Review* 22 (1976): 19–20.

Bell, Pearl Kazin. "American Fiction: Forgetting Ordinary Truths." *Dissent* (Winter 1973): 26–34, passim.

Bergman, Linda S. "On *Out*." *Chicago Review* 25:3: 9–12.

Bogue, Ronald, and Marcel Cornis-Pope, eds. *Violence and Mediation in Contemporary Culture*. Albany: State University of New York Press. 1995.

Bolling, Douglass. "Some Observations on Contemporary Fiction." *Northeast Review* (Winter 1975–76): 14–16.

Bradbury, Malcolm. *The Modern American Novel*. New York: Oxford University Press. 1983.

Broderick, Vincent A. "Disruptive Participants: Observations of Works by Sukenick and Sorrentino." *Kobe College Studies* (1978): 39–68.

Brooke-Rose, Christine. "Where Do We Go From Here?" *Granta* 3 (1980): 168, 176–82. Rpt. in *New Realism in Contemporary Fiction*. Oxford: Oxford University Press, 1981.

Butler, Christopher. *After the Wake*. Oxford: Oxford University Press, 1980.

Caramello, Charles. "Ronald Sukenick." *Contemporary Novelists* (November 1986): 5.

———. *Silverless Mirrors*. Tallahassee: University Press of Florida, 1983.

Chabot, C. Barry. "Fiction, Truth and the Character of Beliefs." *Georgia Review* 37 (Winter 1983): 835–43.

Cheuse, Alan. "Way Out West: The Exploratory Fiction of Ronald Sukenick." *Itinerary Criticism #7: Essays on California Writers*. Ed. Charles Crow. Bowling Green, Ohio: Bowling Green State University Press, 1978. 115–21.

Cohen, Keith. *Writing in a Film Age*. Boulder: University Press of Colorado, 1991.

Cornis-Pope, Marcel. "Postmodernism Beyond Self-Reflection." *Mimesis in Contemporary Theory*, Vol. 2. Ed Ronald Bogue. Amsterdam: John Benjamins, 1991.

———. *Narrative Innovation and Cultural Rewriting in the Cold War Era and After*. New York: Palgrave, 2002.

———. "Narrative Innovation and Cultural Rewriting: The Pynchon-Morrison-Sukenick Connection." *Narrative and Culture*. Athens: University of Georgia Press, 1994. 216–37.

Docherty, Thomas. *Reading (Absent) Character*. Oxford: Oxford University Press, 1983.

Federman, Raymond. "In." *Partisan Review* 41:1 (1974): 137–42.

———. "Self Reflexive Fiction." *Columbia Literary History of the United States*, New York: Columbia University Press, 1988.

Foley, JR. "Fiction Collective Two." *Poets and Writers Magazine* (September/October 1996): 35–43.

Friedman, Melvin J. "Dislocations of Setting and Word: Notes on American Fiction Since 1950." *Studies in American Fiction* 5 (Spring 1977): 79–98.

———. "To 'Make It New': The American Novel Since 1945." *Wilson Quarterly* 2 (Winter 1978): 133–42.

Friedman, Melvin J., and Ben Siegal. *Traditions, Voices, Dreams: The American Novel Since the 1960s*. Newark: University of Delaware Press, 1995.

Hassan, Ihab. *Paracriticisms*. Urbana: University of Illinois Press, 1975.

———. "Reading Out." *Fiction International* 1 (Fall 1973): 108–09.

Hicks, Jack. *In the Singer's Temple*. Chapel Hill: University of North Carolina Press, 1981.

Hornung, Alfred. "Absent Presence: The Fictions of Raymond Federman and Ronald Sukenick." *Indian Journal of American Studies* 14 (1984): 17–31.

Hutcheons, Linda. *Narcissistic Narrative*. London: Methuen, 1984.

Kawin, Bruce F. *The Mind of the Novel*. Princeton, N.J.: Princeton University Press, 1982.

Klinkowitz, Jerome. *The American 1960s*. Ames: Iowa State University Press, 1980.

———. "Getting Real: Making It (Up) with Ronald Sukenick." *Chicago Review* 23 (Winter 1972): 73–82.

———. "Innovative Short Fiction: 'Vile and Imaginative Things.' " *In Innovative Fiction*. New York: Dell, 1972.

———. "A Persuasive Account: Working It Out with Ronald Sukenick." *North American Review* 258 (Summer 1973): 48–52. Rpt. in *Seeing Castaneda*, ed. Daniel Noel. New York: Putnam's 1976, 131–39.

———. *Literary Disruptions*. Urbana: University of Illinois Press, 1975.

———. *The Life of Fiction*. Urbana: University of Illinois Press, 1977.

———. *The Self Apparent Word*. Carbondale: Southern Illinois University Press, 1984.

———. *Literary Subversions: New American Fiction and the Practice of Criticism*. Carbondale: Southern Illinois University Press, 1985.

———. *Keeping Literary Company*. Albany: State Univeristy New York Press, 1998.

Kutnik, Jerzy. *Fiction as Performance: The Fiction of Ronald Sukenick and Raymond Federman.* Carbondale: Southern Illinois University Press, 1986.

LeClair, Thomas. "Avant Garde Mastery." *Tri Quarterly* 53 (Winter 1982): 259.

Levenston, E. A. *The Stuff of Literature.* Albany: State University of New York Press, 1992.

Martin, Jay; Tanner, Tony; and Tytell, John. "Composure and Decomposition: Three Pieces on the Fiction Collective." *Partisan Review* 2 (1979): 287–88, 295–97.

McCaffery, Larry. *The Metafictional Muse.* Pittsburgh, Pa.: University of Pittsburgh Press, 1982.

McHale, Brian. *Constructing Postmodernism.* New York: Routledge, 1992.

———. *Postmodernist Fiction.* New York: Routledge, 1987.

Mellard, James. *The Exploded Form.* Urbana: University of Illinois Press, 1980.

Nealon, Jeffrey T. *Double Reading.* Ithaca, N.Y.: Cornell University Press, 1993.

Noel, Daniel. "Tales of Fictive Power: Dreaming and Imagining in Ronald Sukenick's Postmodern Fiction." *Boundary* 2:5 (Fall 1976): 117–35.

Pearce, Richard. *The Novel in Motion.* Columbus: Ohio State University Press, 1983.

Primeau, Ronald. *Romance of the Road: The Literature of the American Highway.* Bowling Green, Ohio: Bowling Green University Popular Press, 1996.

Putz, Manfred. *The Story of Identity: American Fiction of the Sixties.* Stuttgart: Metzler, 1979.

Quartermain, Peter. "Trusting the Reader." *Chicago Review* 32:2 (1980): 71–73.

Roberson, Matthew. *1998.6.* Normal/Tallahassee: FC2, 2002.

———. "Moinous Li(v)es." Ph.D. diss. University of Wisconsin-Milwaukee, 1997.

———. "Ronald Sukenick's Narratypography." *Electronic Book Review* 7:2 (Summer 1998): <http://www.altx.com/ebr/ebr7/7roberson/7rober.html>.

Russell, Charles. "Individual Voice in the Collective Discourse: Literary Innovation in Postmodern American Fiction." *Sub-Stance* 27 (1980): 30, 32–33, 35–37.

———. *Poets, Prophets and Revolutionaries: The Avant-Garde from Rimbaud to Postmodernism.* Oxford: Oxford University Press, 1985.

———. "The Vault of Language: Self-Reflective Artifice in Contemporary American Fiction." *Modern Fiction Studies* 20: 3 (1974): 355–56.

Saltzman, Arthur M. *The Novel in the Balance.* Columbia: University of South Carolina Press, 1993.

Stone, Albert E. *Autobiographical Occasions and Original Acts*. Philadelphia: University of Pennsylvania Press, 1982.

Tatham, Campbell. "Mo-Sukenick." *New Novel Review*. Forthcoming.

Thiher, Allen. *Words in Reflection: Modern Language Theory and Post Modern Fiction*. Chicago: University of Chicago Press, 1984.

Tytell, John. "Epiphany in Chaos: Fragmentation in Modernism." *Fragments: Incompletion and Discontinuity*. Ed. Lawrence D. Kritzman. New York: Literary Form—City University of New York, 1981.

Waugh, Patricia. *Metafiction*. London: Methuen, 1984.

Werner, Craig Hansen. *Paradoxical Resolutions*. Urbana: University of Illinois Press, 1983.

White, Curtis. "Writing the Life Postmodern." *Review of Contemporary Fiction* XVI:1 (1996): 112–21.

Wilde, Alan. *Horizons of Dissent*. Baltimore, Md.: Johns Hopkins University Press, 1981.

Wolfe, Tom. "Why They Aren't Writing the Great American Novel Anymore." *Esquire* 78 (1972): 152–58, 272–80.

Zavarzadeh, Mas'ud. *The Mythopoeic Reality*. Urbana: University of Illinois Press, 1976.

Contributors

Mark Amerika's first novel, *The Kafka Chronicles*, is now in its third printing and his most recent novel, *Sexual Blood*, is already being translated into three other languages. Amerika, who is the Publisher of Alt-X, which Publishers Weekly recently referred to as "the literary publishing model of the future," has published two anthologies, *Degenerative Prose: Writing Beyond Category* [co-edited with Ron Sukenick] (Fiction Collective Two/Black Ice Books) and *In Memoriam to Postmodernism: Essays on the Avant-Pop* [co-edited with Lance Olsen] (San Diego State University Press).

Nancy Blake is professor of comparative literature at the University of Illinois. She is the author of *Henry James: Ecriture et absence*, as well as essays on Gertrude Stein, John Barth, Wallace Stevens, and contemporary American poetry. She has translated numerous American literature texts into French and is presently working on Marianne Moore and an overview essay on Robert Steiner.

Marcel Cornis-Pope is professor of English and comparative literature at Virginia Commonwealth University. His publications include *Anatomy of the White Whale: A Poetics of the American Symbolic Romance* (Bucharest: Univers, 1982), *Hermeneutic Desire and Critical Rewriting: Narrative Interpretation in the Wake of Poststructuralism* (London: Macmillan; New York: St. Martin's, 1992), *Violence and Mediation in Contemporary Culture* (co-edited with Ronald Bogue; Albany: State University of New York Press, 1995), *The Unfinished Battles: Romanian Postmodernism Before and After 1989* (Iasi, Romania: Polirom, 1996), and *Narrative Innovation and Cultural Rewriting in the Cold War Era and After* (New York: Palgrave, 2002). Cornis-Pope has also published numerous articles on postmodern theories and practices and has recently finished a book on *Narrative Innovation and Cultural Rewriting in the Cold War Era and After*, with chapters on Coover, Pynchon, Sukenick, Federman, and Morrison. His awards include the Romanian Writers' Award for best book translation into English (1975), the Romanian Writers' Award for best book of criticism (1982), a Fulbright teaching and research grant (1983–85), an Andrew Mellon Faculty Fellowship at Harvard University (1987–88), the College of Humanities and Sciences (Virginia Commonwealth University) Scholarship Award (1991; 1993), and CELJ's Phoenix Award for Significant Editorial Achievement (1996).

Charles B. Harris is author of *Passionate Virtuosity: The Fiction of John Barth*, *Contemporary American Novelists of the Absurd*, and *Humor and the Recent American Novel*, as well as of numerous essays on contemporary fiction and the profession of English studies. Co-publisher of *American Book Review*, he directs the Unit for Contemporary Literature at Illinois State University. In 1997, the Modern Language Association honored him with the Francis Andrew March Award for Exceptional Service to the Profession of English.

Ursula Heise is associate professor of English and comparative literature and Director of Graduate Studies for Comparative Literature at Columbia University. She specializes in postmodern literature and literary theory; her major fields of interest are theories of modernity and postmodernity, ecology and ecocriticism, literature and science, narrative theory, science fiction, and the intersection of twentieth-century literature with other media (film, television, performance, computer). She has published articles on Renaissance theater and various contemporary authors. Her book on the postmodern novel *Chronoschisms: Time, Narrative, Postmodernism* was published by Cambridge University Press in 1997. She is currently working on a project called "Technology, Ecology and Utopia: Postmodern Literature and the Challenge of the Environment."

JR Foley is Fiction Editor of *Flashpoint: A Multidisciplinary Journal of the Arts and Politics* <http://www.flashpointmag.com/>.

University of Northern Iowa Distinguished Scholar and professor of English, **Jerome Klinkowitz** is the author of forty books of criticism and fiction. His work on Ronald Sukenick began in 1970 and was first collected in his book *Literary Disruptions*.

Larry McCaffery is professor of English at San Diego State University. He has published four volumes of interviews: *Anything Can Happen*, *Alive and Writing*, *Across the Wounded Galaxies*, and *Some Other Frequency*, and edited several texts, including *Federman: From A to X-X-X-X*, *Postmodern Fiction: A Bio-Bibliographic Guide*, and *After Yesterday's Crash: The Avant-Pop Anthology*. His book, *The Metafictional Muse*, was one of the first to examine American metafiction of the 1960s.

Brian McHale is professor of English at Ohio State University. His publications include, among others, *Postmodernist Fiction* and *Constructing Postmodernism* (both from Routledge).

Lance Olsen is the author of several novels, including *Time Famine*, *Burnt*, *Tonguing the Zeitgeist*, *Live from Earth*. He is also the author of a textbook on writing fiction, *Rebel Yell: Writing Fiction*, and several books of criticism, including *In Memoriam to Postmodernism: Essays on the Avant-Pop*, co-edited with Mark Amerika, *Lolita: A Janus Text*, *Surfing Tomorrow: Essays on the Future of American Fiction*, editor, *William Gibson*, *Circus of the Mind in Motion: Postmodernism and the Comic Vision*, *Ellipse of Uncertainty: An Introduction to Postmodern Fantasy*. His short story collections include *Sewing Shut My Eyes*, *Scherzi, I Believe*, and *My Dates With Franz*. He has published a poetry chapbook, *Natural Selections*, co-authored with Jeff Worley, and has had over sixty short stories in *Iowa Review*, *Mississippi Review*, *Nobodaddies*, *California Quarterly*, *Alaska Quarterly*, and various anthologies. His poems have appeared in *Willow Springs*, *DoubleTake*, *Alaska Quarterly*, *Kansas Quarterly*, and *Bellingham Review*.

Matthew Roberson is the author of a novel, *1998.6*, and his reviews, articles, and stories have appeared in *Postmodern Culture*, *The Review of Contemporary Fiction*, *American Book Review*, *electronic book review*, *New Novel Review*, *Federman: From A to X-X-X-X*, *The Nightshade Reader*, and *Porcupine Literary Arts Magazine*.

Charles Russell is a professor of English at Rutgers Univeristy-Newark. He is the author of *Poets, Prophets and Revolutionaries: The Literary Avant-Garde from Rimbaud through Postmodernism* (Oxford University Press) and *The Avant-Garde Today* (University of Illinois Press).

Campbell Tatham has published over two dozen critifictions in such journals as *Diacritics, Chicago Review, boundary 2, Genre,* and *Paradoxa.*

He is currently working on the scholarly adventures of Professor Arthur Challenger in *Critifiction 3: The Text.* He is associate professor of English at University of Wisconsin-Milwaukee.

Steve Tomasula's fictions and essays have appeared in *Fiction International*, *New Art Examiner*, *Leonardo*, *American Book Review, The Review of Contemporary Fiction*, *Emigre,* and *Black Ice*. He recently guest-edited an issue on narrative theory and image for *electronic book review*, and is the author of a novel, *Vas: An Opera in Flatland.*

Index

Short fiction and essays

Books